Bloggers Boot Camp

Bloggers Boot Camp

Learning How to Build, Write, and Run a Successful Blog

Second edition

Charlie White and John Biggs

Focal Press
Taylor & Francis Group

NEW YORK AND LONDON

First published 2012 by Focal Press

This edition published 2014
by Focal Press
70 Blanchard Road, Suite 402, Burlington, MA 01803

and by Focal Press
2 Park Square, Milton Park, Abingdon, Oxon OX14 4RN

Focal Press is an imprint of the Taylor & Francis Group, an informa business

Notices

Knowledge and best practice in this field are constantly changing. As new research and experience broaden our understanding, changes in research methods, professional practices, or medical treatment may become necessary.

Practitioners and researchers must always rely on their own experience and knowledge in evaluating and using any information, methods, compounds, or experiments described herein. In using such information or methods they should be mindful of their own safety and the safety of others, including parties for whom they have a professional responsibility.

Product or corporate names may be trademarks or registered trademarks, and are used only for identification and explanation without intent to infringe.

Library of Congress Cataloging-in-Publication Data

White, Charlie, 1956–
Bloggers boot camp : learning how to build, write, and run a successful blog /
   Charlie White and John Biggs. — Second edition.
     pages cm
   Includes index.
   1. Blogs.   I. Biggs, John, 1975–   II. Title.
   TK5105.8884.W48   2014
   006.7'52—dc23   2013048420

ISBN: 978-0-415-73714-2 (pbk)
ISBN: 978-1-317-81619-5 (ebk)

Typeset in Caecilia
by Apex CoVantage, LLC

Printed and bound in the United States of America by Sheridan Books, Inc. (a Sheridan Group Company).

Bound to Create

You are a creator.

Whatever your form of expression — photography, filmmaking, animation, games, audio, media communication, web design, or theatre — you simply want to create without limitation. Bound by nothing except your own creativity and determination.

Focal Press can help.

For over 75 years Focal has published books that support your creative goals. Our founder, Andor Kraszna-Krausz, established Focal in 1938 so you could have access to leading-edge expert knowledge, techniques, and tools that allow you to create without constraint. We strive to create exceptional, engaging, and practical content that helps you master your passion.

Focal Press and you.

Bound to create.

We'd love to hear how we've helped you create. Share your experience:
www.focalpress.com/boundtocreate

Contents

Contents

Acknowledgments

John:

I'd like to thank my eternally patient family for allowing me to take on yet another project, and my indulgent colleagues at *TechCrunch*, Matt Burns, Natasha Lomas, Ryan Lawler, Anthony Ha, Matthew Panzarino, Chris Nesi, Catherine Pickavet, Jordan Crook, Ingrid Lunden, Greg Kumparak, Eric Eldon, Greg Ferenstein, and Alexia Tsostis and the rest for putting up with my distraction. Thanks to the old TC/AOL team, Heather Harde, Michael Arrington, and all the rest and the new team led by Ned Desmond. Thanks to Sharona Jacobs of SharonaPhoto.com for her help.

Special thanks to Mayer Reich of RankAbove for his help with SEO and the bloggers I spoke with, including folks from *F*ckedInParkSlope*, *TheBikeSnobNYC*, and *Gizmodo*. Special thanks to Joel Johnson for making me the blogger I am today.

Finally, I'd like to thank all of my readers and especially JOSH, Weatherman, and bonafortuna. You guys help me get up in the morning and make me want to keep doing this late into the night.

Also, thanks to my wife and kids who have put up with me all these years.

Charlie:

I'd like to thank my writing partner and friend John Biggs for giving me my first break in the blogosphere, trusting me to copy edit *Gizmodo* when he barely knew me. Thanks to former Focal Press publisher Elinor Actipis for her enthusiasm for this project, and thanks to our editors David Bevans and Catharine Steers and project manager Matthew Scotti for their steady guidance and gentle revisions. Thanks so much to our intrepid, eagle-eyed project manager Mae Lum of Apex CoVantage, and our tireless editorial assistant, Max Rohrig, both of whom helped us polish the text to a dazzling shine. I'd also like to thank our production editor Emma Elder for keeping everything moving along so smoothly. I'd especially like to thank my longtime pal and colleague Stephen Schleicher for his comprehensive counsel. Most importantly, I'd like to thank my lovely wife, Denise, for her unwavering support.

Introduction

Welcome to the second edition of *Bloggers Boot Camp*, where we keep all the coolness from the first edition, and add everything we've learned since the last edition hit the shelves three years ago. In Internet time, three years is like thirty years in less innovative fields. So much has evolved and changed since we first penned the original *Bloggers Boot Camp* in 2010 that we're going to have lots to write about, and we're glad you decided to join us.

First, we've added a new chapter that will interest many of you: how to get a job at a big blog or website that already exists, using the knowledge you've gained in this book to hit the ground running at a high-traffic, major-league website. We'll show you how to build your brand, spread the word about your new adventures, and make that leap from one career into this new world of always-on communication and personal expression.

We'll talk about how blogging has gotten even closer to the mainstream media, making the divide between them almost imperceptible. We'll show you new ways to get your blog online and find the best designs for your blog, introduce you to new ways to use photos and graphics, and show you how to integrate podcasting into your media empire.

One of the biggest growth areas has been social media, and we have decided to add a great deal more to this edition. We're going to reveal techniques we've learned for promoting your work on Twitter, Facebook, Google+, and other platforms that can make a post explode. We'll talk with experts to give you further insights into leveraging social media into your blogging strategy. And we'll warn you of the dangers of social media, alerting you to the booby traps we've seen too many great writers fall victim to. We even have three key rules for spreading the word, and a new Golden Rule of Blogging that you'll want to always remember.

At the same time, as we've always done in this book, we're going to teach you the most important skill of all: how to write for blogs and online publications. More specifically, you'll learn how to write content geared toward today's readers, and we've learned boatloads of new tips and techniques for that, discovering to an even more refined degree what works and what doesn't.

Blogs are a new medium. They're powerful and deserve to be taken seriously. Your own blog and your own writing can change the world or flounder in obscurity. It's up to you, but we're here to help.

Introduction

Bloggers can make money doing what they love, but it is hard work. It usually takes a lot of time to develop an audience. It requires the serious initiative of a self-starter. Not everyone can be a successful blogger, although we hope to give you the tools necessary to get a running start.

If you're already blogging now, we'll show you techniques that will help you become a better blogger and a better writer in general.

Blogging requires regular and daily effort. A blog is like a shark—it stays alive only if it keeps moving. You can't write just one blog post per week and expect people to keep returning. We'll teach you some tricks to keep the content fresh and constantly flowing from your keyboard. More importantly, we'll teach you how to monetize your hard work.

There is no magic bullet for creating a successful blog, especially if your goal is not overtly commercial and is instead a desire to share your viewpoint with the world.

We're not here to help you make a million dollars a year blogging, but we want to give you the tools necessary to give you an exponentially better chance of success.

Why us? We know why blogs fail and we know why they succeed—we have extensive experience in many forms of online media and feel it's time to start sharing some of our expertise with other prospective bloggers.

The good news is that your barrier to entry is easy to break through. What will you need? At the very least you will need a computer with an Internet connection, ideally a fast one. Even that is not set in stone anymore, because now users of mobile devices may find that they will be able to blog from the streets of their cities as easily as they do from their desktops, snapping pictures to illustrate their stories directly from those mobile devices. There are almost as many blogging tools as there are bloggers.

Here's the best news: You won't have to start from scratch, because we've already made the mistakes, found the successes, and learned what works and what doesn't in the blogosphere.

We'll show you the ropes. We'll show you how hot sites like *Mashable*, *Gizmodo*, and *TechCrunch* work their magic to attract millions of readers every day. We'll show you how we create our own microblogs and gain hundreds of readers overnight. We'll show you how to think about the strange calculus of audience, content, and reach.

But first, who are we? We'll be writing this book as "we," but for the introductions, allow us to write individually.

John Biggs is the East Coast editor of *TechCrunch*, a tech website owned by AOL, and Charlie White just finished a two-and-a-half year stint at *Mashable*, a social media news site. We have worked with teams of up to thirty writers, and we both bring in millions of pageviews a month—about 100 million at last count. In the world of modern pro-blogging we're about as big as you can get without being CNN. We've written—and still write— more than forty posts per month on topics ranging from politics to the latest smartphone.

How did we get here? That's a funny story.

John's Fall and Rise

The late 1990s and early 2000s brought a new world where the business section of the newspaper turned from a one-page add-on at the back of the sports page into a full-fledged section detailing the deals, IPOs, and flame-outs of the "dot-com" era. Tech news was now a big part of the landscape, and the old magazines—*PC Magazine*, *PC World*, *Newsweek*, *Fast Company*—were shrinking in size and revenue. Business meant technology now, not just stuffed shirts making decisions over pensions. More importantly, news was appearing online faster than ever before. Websites were eviscerating newspapers at a clip that no one could have expected a decade before, but no one trusted blogs.

It was the summer of 2004, mid-August. I was working at *Laptop* magazine, a print title that reviewed the latest laptops, cellphones, and tablets. There were hundreds of new devices rolling out every year, and each needed a few thousand words written about it. Everything got a long, 5,000-word feature article, or, barring that, a shorter 1,000-word review. Brevity was not the soul of wit at *Laptop*. It was, in fact, the enemy. For all this work, the auditors were able to assess that *Laptop* was the top-selling magazine in the Honolulu airport. That's right: we were primarily popular in touristy island newsstands in the Pacific. It wasn't a very heartening situation.

I had been blogging—a fancy term for putting things on the Internet—for most of four years, starting with a site I ran called *BigWideLogic*. It was my personal site, a goofy collection of links that I rarely updated. I also started a watch website called *WristwatchReview* in 2003, making me one of the first watch bloggers in the world. That is not to say that either of those ventures was particularly good, serious, or lucrative. I made little money from advertising—perhaps $10 a month—but I had free Internet hosting from a friend, so at least the only thing I spent was time and attention.

However, the process of preparing stories for the sites—posts—taught me a great deal about what to look for in a good, short piece. I was just giving things a try, and back in those heady days, there was no guarantee of success. A tech site, *Gizmodo,* was about a year old, written by a snarky kid named Joel Johnson who took over after its founder, Peter Rojas, bolted for another site, *Engadget.* Meanwhile, there were ideas sprouting on the blogging landscape. The Julie/Julia Project, the precursor to *Julie & Julia*, begun in early 2002, was beginning to gain a small following that led—years later—to fortune and fame for its heretofore-unknown author. The only "cool" online news source of note was *Salon,* and in 2003, shares of the company were selling for 5 cents in over-the-counter markets. There was, in a way, no reason to think anyone on the Internet could go pro.

One August morning my editor walked into my secluded back office and asked me to clear out my desk. I was being laid off. The technical magazine I worked for no longer needed a technical editor to read over the pages to ensure technical accuracy. It was facing a downturn in readership and value that almost led to the title's demise.

I left for home, dumbfounded. I was a tech guy at heart. I studied IT in college, and I had quit a semi-lucrative but soul-sucking job as a computer consultant in 2000 to get a master's in journalism from New York University. Now, in my first real journalism job, they made me redundant. Luckily, that week I emailed Joel at *Gizmodo*, who invited me to interview for a "reporter" position for the site. I drove to meet Joel in Brooklyn's hip Greenpoint district, and we ate Polish food. There he laid it out for me: His day consisted of long hours spent in a chair, poring over the Internet for stories to write. Some days he did nothing but rewrite press releases. He was tired and he looked burned out, nervous, and edgy. In fact, lunch was taking too long. He needed to get back to his computer, so we cut the interview short and he told me that he had ten more posts to write before he went to bed.

This didn't sound like any journalism job I'd ever heard of. In fact, it sounded, at first, like heaven: no editors, no deadlines, no workflow. It was, at its core, the purest form of a "beat" I had seen. It was first-thought-best-thought, writ large. The job, in short, consisted of writing about cool things all day, as quickly as possible, and being funny about it.

Introduction

I got the job mostly because I was free. I got lucky. I was up against writers from the *New York Times* and tech gurus from the rapidly shrinking tech magazines. In fact, blogging for *Gizmodo* wasn't like writing for a magazine. I was up in the morning at 7 a.m. and writing until 10 p.m. There was no real work/life balance—a trap I fell into early—and there was no sense that the job ever stopped. I started working with Joel, producing twenty-eight stories a day, and then when Joel left I hired a few other writers, including Charlie White. By the time I left, the site was bumping up against the 18 million pageview-per-month mark. Now it is topping out at more than 100 million.

I never went back to print. Today, ironically, *Laptop* now makes its money from the web. The paper version is no more. A few years later Joel got rid of me at *Gizmodo*—they wanted to hire a writer from hoary old *Wired* magazine to replace me—and I wrote a good-bye post that still exists on the site. A few days later I got a call from a brusque man who lived in San Francisco. "I want you to start a gadget site for me," he said. His name was Michael Arrington, and he owned a start-up business blog called *TechCrunch*.

He invited me to visit him at his ranch-style rental in Atherton, California. I arrived late—around 2 p.m.—and he was just waking up, having spent all night blogging. He took me to Costco to buy wine for a party he was having that night, and he asked me a few questions. A few days later I was running *CrunchGear*, my own site. I hired a kid who IMed me out of the blue one day—Blake Robinson—and grew the team with ex-*Gizmodo* writers and a few hotshot freelancers. It felt like the best time of my life.

A few years passed and AOL bought *TechCrunch*. *CrunchGear* folded into the main site, and I got a great team of gifted writers who have made my job even better.

I got lucky . . . again.

Why did I tell that story? Well, we have been blogging since the beginning of the blogging revolution. Combine our years spent behind the keyboard and you'll find that we've been blogging longer than almost anyone in the world.

Charlie and I grab more than 100 million pageviews per month on multiple sites. We've written more than 20,000 blog posts between us, launched wildly successful blogs, dealt with all of the intricacies of the new medium, and reveled in our success. Now it's time for us to pass this hard-won knowledge along to you, letting you learn from our triumphs, while helping you avoid our mistakes.

Charlie's Tale

I'm Charlie White, and in the midst of a thirty-year career producing and directing television broadcasts, I started writing about technology on the web in 1994. The web wasn't much to look at back then. If you've been around that long, you'll remember those ancient days when Mosaic was the most popular browser, Bill Clinton was president, and Windows 95 was considered futuristic technology. Five years later, I was spending most of my time (while working two full-time jobs) writing about technology for a group of websites called *Digital Media Net*. One day at a trade show in 2000, several of my journalist cohorts and I decided to write short two-paragraph news stories about what we'd just seen and experienced on the show floor. The immediacy of these punchy paragraphs caught on quickly with readers, and suddenly we realized that this could turn into an entirely new medium.

Unfortunately, my short-sighted managers disagreed, so the concept lay dormant, and I continued working in the web journalism environment of the time. That revolved around webzines and portals—megasites that linked to numerous affiliated sites, all under the same umbrella. And all their content consisted of longish, magazine-like articles, product reviews, editorials, and features. They weren't blogs yet.

After toiling away at that business model for a few years longer, by 2005, a technology and gadget blog *Gizmodo* caught my attention. Its traffic was starting to eclipse the numbers of the large portal for which I was working. What kind of site could garner such impressive numbers, I wondered. Surely it must have involved a staff bigger than that of *Digital Media Net*—a dozen writers or more? Hardly. All that content, some thirty posts daily, was cranked out by a quick-writing, wisecracking crew the size of a pickup basketball team. These four hungry journalists had a nose for news and a love of gadgetry and high tech. They wrote as a group, using a unique and cohesive style, where all were able to express a similar and astute brand of humor. It was working—they had amassed a rabid following. I wanted to get myself mixed up with such excitement, so I contacted the site's editor, my future writing partner and the other author of this book, John Biggs, who invited me to join the blogging revolution. "I'll hook you up," he typed into an instant message. "Start tomorrow." It was that easy. I got lucky, too.

Two years later, I had banged out 4,442 articles on that eclectic gadget site. Over those years, the site's traffic grew from 7 million pageviews per month when I started to 83 million when I left in 2008. But the money was decidedly unsatisfying, so my next stop was NBC Universal, where the mainstream media giant lured me into writing more than 2,500 blog posts, reviews, and features for the SyFy-powered blog *DVICE* over the next three years.

My next stop was *Mashable*, one of the five most influential blogs in the world with more than 25 million unique visitors each month. John recommended me for the job one weekend after a headhunter had called him to poach him from *TechCrunch*. In short order, the headhunter was calling me.

As senior editor there, I wrote 1,433 posts, reviews, and features, resulting in the highest traffic numbers anyone has ever achieved at that site. I edited every word published on the site each weekend, and learned even more about blogging, journalism, what readers want, and how to identify and measure success, and perhaps most importantly, how to create compelling social media. I figured out what has made *Mashable* such a roaring success.

Look: we got lucky. There are no two ways about it. But we got lucky because we were ready when the call came. You can get lucky, too. Online personalities are becoming a more important part of the media landscape. **You can take part in the conversation, and you can lead the conversation**, whether through the written word, photography, or video.

One blogger, our buddy Scott McKenzie, parlayed his love of books into a successful site about the publishing industry and used his contacts there to score a contract with two major publishers. Blogger Cali Lewis became famous for her no-nonsense video reviews of new technology. Political blogger Ana Marie Cox turned into a well-known Beltway pundit after scribbling for *Wonkette*. One thing made these bloggers stand out and gave them success: **perseverance and a strong impulse to produce—whether it's a post, a video, or a rant—daily and well.**

We are not social media snake oil salesmen. We are not affiliate marketers. We don't want to offer you a four-hour workweek. We are real journalists breaking real news. If you want a get-rich-quick scheme, the Internet is rife with them. Hit Google. If you think blogging is a sure-fire way to get free stuff from companies for being an influencer, then you'd best pack up now. However, if you want to learn how to run a successful news business and maybe make some money in the process, we're here for you. But that's not all. We can also teach you how to become a giant in your field. We can teach you how to become a more valuable employee, how to use blogging to get a better job, and how to become important online.

When we say we're here for you, we mean that. Check the end of this book for ways to contact us to ask questions, make recommendations, and to just keep us abreast of your doings. Just because this is a paper book (or ebook) doesn't mean the learning has to stop at the last page.

Enough about us. Who are you?

If our assumptions are correct, you have something to say and you want everyone else to know what it is. But there's a big problem right now: There are billions of other blogs competing for the attention of your prospective readers. We'll show you how to grab their attention. We'll show you how to find the best stories, and what to do with them after you find them. We'll show you how to make your blog stand out from all the rest.

If you can write and you have passion about your topic, blogging is easy. It should be noted that the difference between being a journal writer and a journalist is stark and important. Bloggers might write about themselves, but they are always seeing the bigger picture. Bloggers might wax euphoric, hold grudges, and display bias, but at their heart they are attempting to bring truth to light in the best ways they know how.

Many high-traffic blogs seem like massive journalistic entities, but, as Joel Johnson once wrote, "most of the time—we're just talking." We're talking about what we like, what we don't like, what we learned today about something you might know little about, or what we stupidly think we understand about something in which you're an expert. Blogging is a form of journalism just as ballet is a form of dance. Journalism is a "process" whereas blogging—electronic writing—is a specific subtype of that process.

Being a *successful* blogger is hard. Not only will we show you how to pick the best blogging platform for your needs and how to drive users to your blog, but also we'll show you all the tips and tricks we've learned along the way, emphasizing quality, finding the best stories, and gathering millions of readers to a blog whose first day had none. Okay, maybe it had one reader—Charlie's dad.

Blogging goes way beyond mere content. It's a conversation between you and your audience. We'll show you the best way to interact with your audience, how to encourage their input, how to deal with unruly commenters, and how to attract the best commenters—which many readers think is the most entertaining part of a blog.

No longer will journalists sit in their ivory towers, comfortable with writing two columns a month. Creating a blog is like riding on a fast-moving train, and to navigate these newfound, gleaming rails of virtual steel, you'll need additional skills that go far beyond writing. We'll show you how to find or create compelling graphics, make a viral video that could spread to millions of viewers, promote your posts with social media, and how to reach a world full of readers with your ideas.

If you are an old-guard journalist, don't forget what you know. However, don't expect the safety net of process journalism to protect you anymore. You are now on your own, and you make or break your story. There's no one else to blame when the support system you had grown accustomed to is gone. There are new ways to find news, and we'll show you how to find out what's happening in the world you choose to cover. With all the electronic tools available, you no longer have to camp out at the police station to get fresh news. This is not your father's journalism. The barriers to entry are lower, the information is a whole lot easier to find, and you'll be able to put together stories and publish them immediately, promote them instantly via social media, and receive feedback from your readers minutes, or even seconds, later. This is ultimately freeing and frightening at the same time.

Maybe you're not trying to become a capital W Writer. That's fine, too. We can show you how to use these techniques to improve your marketing efforts and head to the front of the pack when it comes to your career, your interests, and your industry. Blogging has helped plenty of people get big, and it's still a great way to get noticed in a crowded world.

If you are reading this, you see the writing on the wall: Formal news and publishing organizations, as they exist today, are disappearing. Aside from the dinosaurs that still roam the earth, limping along and wondering what hit them, the daily local newspaper is on life support. Magazines are hitting the iPad, and some titles exist in the ether entirely. The closest analog to what you will be doing while blogging is the old-fashioned wire service that required a unique combination of talent, skill, and precision. But it's not all about writing. It's about video, it's about audio, it's about being a one-man-band at a trade show while the rest of the "mainstream" journalistic community has the force and resources of a large news-gathering organization at their backs.

We are also not saying that the so-called mainstream media is in any way our enemy or beyond our reach. Blogs are the mainstream media for a vast group of Internet-savvy news readers. You might have heard that 60 percent of teenagers pay no attention to mainstream news, but most will be more than happy to watch Jon Stewart on *The Daily Show*. Attention spans are shorter, and they're looking for new points of view aside from the old guard. The good news? There are millions of readers hungry for fresh, punchy info, and willing to find it from almost any form of niche blogger imaginable.

This is where you come in. We are offering the beginning and intermediate blogger our secret formula that we've learned through years of experience at the most powerful blogs in the world: the key to building a more active, interesting, and widely read blog, as well as expanding your reach and voice to create a unique online identity. We'll show you why this new medium is different from magazines, newspapers, and video, and we'll show you how to successfully attract an audience. Advanced bloggers will be able to use this book to learn a few best practices from guys who have been doing this longer than anyone else. No one has codified the rules of blogging, and so that's what we set out to do.

To be a successful blogger, you need to concentrate on content production and audience gathering. There are many tools in a blogger's arsenal, but the most important is perseverance and understanding of your topic. You can blog about anything you want, and obviously you're approaching this effort from a professional standpoint. Lots of people say that bloggers write about what they're having for lunch and their cats. But, if you create a successful food blog—see *Julie & Julia*—or a site dedicated to lists of funny pictures covering everything from cupcakes to cats—BuzzFeed.com—you can create a successful niche, turning what used to be considered one step below journal-keeping into a lucrative and exciting business.

Let's get started!

The Niche
Laying the Foundation

What's Your Name, Private?

If you're reading this you want to be a blogger. Maybe you're working a full-time job that is ultimately unfulfilling to you, and during your free moments you're musing about something entirely different. Or you're a journalist who wants to get in on the blogging revolution, and you've discovered a niche with little or no competition thus far. Or maybe you read a lot of blogs, consistently convinced you could do a better job yourself. Or you're working on becoming an expert in a specific field and you need a body of work that you can point to in meetings. Bam! You're on the road to conceiving a blog.

Many blogs exist because a fan or expert is tired of reading wrong things written about his or her topics of interest. While in the old days you would call these people "crackpots," now they are called bloggers. However, you're going to perform this service considerably more intelligently and intelligibly than some old-timer railing against the government in the editorial pages. You're going to cover the story using your unique point of view and skill set.

So what are you up against? What is blogging? What is a blogger? And, most important, how can you become one?

Blogging is journalism on a thirty-minute deadline. That's the easiest way to explain it. While there are all sorts of blogs online, the best ones cover news and cover it quickly, adding a bit of fun, quirk, or extra information. **Blog posts can also be reviews, essays, infographics, and the like, but if you're covering a niche you need to be fast, right, and readable.**

A blogger is a journalist. To say otherwise is to demean a medium that has fought long and hard for a place at the media table. The best bloggers run circles around "professional" journalists.

Blogging is still the domain of the dedicated amateur. Let no one tell you differently—blogging is run by the little guy. Sure there are big blogs, but they are most often written by folks who are just starting out in the writing business. There's a difference between an amateur and *amateurish* work, however. Amateurs grow and change and improve, and that's what we're here to do: to help you move from beginner to expert in a few steps, and to make sure you understand that dedication, hard work, and drive are all you need to become a successful blogger.

If you're currently blogging, describe what you're blogging about in one complete sentence. It should be unerringly simple. If you're blogging about technology, you'd write, "I cover mobile phones with an emphasis on devices for older Americans." If you're writing about romance novels, you'd write, "I blog about romance novels set in historical time periods and with a strong heroine." You'll notice the level of focus you should have in your blogging experience. You are an individual writing about a certain topic with a certain expertise. If you're an older technology blogger, write for your age group. If you're a mother, write about bicycling for moms. The key here is *niche* or, if you're thinking in terms of old media, a premise.

You don't have to stick to the premise throughout your career, but, on your first day at the keyboard, this premise should be the first thing on your mind. Think "I'm a blogger who writes for left-handed philatelists who collect Mauritanian air mail stamps" rather than "I write about cool stamps."

These niches don't have to be ephemeral, either. You can cover the war in Syria. You can cover terror plots in the news. You can cover bioscience. You can cover diseases. Anything is fair game.

We'll discuss this in depth further on, but our goal now is to find your focus. What do you write about? What are you passionate about? What topic will carry you along through the trials and tribulations that come with blogging?

If you haven't started blogging yet, you're actually lucky. So far, your blog is only the germ of an idea, and what you're doing right now might not feel important. That is not true. Whether you realize it or not, right now, you're doing the most vital work that will ever be done for your blog: that is, you're choosing the direction the site will take from now on. You're carving out the niche for your blog, and what you decide now will ultimately determine whether your work will be successful.

What do you need to be a good blogger? Besides the technical equipment, you'll need to possess a way with words and, more important, perseverance. The Internet is littered with dead blogs that had little of those two characteristics. Of the millions of blogs currently in existence, many are dormant, many are unread, and many are just plain bad. Our goal, in short, is to help you avoid the pitfalls many bloggers fall into, and in the process, make a little—or a lot—of money doing what you love.

You must define your goals before beginning a career in blogging. Do you want to make money? Do you want recognition? Do you want to research a topic? Do you want to become an expert? Your answer should be a permutation of any of the aforementioned questions. Perhaps you are a researcher who wants to find a new job by becoming an expert in a new field. Perhaps you are tired of the grind and want to expand out of your cubicle. Maybe you're looking to improve your private consulting operation by becoming well-known in your profession. Perhaps you just graduated with a journalism degree and you don't want to live at home. Before we go any further, write down your goal. This is of utmost importance, young blogger, and will guide your career.

What the Heck Is Blogging?

Blogging at its most basic level is the keeping of an online journal. At its most transcendent, however, a blog encompasses the journalism every nonfiction writer aspires to, an achievement this book will help you embrace.

A *blog* is a website that's organized in usually short articles called *posts*. Don't call the articles themselves "blogs"—if you must put the word "blog" in there, call them blog posts. The newer entries are always placed at the top, while older entries scroll down as each new one is added. As time passes, your readers encounter each story laid out in this reverse chronological log format.

Why is it called a blog? A writer and programmer named Dave Winer created the first "web log" when he built a site called Scripting.com. The site featured the reverse chronological (newest stories first) arrangement. A web log, then, would be similar to a captain's log—a place to store snippets of information. Winer's idea quickly became known as a *weblog*, a term that has since evolved into its shortened and most familiar form, blog.

Winer created a basic system for distributing his ideas about programming and hardware, and incorporated something called Really Simple Syndication or RSS, allowing readers to access his posts from programs called *newsreaders* (we'll talk about those in Chapter 5). This, in a sense, divorced the blog from the website on which it was hosted. Blogs themselves have become part of many static websites and are now a way for developers and CEOs to send little missives from inside a company or organization. In fact, organizational blogs by Google and Apple have replaced many official news repositories. Blog posts have quickly replaced staid, boring press releases on corporate sites—a welcome change.

True blogging did not take off until a Silicon Alley (New York City's answer to California's Silicon Valley) rivalry began between Nick Denton, a former *Financial Times* journalist, and Jason Calacanis, the publisher of *The Silicon Alley Reporter*. Denton began a site called *Gawker* and focused on New York gossip. When that site grew popular, he expanded his empire, starting a technology and gadget site called *Gizmodo*, where both your humble narrators began their blogging careers in the mid-2000s.

At the same time, Calacanis was creating a rival blog network called Weblogs, Inc. His goal was to saturate the market with niche blogs written by low-paid but dedicated editors. Both companies grew out of the ashes of the dot-com bust, and both publishers found themselves with a surfeit of talent. Calacanis, however, poached one of Denton's writers to start *Engadget*, and when Weblogs, Inc. was sold to America Online, the first blogging millionaires—and the first blog rivalry—was born.

Weblogs, Inc. and Gawker Media were the first to meld content management, advertising, and cheap labor to create a blog network designed, through synergistic linking, to build traffic. In fact, it can be argued that Weblogs, Inc. and Gawker Media were the first sites where "traffic" was a main concern, in contrast with the years preceding the founding of these organizations, when media operations saw the web as, at best, a distraction.

Gawker Media, and to an extent, Weblogs, Inc., defined a methodology and style that critics excoriated and eventually adopted. The goal of the blog was a stream of content so overwhelming that it required frequent updates. This was coupled with a conversational style that spoke of "outsider" journalism, a suggestion that the writer was in a beleaguered underclass, not beholden to the vagaries of the entrenched media. This plan worked well for years until, of course, blogs became entrenched media.

The entrenchment reached a fever pitch in September 2010, when America Online went on a buying spree. It first extended its reach by spending about $40 million to buy Michael Arrington's *TechCrunch* (including *CrunchGear*, the site John Biggs was editing at the time). A mere five months later, it acquired the jewel in its New Media crown, the #1 blog in the world, *Huffington Post*, for $315 million in cash. In a matter of less than a half a year, AOL, a former laughingstock of the tech world that became known for mailing millions (billions?) of useless CDs to countless mailboxes throughout the world, was back on top as the world's blogging juggernaut.

If this is all too "inside-baseball" esoteric, rest assured that it's important to understand who the major players are in this space and how they operate. You can learn a great deal, for example, about how *The Verge* covers a technology press conference or how *Politico* handles an election. If there is one rule to live by, however, it's this: **Everything about blogging is being made up on the fly**. As successful as these sites are, there are few "best practices" to follow, and the ones that exist we will outline in this book. Blogging has moved far too fast to codify any sort of "style guide" or list of do's and don'ts, which is why we decided to write these chapters.

Although there are plenty of more popular blogs these days, sites like *Gawker* and *Gizmodo* defined an entire genre of writing—a snarky, New York–centric voice that speaks to both the experts in technology, media, and sports and the dilettantes. Great bloggers are good at making readers feel like they are part of a privy conversation full of gossip, lore, and insider knowledge. Anything less and you're basically reading a newspaper clipping. Many of the same bloggers who began at *Gizmodo* are now heading up major blogs elsewhere. The talent pool that came out of these early years is still controlling the web.

Calacanis and Denton got rich with their blogging empires, but this is not to say everyone involved in those early years of blogging got rich quick. There were plenty of bloggers—millions—who made absolutely no money and accomplished nothing. This book will give you the tools to avoid that frustrating fate.

However, by taking the Denton/Calacanis model and expanding it, many blogs have found their niche and discovered a potent advertising model. The result? **In less than a decade, a new medium was created.** The most exciting part of this revolution is the way it's harnessed the immediacy of the web, and given a voice to those who might not have had such an opportunity a mere ten years ago.

Think about it: At the turn of the century, the majority of people had no far-reaching voice to reach the masses. They could try to be published in journals or magazines. Their quests for stardom were often driven through attempts at being in the "it scene" or sending out demo tapes to bored A&R men. Now, however, the average Joe or Jane (or Justin or Jenna) can become an Internet sensation overnight. Bloggers are brought on as experts in mainstream news programs, and blogs often force mainstream journalists to get off their duffs and actually research a story. For instance, a blogger broke the Bush-Gore recount, and blogs helped aggregate the Afghan War documents released by Wikileaks. Now, even more stories are broken on Twitter, which is tightly intertwined with blogs, as well as Facebook, big media websites, and newscasts. Blogging is still a new medium, and it's competing with the big guns of media. All media are using Twitter and Facebook to drive traffic to sites and blogs, breaking big stories. And it's all happening in fast motion compared to a few short years ago.

The blog is a powerful medium when used correctly. Blog formats give writers tremendous flexibility. That means you can be your own boss and write about anything you want. It's all in your hands, but you can't just write at random. Your goal is to introduce your readers to the most compelling topics in your world at that moment, and then bring your own unique insights to those topics. Add more facts you've found elsewhere in your world, or blurt out those nagging notions you have rattling inside your head. Mix in some of your own perspectives that readers might not have ever thought of on their

War Stories   Old News vs. New Media

News organizations are still floundering in the shoals of misunderstanding and assessing new ways of selling content in a world where content is free. Blogging is changing the way we think about news and opinion, and it's moving eyeballs away from established news sites and toward upstarts. This, then, is the opportunity for you to capture–and it's also the juggernaut you're up against. Even as they deride the blog revolution as the work of amateurs piggy-backing on their expensive content, media organizations are trying desperately to copy the magic that defines many of the biggest and best blogs in the world. They will, in short, fail, for a few simple reasons.

First, most news organizations are "too big" or at least entrenched in an older newsroom mentality. We will discuss this mentality–and its usefulness–in later chapters, but as it stands large news organizations don't have the flexibility to mix fact, opinion, and original reporting in a way that tracks with their original mission. This could obviously change–and it will over time–but until it does, there are many blind spots to take advantage of in the blogosphere.

One prominent example of a news organization's attempt to embrace new media was *The Daily*, produced by News Corp. and created as the world's first well-funded online-only news magazine/newspaper (think of it as *Newsweek* meets a tabloid newspaper). Rupert Murdoch invested $30 million in *The Daily's* creation and maintenance. Configured like a walled garden behind a paywall, it wasn't accessible from the web. Murdoch is an old-school thinker, determined to collect a fee for any content he creates.

It was a failure. Why? Because the market it tried to grab–bored bankers on Wall Street who wanted a little news with their sports coverage–was saturated. The readership usually took their phones to the bathroom at work, not their iPads. Thus a tablet-only tabloid was doomed to failure.

In short, blogs and bite-sized content spelled the end of a news organization that had millions to spend and some great writers at the helm. If that isn't scary then we're not sure what scary is.

own. Entertain and surprise them with your wit, your personal experience, and your well-supported opinions.

Researchers take note: **Becoming a blogger is the fastest way to become an expert on a particular topic or niche.** You are immediately seen as someone in-the-know, and with a big enough audience, you can turn that experience into ad dollars, a book contract, or simply a completed thesis. **Most popular blogs were created by writers who wanted to share what they knew.** Just ask Steve Huffman and Alexis Ohanian, founders of Reddit. They thought there were so many sources of information on the web that somehow it all needed to be aggregated into one place. "It seemed like the Internet was going to need a new front page," said Alexis Ohanian. "Because content was being created, even back in 2005, by such a broad array of sources."

Steve Huffman said the two college seniors decided to combine the mechanisms of Delicious, which had the most popular content on the web, and Slashdot, which had a knack for finding high-quality content. The combination of quality and popularity would prove itself to be worthy of being called the new front page of the web. Huffman and Ohanian created something that didn't exist before, a site that the web needed in the worst possible way. That's what you need to do with your blog. Identify a niche—an idea or topic or service that people need, but they don't even realize it yet. Fill that niche, and you will be a success.

What Is a Blogger?

Let's get a handle on what bloggers really are, and what they actually do. Are they stars, journalists, dilettantes, rabble-rousers, hacks? Yes, but not all at the same time. They're mavens, critics, opinion leaders, and inciters of riots. Some are whiners and complainers, naysayers and contrarians. Some are lovers, others are fighters; many are both. But before they can earn any of those labels, first of all, they must be **filters**. The best bloggers are able to sift through enormous volumes of information every day, and pick out the few shiny nuggets that will fascinate their readers. Bloggers know where to find the best stories, and who to ask that all-important question, "What's up?" They know how to filter out topics that are of no consequence, and zero in on those that will grab attention. Even if you are the greatest writer in the world, if you choose topics no one cares about, you will have few readers. The bottom of traffic lists of the world's most popular websites are populated by many great writers who have no idea what their readers want.

The closest analogy we've been able to find for a blogger to a real-world professional—and this is not to say that blogging cannot be a job—is that of a wire reporter. In the old days, the news wires supplied a steady feed of information to readers around the world and almost everything of import was reported over them. Ironically, with the rise of blogging, wire reporting actually makes up most of the content that appears in daily newspapers, and thanks to reduced staff sizes and budgets, many papers are going online-only. It is online, where the price of paper and ink is immaterial, that a news organization can really shine—or flop.

Bloggers are also editors or, if you want to stray from journalistic terms, curators. Just as a magazine needs someone to pick out the stories that appear in its pages, bloggers select the stories that will appear in their feed. Much has been said about bloggers "copying" other news stories. This is not true. At worst a blogger will cut out a paragraph from another story and add a bit of commentary. At best, a blogger will make a story his or her own. Better yet, a blogger will write his or her own story that will guide the conversation. This is done by news organizations all the time: One magazine or newspaper will release an exclusive, and hundreds of other organizations will "report around" the original story, publishing their own angles. Read any of the best news sources—the news is usually old. It has been reported elsewhere and expanded by a reporter.

Then we have the second statement: that bloggers are not journalists. To suggest that bloggers steal and newspapers "report" is disingenuous, especially considering the budgets and manpower available to both organizations (read "none" and "decades of talent and hundreds of individuals dedicated to the newsgathering profession"). This isn't to say that bloggers have license to be sloppy. On the contrary, bloggers have the time and energy to get things right, interesting, and well-phrased—and they have an endless amount of space in which to tell their story.

Blogging gives you a chance to show your readers everything you know (and expose everything you have yet to learn) about your topic of choice, but that's just the beginning. Immediately after you've published your blog post, the conversation continues when your crowd of readers responds with everything they know about your post's chosen topic. The result is a body of knowledge—sometimes brand-new—that's a combination of the topic you've introduced and the collective knowledge of your readers. When you're talking about thousands of readers, their collective knowledge far surpasses that of any one person. It's called crowdsourcing, and it encompasses so many facts, figures, and details that it can be daunting.

Our official definition of blogging: **It is journalism written on a short deadline**. If you are a blogger, you are a journalist. Soon, the reverse will be true. Just like journalism, blogging requires dedication and accuracy, but unlike journalism, bloggers in most cases do not have the old-fashioned safety net of the editorial process to fall back on. In the old days, a newsroom featured "writers," "editors," and "photographers"—we put all of those in scare quotes because most of those positions were staffed by people with no business being in those positions—and "layout" people. The writers sent text to copy editors, who fixed the text. Photographers took assigned photos, and everything went to the layout team, who then sent things to the printer. As you can imagine, the business of producing anything was fraught with difficulty, and major news organizations were large because of this long chain of command required to produce one issue.

Now, however, the blogger does all of those things and more. The blogger is a one-man band—a lone news organization. If your goal is to write about your kittens or your life, you are not a blogger. You are a diarist. However, if your goal is to cover news that no one else is covering within your niche, you are a journalist and you are expected to run like a journalistic organization. While your readership will not mention it at first, the assumption is always there: "*This person is someone whose work I'm reading because of his skills and expertise.* I expect the writing to be strong and clear, the pictures to be sharp, and the layout to be conducive to long reading." At the very least, this is what is expected of a beginning blogger.

The Four Questions

Before you start blogging, you need to ask yourself four simple questions. Answer them as truthfully and as specifically as possible. Remember: what you decide to write about is what you will be thinking and dreaming about 24 hours a day, 7 days a week. There are no vacations for bloggers.

- Who are you?
- What do you know about?
- What are you passionate about?
- What are you going to write about?

These are the four questions you must spend lots of time contemplating. Let's start dealing with those questions in reverse order, ultimately arriving at the answer to the first one.

Question 1: Who are you? Yes, older readers are now humming that song by The Who, perhaps helping them focus on this crucial point. *Who, who, who, who? I really wanna know.* To be a successful blogger, you must be a self-starter. You need to be a quick thinker, organizing your thoughts and expressing them immediately. And you need a thick skin, because invariably, visitors to your blog will disagree with you, and express their dissenting opinions in the cruelest possible way in your comments section. In short, they will tear you apart. If you've lived a life where everyone constantly expresses approval of everything you do, you might be in for a rude awakening when you start writing your new blog. Are you tough enough to take it? Do you have the consistency to regularly update your blog, giving readers a good reason to return day after day? Figure out who you are, and decide if you are really a blogger. Do you have the time? Do you have the energy? Blogging is a daily endeavor and is often unrewarding—until it's surprisingly rewarding.

Question 2: What do you know about? Expertise gives you an enormous head start over any competitors. For example, if you can identify any phone on sight, and you know the model numbers of each of the 3,997 Android phones available when we wrote this (no kidding, according to David Pogue of Yahoo (and formerly *The New York Times*); www. nytimes.com/2013/08/07/technology/personaltech/the-moto-x-from-google-iphones-latest-challenger.html), you're going to be way ahead of hapless competitors who've decided to write about smartphones and are knowledgeable only about the one they happen to possess. You're the one who should be writing about smartphones. If you don't know more about a topic than almost all your readers, what exactly do you plan to bring to the conversation? In an ideal situation, your own wealth of knowledge and personal experience will be enlightening for your readers. If you have neither, you might want to either learn everything there is to know about your topic, or choose another.

Your expertise can be wildly obscure. There is room for everything on the Internet. If you are a radio technician, don't be afraid to write about your career. If you're a horse breeder, share with your readers your experiences with the stallions on your ranch. If you've discovered parenting tips that no one's ever attempted but you've seen working wonders, you might strike gold with your own mommy blog. If you love to cook ancient Hungarian recipes, perhaps you can find a niche writing about your paprika experiments. Do you love raising huge goldfish? I assure you there is someone out there who wants your input. Someone somewhere will want to know something about what you do.

This is especially true if you run a business—by adding a blog to your business home page you can quickly and easily create a captive audience of people who want to hear what you have to say. For example, Northern Brewer (NorthernBrewer.com), a brewing supply company in St. Paul, Minnesota, created a blog and video podcast based on brewing. With a camera and a little free time, the company's bloggers built "Brewing TV," giving them a way to share their point of view and expertise with their customers. In fact, it's smaller organizations that benefit most from the existence of a personal blog. While we have decided not to focus on "corporate blogging" in this book, understand that the techniques and attitudes we espouse here are applicable to almost any situation in which an expert wants to get his or her point across.

If we want to stress anything in this section, it's that "general" blogs rarely work. If you have incendiary political opinions, for example, focus on one aspect of policy that interests you most. Do you love to travel? Focus on one area of the world or one state. Do you like to collect stamps? Focus on rare and odd stamps that may keep a reader coming back for more. The goal here is to reduce and focus your target and ensure that all of your content will be readable and understandable, and contain enough context to hook new readers and satisfy the whims of fans.

"Topic" blogs—like a general blog on watch collecting or amateur flying—can succeed simply because you may need to expand your news gathering to find enough content for daily posts. However, the more focused the better. Instead of a "watch" blog, why not outline your own collection of quartz watches from the 1980s while bringing in interesting news about other 1980s watch brands? Until you're comfortable, think small, not big. **Think niche.**

Question 3: What are you passionate about? No matter how good your writing is, it will lack that fascinating spark if there's no passion underneath. Write about what you love, and about what you know. If you've decided to write about politics, for example, make sure you're someone who lives, eats, sleeps, and breathes politics. When there's a big political story breaking, do you immediately have a strong opinion about it? Do you start gritting your teeth with anger before you've finished reading the first story you've seen about it? Do you talk to everyone you know about the story, finding out everything there is to know about the topic, and then fume over each development with which you disagree? Does it make you angry to think about certain aspects of politics? Does it dominate your thoughts? That's passion. That's the engine that can drive day after day of writing, asserting your opinions, and ultimately setting yourself apart from all the others.

You'd better be in love with your topic of choice. There is no other way to succeed. If you're bored or distracted by other hobbies and you allow your blog to languish, you're essentially throwing away sweat equity. The longer you run a blog and the more you update it, the better the chance you'll succeed. For instance, if you're only mildly interested in birdwatching, don't start a birding blog. However, if you live for birdwatching, treat the blog as an extension of your hobby. Grow your blog along with your hobby and become an expert in your field. Your readers will be able to sense that you're growing with your passion and you're expanding into new territory as you become more comfortable with the topic.

If you're not writing about something you're passionate about, you're going to run out of steam. In our experience, the best blogs are about one specific topic. Niche blogs are far more valuable and will gather more readers than general interest sites. Instead of creating a tech blog, focus on an aspect that interests you and that you have experience with. Are you a frequent business traveler? Why not write about the indignities and pleasures of various aspects of your travels? Do you like cellphones? Focus on one manufacturer or carrier. Covering too much too soon ends up in frustration and will overwhelm a beginning blogger.

Focus on a niche that you can write about daily and with great intensity. There are plenty of blogs already, and making yourself stand out is of utmost importance. You are creating a place for yourself on the Internet, and by updating this place regularly you will encourage an audience and a potential source of income.

Don't think of yourself as a news source. You are not *Reuters* or *The New York Times*. You're a single person with an obsession, and we're going to tell you the best way to have fun and get noticed with that obsession.

The best blogs are explorations. Most major bloggers began their sites in an effort to learn more about a topic. Michael Arrington of *TechCrunch* started his site to gather information about potential investments. Many political blogs began as personal blogs that morphed into public commentary. Watch bloggers like Ariel Adams of *ABlogToWatch*.com started their sites to educate a potential audience on the vagaries of the watch world and to learn quite a bit in the process. Through dedication, all of these bloggers turned a labor of love into a source of income.

Question 4: What are you going to write about? Now that we've gotten the metaphysical out of the way, let's focus on the concrete. Answering the three previous questions will help you get close to answering this last and most crucial of our quartet of questions.

Being passionate about sports does not make you a good candidate to write a general sports blog. Instead, focus on the sport or team that most excites you. Focus your energy instead of dispersing it willy-nilly. The question is what *specifically* do you want to write about?

Spend a few days poking around the web, and if you find a blog that covers exactly the same topic you've chosen for yourself, that doesn't mean you should give up and consider another. Study those blogs that are similar to what yours will be, and learn. What are they doing wrong? Why are they successful? Another important point to consider: Is there a glut of blogs covering your chosen topic? If the market is already saturated, it will be that much more difficult for you to stand out above the rabble. Once you've extensively researched the competition in the area you're considering, think of a unique angle your blog could take on the topic. Will you be able to bring a fresh perspective to the conversation? Choose your topic carefully, and half your battle will already be won.

Does this mean you always have to blog on the same topic forever? Absolutely not. Your site can expand and grow as you grow as a writer. Our goal here is to give you a chance to succeed on a smaller scale while expecting big things in the future.

Once you've answered these questions, you need to understand some fundamental rules about blogging.

The Two Rules

Ignore these two rules at your peril. Understand that blogs take on a life of their own, and if your goal is to blog to make money, or you are blogging as an extension of your interests or job, these two rules—part of what we would call a "blogging plan"—are absolutely paramount. Blogging is a job. It may be your second job, but it is a process that takes hard work and discipline. We have been blogging for a decade, and it's a constant struggle as well as a source of constant reward. Our days begin at 8 a.m. and end whenever the last news item flickers across our screens.

Rule 1. Always Be Blogging

The best blogs are updated daily, if not hourly. There is nothing worse than a ghost blog, a site that seems to be updated sporadically at best. Readers are becoming experts at sensing the freshness of content. If you leave your blog sitting for weeks at a time with no new posts, they'll catch on quickly and your audience will migrate elsewhere.

Keep posting! What do you mean, there's nothing to write about today? Of course there is! Some finely targeted niches won't have something to write about every hour, but there's always something going on that would interest your readers each day. Your goal is to be the person "in the know" about all things involved in your topic. If you truly love what you're writing about, you won't have any problem writing something at least daily. If you find you're having trouble, you may be facing a serious problem in your choice of topic. There is no topic too mundane that you can't pull a post out of it. Can't find news? Post some pictures from a recent activity related to your topic. Talk about what other bloggers in your niche are doing. Prepare a round-up of news from other sources.

Your posts don't always have to be news. They can be a personal story, a reaction to the news of the day, or a simple link to another site with information you enjoyed. However, if you find yourself getting lazy and failing to post, you've broken the first cardinal rule of your blogging plan.

However, don't fall into the "personal blog post" trap. Don't tell the story of your problems at the DMV or your relationship issues. Don't tell us what you had for dinner last night (unless you're a food critic), or fill us in on every detail of that dream you had last night. Don't spring your heartfelt musings on your unsuspecting audience. But if you can somehow creatively weave some personal experience into your posts, that could be the very thing that makes the story yours.

Lacking inspiration? Create a calendar for yourself and a to-do list. Add items to the to-do list as you think of them and then add them to the calendar. These "evergreen" post ideas can be published at any time. If you find yourself frustrated or facing the dreaded writer's block, simply go to this list of items you haven't gotten around to yet and do one.

That doesn't mean you'll have to sit in front of your computer 24 hours a day. A lot of blogging is thinking, observing, and discovering a fresh angle on a topic that's already been covered elsewhere. If you keep your blog top-of-mind, you'll find yourself coming up with ideas wherever you go. Who knows where you'll find inspiration? Beethoven went for daily walks, and heard a bird singing the first four notes of his *Fifth Symphony*. Occurrences, people, objects, and new experiences that have great potential to be turned into blog posts are everywhere, and it's up to you to tease them out, write about them, make them interesting, and grab your readers with them.

Rule 2. Find Your Voice but Don't Forget the Rules of Language

What sort of voice will your blog have? You want readers to become familiar with the way you do things, the way you express yourself, and the way your blog is laid out. Do you want to do long posts, daily? Many short posts each day? Digests of news with simple links? Videos? Lots of pictures? Podcasts? There's a variety of ways to build a blog, and most of us would choose a scattershot approach to posting daily. However, if you find you enjoy writing longer posts, you may want to stick with that style. It gives your readers plenty to chew on on a regular basis, and you can still add shorter posts in between. Establish your style at the beginning, and keep it consistent.

Having a style doesn't mean you have to be snarky, mean, or silly. It means you need to be clear and concise, and you need to stand out in a vast sea of "me-too" content. Be the person people link to when they want to prove a point. Be the expert other experts trust when it comes to matters of technical accuracy. Pride yourself on a consistent and readable style. And make it sound like you.

However long your posts will be, it's most important to decide on a writing style. Will you embrace vulgarity with your site, cussing like a sailor in every sentence, or will you be prim and proper? Will you attack your topics with sarcasm and aggressive humor, or will you play it straight? Will you have a happy, carefree, and uplifting approach, or will you incite your readers to share your anger? Will you find a way to be different, standing out from the crowd of blogs blanketing the earth with your dazzling insights?

Maybe you're funny. However, comedy, as they say, is hard. One of the pitfalls we've seen in new bloggers attempting a snarky style is the descent into meanness for meanness's sake. When you focus on a topic with any intensity, you "go native" and allow things to affect you more than they should. The antidote to this is to write everything in a hard news style or a more conversational style. Also avoid lashing out at figures and major players in your niche. And remember, a bit of self-deprecating humor and personality goes a long way.

Don't forget to make it personal. The one thing the "big newsrooms" can't do is inject personality into their work. Sure, there are some exceptions, but on the aggregate many news sites are stale and boring by dint of their mission. Will this be a log of your experiences and opinions? Unless you're going to be simply rewriting news stories, or doing straight reporting, you'll probably insert many of your experiences and opinions into your writing. In the early days of blogging, much of the writing was a lot like the early days of Twitter, where writers would talk about everyday trivialities such as what they just ate for breakfast. Now, writers have taken it way beyond that level, by orders of magnitude. If you're a solo act, let the readers inside and bare your soul. That's entertainment!

If you're writing a blog with a group of colleagues, your blog style will need to reflect the fact that there is a group of people working together. Referring to yourself as "we" is probably the best idea here, but that's not to say you can't use the proverbial "we" when you're writing a solo blog, either. This is an important element of your blog style: Will you write as a group or as a collection of individuals? You can choose whether each post will reflect the separate opinions and attitudes of individual writers, where all the writers in your group strive to set themselves apart. Or you can work as an editorial team, akin to how newspaper editorial boards write, and speak as a group.

We've asked you a lot of questions in this first chapter, and we would suggest you carefully contemplate each one and come up with solid answers for yourself. Be honest. If you do this, you'll be on a sturdy foundation for starting up a successful enterprise.

Pro Tip   Danger, Young Blogger

Go ahead, break all our rules. Write a blog about yourself and fail to find a niche. Focus on how cute your hamsters are—we're sure the hamster-fan blogosphere is booming. However, in our experience the best bloggers have a niche, write as if they were writing for a paying audience, and offer more than just a link and a smiley face emoticon.

To treat blogging as anything other than journalism—to say it's a hobby or a self-indulgence—is to completely miss the point, and in the end, it is an insult to the hard work of pioneer bloggers who fought long and hard to gain access and respect in an entrenched industry. Bloggers are members of the mass media.

The news cycle is so fast that the only way to get a message across will be through short-form posts and the occasional longer piece. This does not mean journalism is dying—it is just evolving. We're here to hasten the change.

Being a blogger isn't all fun. Be prepared to bask in the iridescent glow of your readers' adoration one day, and wallow in the snake pit of their hatred the next when they all disagree with you. Posts you thought might be blockbusters fall flat, with no one commenting at all. Another you thought might just be a throwaway turns out to be a tremendous hit. Most days fall somewhere in between those extremes. Either way, while you're probably not an expert on everything you'll be writing about, chances are one of your readers is an expert. Take special care to get your facts straight with everything you write, because there are always multitudes of readers who are more than eager to set you straight.

After you've gone through that period of self-examination, you might be thinking that this sounds like a lot of work. You would be right. In fact, writing might seem easy to you, but the daily dedication needed for a successful blog is hard. You must summon all your energy and enthusiasm, applying a steady and dedicated work ethic to this venture. Set yourself realistic goals, and meet them every day, and you'd be surprised how even a small amount of work—applied consistently—will turn a series of seemingly small efforts into a monumental achievement.

Getting Started
The Field Guide to Blog Warfare

Before we dive into writing for your blog, first we must gather the tools to build your blog into a galactic force of epic proportions, raining down wisdom and enlightenment on all who encounter it. In other words, let's get some hardware, software, and a place on the web where you can park all that scintillating prose you're about to inflict on the world.

Blogging today is easier than ever. New software and services make it possible for anyone to create a new blog in seconds—and we mean this quite literally. If you're just starting out and you're not entirely sure you want to stick with this blogging dodge forever, you can choose to begin developing your blogging chops with one of the free services such as Blogger, LiveJournal, Tumblr, TypePad, or WordPress. Some services, like Square-Space, cost a bit but allow you to add tools like image viewers and shopping carts to your blog posts. Signing up with all of these services is free, and you won't believe how easy it is. It's a simple matter of opening up an account and picking a username and password, and after a quick email confirmation you're ready to start blogging right away.

These free blogging sites also host your files—all your text, graphics, videos, and any other elements reside on that service's servers. They all offer a blogging platform, making it easy for you to write your posts, insert graphics and video, and receive comments from your readers. Most offer basic "themes" that let you personalize your site, and after you've added your own graphics, you can end up with a site with basic structure that's similar to many others, but with your own unique graphics on board.

We will explain basic HTML and CSS for bloggers, and point out two blogging platforms that we particularly like in the next section. If you are already familiar with HTML coding, know about CSS, and are comfortable with setting up a blog, feel free to skip ahead. However, we don't want anyone to feel left out, so here's a quick run-through.

Basic HTML for Bloggers

Although most blogging platforms bend over backward to help you avoid writing HTML (HyperText Mark-up Language) code, it's not completely avoidable, nor is it particularly difficult. Here are a few simple HTML tags you *must* know in order to blog. HTML allows you to change text formatting using codes that are readable by your browser. Each "open" tag has to have a "close" tag. For example, to make something **bold** you must have an open bold tag <strong> and a close bold tag </strong>. So it would look like this.

```
<strong>Good morning!</strong> How are you?
```

Which would look like this on the page:

Good morning! How are you?

By the way, HTML tags can be in either upper- or lowercase. It makes no difference. In addition to bold, above, you can use:

```
<I></I>—Italics

<U></U>—Underline

<IMG SRC="[URL where image file is located, without these brackets]">—
This inserts an image into your post. Be careful not to use smart
(curly) quotes inside HTML tags, or they won't work properly. This is
a problem we would run into at Mashable, where the code was broken
and it was difficult to figure out why. If you're creating HTML in a
word processor like Microsoft Word that automatically turns straight
quotes—otherwise known as inch marks (")—into smart quotes, you'll
need to either turn off that autoformatting in Word or type your HTML
in a text editor or inside your blogging platform itself.

<A HREF="[link]">Link Text</A>—This adds a link inside a post.
```

Will you ever use actual HTML code in your everyday writing? Probably not. However, you should get in the habit of working with it, because sometimes things go wrong, and you'll need to get into the code and try to determine what happened. Or you often need to make quick modifications that are easier to execute by adding a few snippets of simple HTML. We don't often dive into the raw HTML anymore, but when we must, it's always quick and easy to search for any HTML tags we can't remember. For example, to find out the HTML for a bulleted list, search for the terms "HTML" and "list," and you'll quickly find the code you're looking for:

```
<ul>

<li>text</li>

<li>text</li>

<li>text</li>

</ul>
```

Many blogging platforms offer built-in word processor–like editors that include spell check and any number of easy-to-use processing tools. However, when you're expected to turn in web-ready copy, always submit a flat text file with HTML tags included, and if possible, prepare and upload your own images to your own private server. If you're unsure how to deliver your finished files, ask. This will save your editor a great deal of time and heartache.

Why should you learn HTML? For the simple reason that it is the backbone of the Internet and it is of utmost importance that you at least understand the concepts involved. It's not difficult to pick up a few tags, and it will make your editor quite happy if you come with a grasp of simple HTML code.

For example, online editors are usually uncomfortable receiving Microsoft Word files. They rarely, if ever, flow correctly into their own content management systems unless all formatting is removed. The best thing you can do is send a flat text file, completely spell-checked, and with embedded HTML tags for links, formatting, and images. A file can look like this:

```
I wrote a book in 2004 about hackers, spammers, and other nerds and
I thought I'd like to share it with the world. It's currently avail-
able on <a HREF="http://www.amazon.com/Black-Hat-Criminals-Scammers-
ebook/dp/B001KU71X8/ref=sr_1_1?ie=UTF8&m=AG56TWVU5XWC2&s=digital-
text&qid=1306850162&sr=1-1">Amazon</a> and <a HREF="http://search.
barnesandnoble.com/Black-Hat/John-Biggs/e/9781590593790/?itm=1&USRI=jo
hn+biggs">B&N</a> and is $9.99 for the print edition and an inexplicable
$9.49 in the Kindle edition. It is apparently not available for the Nook.
  The book is nine years old and is nearly out of print. It is about
spammers, hackers, and viruses, and I wrote it for a general audience
like my dad who may or may not be all that technically savvy. It's not
a How-To as much as an exploration of the personalities in hacking.
  According to Bookscan I sold 0 copies in the past few months and
rather than allow it to molder, I've decided to give it away, with
some caveats.
  MANDATORY STEP: Let me know you downloaded it. Email me at john @ big-
widelogic.com or tweet me at <a HREF="http://twitter.com/johnbiggs">@
johnbiggs</a>
```

You'll notice the most complex HTML we used in that example was a few simple links to book sites on the web. If you can read this code then you can read 99 percent of the HTML on the Internet. It's easy and worth learning.

CSS and the Single Blogger

Cascading Style Sheets, also known as CSS, is a way to define various parts of a web page using straightforward and very easy-to-understand tags. These tags supersede the common styling used by HTML—they allow you to set various fonts, colors, and text styles. Think of them as a sort of instruction manual for an entire site. They allow designers highly granular control over most aspects of a site's design.

Most blogging platforms use a file called style.css that contains all of the style settings for a certain site and, rather than modifying each file, you can simply change a CSS setting and see the style change immediately.

For example, take a look at this simple CSS from W3Schools.com, a tutorial site.

```
<!DOCTYPE html>

<html>

<head>

<style>
```

```
body

{

background-color:#d0e4fe;

}

h1

{

color:green;

text-align:center;

}

p

{

font-family"Times New Roman";

font-size:20px;

}

</style>

</head>

<body>

<h1>CSS example!</h1>

<p>This is a paragraph.</p>

</body>

</html>
```

This is actually an embedded style sheet that changes some very basic properties of the page. For example, it changes the <p> or paragraph tag, setting the font family to Times New Roman and the font size to 20 pixels (px).

```
p

{

font-family: "Times New Roman";

font-size:20px;

}
```

You could also add a line like "color:green;" to set the text color to green. Note each line should end in a semicolon. If you can't find the CSS, look for a line similar to the following one in the HTML code for your site. It points to an external CSS file (usually "style.css").

```
<link rel = "stylesheet" type = "text/css" href = "mystyle.css">
```

Will you ever need to edit CSS? Probably. You'll find that a WordPress theme is acting up or that you'd like to change the headlines on your site to orange or pink for a special occasion. This is very easily done in CSS but far beyond the scope of this chapter. We'd recommend picking up a good book on web design to help familiarize yourself with these concepts.

Pick a Domain

Even if you're not planning to start up your own self-hosted website right away, you might as well find an available domain name and snap it up now. And don't worry, most available domain names aren't super expensive, with some .com names going for as little as $11 per year at sites such as namecheap.com. Other services will give you a domain name free if you host your site with them. Go ahead, stake your claim!

But wait a second. This is going to be your place on the Internet from now on, so choose carefully. Your goal is to make it memorable and topical. We have seen too many blogs saddled with accidental and unfortunate names—Mashable.com is one notable example—to tell you not to think long and hard about what you want your place on the Internet to be called.

The best blogs have their own domain names. Obviously it won't be a picnic finding a good domain name; millions are already taken and almost every word you can think of already exists as some sort of site, be it a legitimate source of news or information or a spam blog (splog) spewing out garbage.

The best domain names are memorable and to the point. It's harder to gain traction with a site that has a made-up word for a title, and we've seen plenty. However, this is not a hard and fast rule. After all, sites like *Gizmodo* and *Engadget* took off, but if you'll notice, their missions are embedded in their names.

Think clever. Try translating the topic into a different language or try a *portmanteau* word—a blend of two words into a new one, for example, GadgetCodger.com—or a name that someone might have overlooked—FoodReviewer.com instead of FoodReviews.com. Feel free to be creative, but remember that clarity is key here.

Pick a name that makes sense to you and your readers. Remember you can add words like "review," "daily," and "digest" to implement keywords in your niche to work around the plethora of domain names already sold and in use. For example, if you like running shoes you can try to grab "runningshoereview.com" or "runnersdaily.com." Ceramicists can grab "kilndigest.com" or "ceramicartdaily.com."

Need help figuring out a name? Try this:

1. Create a list of nouns and synonyms associated with your topic.
2. Create a list of adjectives that can describe your topic.
3. Create a list of verbs that your topic is associated with.
4. Find a list of foreign words that may be familiar to fans of your topic. For example:

<u>Nouns</u>
Needles
Knitting
Yarn
<u>Adjectives</u>
Jolly
Contented
Happy
Quick
<u>Verbs</u>
Purl
Knit
Crochet

5. Put these terms together. For example:

    Jollypurler.com
    ContentedKnitter.com
    KnittingNeedleLover.com
    Also, try to have fun:
    Yarnbirds.com
    Purldivers.com

Be careful when putting together two words for a domain name. For instance, if you want your "Pen Island" site to be called PenIsland.net, you might want to pick a different domain name. It won't always be seen with those nifty drop-caps. Look at it this way: penisland.net. Oops.

Also avoid dashes in names. Popular-Birdwatching.com may be available but I assure you someone already owns PopularBirdwatching.com and you'd just be sending traffic their way. Could you also use .tv, .net, or .org names? Check for the .com first. It may be owned by a similar type of site or blog, and you don't want to risk the ire of KittenPhotography.com if you register KittenPhotography.net.

After all that ruminating, did you find the one domain name that's absolutely perfect for your plan, but it's already taken? Is there no variant that will possibly do? Get out your checkbook, because you'll have to buy your fave domain name from whoever owns it, and depending on the name, that can get expensive. For example, the domain name Insure. com[1] sold for $16 million in 2009.

Once you've decided on a domain, now all you have to do is register it. You'll be asked to pay for that registration by the year, and there's a discount for signing up for multiple years.

Even though it's received negative publicity for the odd behavior of its CEO, we've had good luck with using the service called NameCheap.com to register our domain names, as well as hosting our sites. If you still haven't figured out the perfect domain name for your budding site, NameCheap offers a handy tool that lets you check to see if your chosen domain name is available. If not, it'll offer you alternatives using the same terms, as well as .net, .us, and others.

Beyond the domain choosing help, NameCheap offers a simple interface and payment system that reminds you when it's time to renew your domain name. Note that domain names expire when you stop paying for them, and can be recycled or co-opted by another organization if you're not careful. Many sites have suffered after not paying attention to the expiration date on their domain. We like NameCheap because it sends emails when your domain is up for renewal.

Ready-Made Platforms

There are far too many services with similar offerings to describe them all, but here are a few of the most popular "ready-made" blogging services. The unfortunate problem with these services is that you barely own your own content. If the service goes belly-up or crashes, you could lose your work. While this is true of any service, hosting your own account is probably the best way to go for professionals.

Tumblr.com

Tumblr.com is a free microblogging service owned by Yahoo that allows you to create a basic but attractive blog in a few minutes. Most importantly, allows you to forward your own domain to your Tumblr account. The service reports that it contains more than 130.6 million blogs (www.tumblr.com/about Tumblr), allows you to post images, text, videos, and audio, and you can post updates via email, SMS, or instant message. You can even create an audio post by calling an 800 number and leaving a message. There are also Tumblr apps for most smartphone platforms.

Tumbler has compelling social features, where users can follow each others' blogs, much like you do with Facebook and Twitter. There's the ability to tag photos to make them easier for others to find them. However, if you have an adult site in mind, Tumblr recently made it impossible to search such content, effectively rendering its porn sites unintentionally private unless that blog's readers already possess the blog's URL.

Each post gives you a choice of video, audio, chat, or text, and gives you an authoring format and resulting page especially suited for that media type. Click the type of content you want to add, and the editing interface appears, presenting the necessary options for the content type you've chosen.

Blogger (Blogspot.com)

Google's blogging platform is easy to set up and has the advantage of hundreds of sites all over the web packed with tips and tricks to help you enhance your blog. Some say using Blogger gives you an "in" with Google, where your posts show up in higher and more prominent positions in Google searches, but we couldn't find any proof of that.

WordPress.com

This service is based on the popular WordPress blogging system. It can import content from most other platforms, and there are lots of cool plug-ins you can use to add sophisticated features to your blog. Standard accounts include yourdomain.wordpress. com access, but you can host your own domains *on* WordPress.com for a few dollars per month. If you're serious about blogging and are seeing some traffic already, WordPress. com hosting may be a good way to go.

Pro Tip   Which Blogging Platform Do I Choose?

Let's focus on the two most popular: WordPress and Blogger. Despite many similarities, the two platforms have their applicable uses.

While both services are free, the hosted version of WordPress has a modular pricing scheme if you want to add on additional services. Meanwhile, Blogger (owned by Google) is completely free.

Blogger has a deeper level of customization when it comes to CSS and HTML, while WordPress's CSS editor costs an additional fee. And unlike WordPress, Blogger doesn't have any plug-in support to speak of. The platform does make up for it with a great library of widgets, something WordPress also has.

The bottom line is that if you're looking for a great hosted service, you're probably better off with Blogger. However, if you want to host the site yourself, WordPress's open-source software, with its myriad plug-ins and variety of theme templates, is tough to beat.

LiveJournal

This service features strong privacy, letting you designate who has access to your posts all the way down to the individual post level. It is useful if you want to hide posts from some readers, a feature that can come in handy in countries where political expression could put a writer's life in danger. Sadly, posts on this service don't appear in search engines and most journals are covered in ads unless you create a paid account.

SquareSpace.com

SquareSpace offers a blogging platform for almost everyone and includes multiple features like templates, analytics, and high-end publishing features. You can host your own domain at SquareSpace if you pay monthly. In July 2012, the site was overhauled, giving users the ability to modify their sites' layouts, and create so-called "responsive" designs that work equally well on mobile devices.

How Do I Pick a Platform?

Once you have a domain chosen you need a place to put your content. For most users, a ready-made domain is more than sufficient. However, you may want to host your own site on your own server, giving you considerably more control over the monetization possibilities for your site. For those starting out, sometimes creating a Tumblr site is sufficient.

Which one is best? It depends on how comfortable you feel with the features, cost, and interface. We suggest trying a few of them—most have a short trial period and Tumblr is free—and then choosing one and sticking with it. While it's not absolutely necessary, you should also keep backups of all your work in a text file and a graphics folder in case you need to switch services. While the process of re-uploading all of that content won't be pretty, at least you'll have a record of your posts for later perusal.

Hosting Traps

Because many of the services we have mentioned allow you to assign your own domain name to your ready-made blog, explaining why you would want to host your own blog on your own server is a bit difficult. Generally, if you're fairly computer savvy, hosting your own blog and controlling your own server makes more sense in the long run, and with the right server provider, can be cheaper. However, if you expect to see lots of traffic, hosting charges could go through the roof, thereby making it more valuable to host on another provider's server. In short, there are three major blogging platforms worth looking at: WordPress, Joomla, and Drupal. All are free to download and run and have armies of fully fledged volunteer support staff who maintain the code and improve the services over time. We recommend WordPress because it's the *de facto* standard for most blogs. We like its huge plug-in and theme collections and extensive user base, encompassing 51.13 percent of self-hosted platform usage among the top million websites. Joomla is in a distant second place with 8.28 percent, with Drupal in third with 6.59 percent (BuiltWith trends, September 2013, http://trends.builtwith.com/cms).

Maintaining your own server is far out of scope for this book, but there are plenty of introductory books on the subject. While WordPress and Tumblr are free, nothing is *really* free, and blog space is no exception. While these services are great sandboxes for you to hone your blogging style and start writing immediately, you'll be doing that on a domain that's not entirely yours—these free hosting services give you a URL where you get to choose only part of its nomenclature—for example, myincredibleblog.blogspot.com. That means whatever your blog is named, it will remain a "subdomain" of Blogspot.com in this example. Oops. That will probably mean a lower search engine ranking for your posts. That's because search engines prefer sites that match keywords 100 percent over those that contain additional terms. For instance, a site with the URL gardening.com would do better in search rankings than gardening.blogspot.com. That's why those single-word URLs are so valuable.

Whichever blogging service you choose, many will place ads on your site that you don't control. Most of the time, that might not matter, but it could get awkward. For instance, what if you're writing about how the pharmaceutical industry is gouging everyone with its overpriced drugs, but the friendly blog host robot detects the word "medications" in your post and cluelessly strings ads for big pharmaceutical companies all along the right side of the page? Yikes.

Another key point to keep in mind with these free services: if your blog becomes suddenly and explosively popular—which we're hoping it will, thanks to the lessons you'll learn in this book—you'll have to start paying a monthly fee for that space on a graduated scale, starting at about $10, and skyrocketing up to hundreds of dollars per month as you build traffic. You didn't think they were going to just dole out gigabytes of storage space and bandwidth free, did you? That's right, they'll charge you not only for the files you place on the server but also for the amount of bandwidth your users suck up when they're reading and viewing your stuff.

Another downside to "free" blogging services is the difficulty of transferring your files to your own domain name when the time comes for you to graduate to the next blogging level. With some authoring packages such as WordPress, it's easy to transfer your files over to your own domain. Others, not so much. On top of that, if you've built a significant readership on one of these free sites, you're bound to lose readership when they can't find your new site.

Another troubling factor to consider: If your blog does gain sudden popularity, that means lots of other sites are linking to various "permanent" pages within your blog. Move that blog to your own shiny new domain and poof! All those links you so painstakingly lured toward your site are broken. Sure, your most loyal readers will follow you, but all those links surely won't. You'll spend months building that popularity all over again. On the other hand, your own domain name is portable, and under your control. All those links on board will still be the same no matter where you park your files.

Finally, if your free blogging service goes belly-up for some reason, your blog might suddenly cease to exist, especially if you can't transfer your files to another host. Sure, they'll probably let you know well in advance if they're going to leave you high and dry, but there's something disconcerting about knowing that you don't have the ultimate control over your site.

Whether you choose to start out on a free blogging service or venture out on your own domain from the beginning is a tough choice that has a lot to do with your seriousness about blogging, your financial resources, your confidence level, and your blogging goals.

If you intend to develop your blog beyond just a hobby, we'd recommend registering your own domain and self-hosting it. That doesn't mean you'll need to buy a server, install it in your home, and hook it up to the web. Rather, it means you'll reserve a domain name, sign up with a hosting service such as Rackspace, Bluehost, or Justhost, and then you'll choose and install a blogging platform such as WordPress, Tumblr, or many others. But if you have any doubts about whether this blogging bug will continue to pique your interest, it might be a good idea to start out with a free blogging service and see how you do. While you're making your decision, it's important to remember that the ultimate success of a blog has more to do with its content than its address.

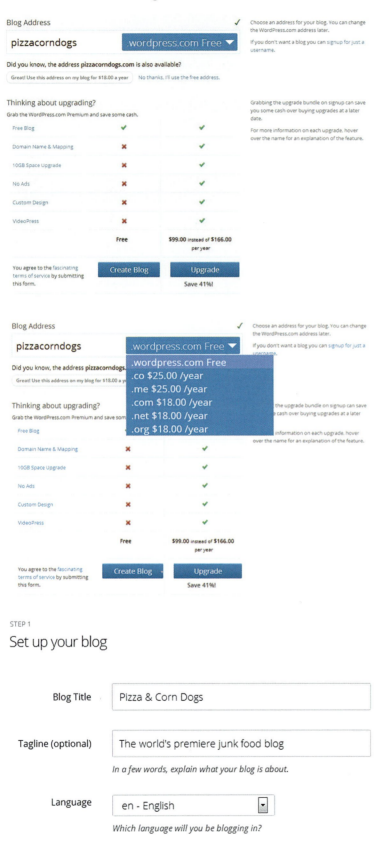

Using WordPress

WordPress is a well-known blogging platform (also known as a content management system, or CMS) that offers a great deal of specialized control over content and posts.

If your mind is set on blogging within WordPress, you'll first need to open an account. Once you fill in your email address and password, create a username. This will be separate from the URL of your blog, which you'll fill out next. You'll want to name your blog something catchy, SEO-friendly, and easy to type. In this case, "pizzacorndogs" is what we've chosen.

Now, here's where WordPress's modular paid services come into play. Through the site, you can register your chosen blog address as an honest-to-goodness hosted website (ex: pizzacorndogs.com), in addition to upgraded storage space, ad-free design, hosted video, and custom HTML and CSS options.

We're not done setting up just yet. After you receive the confirmation email, you'll be asked to title your blog, give it a tagline, and select the language you'll primarily be blogging in.

From there, you'll be asked to choose a theme. WordPress has an extensive library of free and paid blog themes, and what you choose should be dependent upon the blog's focus and your personal taste.

Once a theme is selected, you'll be asked if you'd like to further customize the theme with background images and the like.

You can also do this customization at any time through the WordPress Dashboard.

Assuming you don't want to compose a blog post right away, you can press "Finish" at any time to go right to your Reader page.

This is WordPress's social media function, in that it will allow you to follow and interact with other blogs.

But let's not worry about that right now. What you should be interested in is the Dashboard. This is where all the blogging magic happens within WordPress. From here, you can look at your statistics, compose posts, customize settings, and add paid content to your blog.

By selecting "Add New" from the "Posts" menu, you can start composing your magnificent posts. Once everything is typed up, there are some cool toys to play with that WordPress gives you by default. "Related Content" searches the posts you've written in the past and displays them at the bottom of the current post to recommend to other readers. "Copy a Post" is handy when you have a format you need to adhere to (reviews and list-based posts spring to mind). "Request Feedback" does just that; it sends a copy of the post to anyone of your choosing via email to ask for feedback.

After you're finished composing your post, you can either publish it right away, or choose a time for the post to go live. And don't forget to tag your post. Tags make it easy to organize your post by subject.

Using Blogger

Setting up an account with Blogger is about as easy as ordering a slice of pizza, especially if you already have a Google account. If you don't already have a Google account, you'll need to register with the search giant before blogging to your heart's content.

25

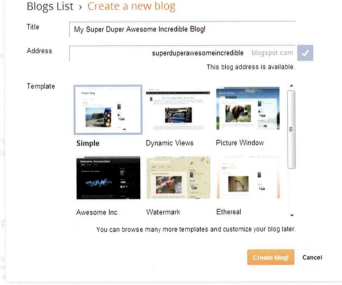

Now that the hard part is over, you're about five clicks away from getting started with your first blog. After visiting the Blogger site and associating the service with your Google account, you're all set.

First and foremost, you'll need to create a blog. It's as easy as finding the "New Blog" button, and clicking it. You'll want to name your blog something unique and interesting that sums up the focus of your blog.

After you have your blog named and a valid URL in place, pick out a theme. You can further customize the look and feel of your blog later, so don't fret if you can't find the perfect theme.

Once your blog has been created, click on that orange pencil button to get writing.

Here comes the fun part: actually writing. Once you're in the Compose view, you'll see that the now-standard text editing functions are all here. If you're familiar with Google Docs, this view should look similar. From here, you can also look at what you're writing in an HTML viewer, which can be handy.

Once you're finished with your post, you can publish immediately, or schedule a specific time for the post to go live. That's all there is to it—we told you it would be easy.

Using Tumblr

Fill in your email address, choose a password and URL for your blog (.tumblr.com extension is added automatically; as in our example the blog's URL will be stripedelephants.tumblr.com).

Registration takes you to the typical verification page.

As your new blog appears, you are prompted to create your first post and upload your portrait photo.

Tumblr guides you through the initial setup process with a stream of pop-ups (closing the first makes the next pop up). You get to title your blog and customize your page by clicking the "Show all appearance options" button.

Here you can customize your blog by providing a description, and adding a custom domain name for your blog.

Choose from hundreds of themes—scroll down for the free ones. If you don't see anything interesting, you can access more by clicking the "Browse more themes" button on the bottom.

You can preview any of the themes, and once you choose one, install it to your blog.

Your new theme comes with specific colors, but if you would like to tweak some background or font colors, you can do that under the Appearance tab.

You may want to add additional static pages to add depth to your blog, using the Pages tab.

The following pop-up facilitates the creation of the new page.

Create the URL by adding the name of your blog—for example, "stripedelephants.tumblr.com/". Provide a Page Title and type the text to appear on this page. You may also add an image using the picture icon on the edit toolbar. Check the box on the bottom to make the link visible on your main page.

The links to your custom pages appear on the top, under the blog name.

You can edit the hierarchy/order of your links by dragging the pages up and down.

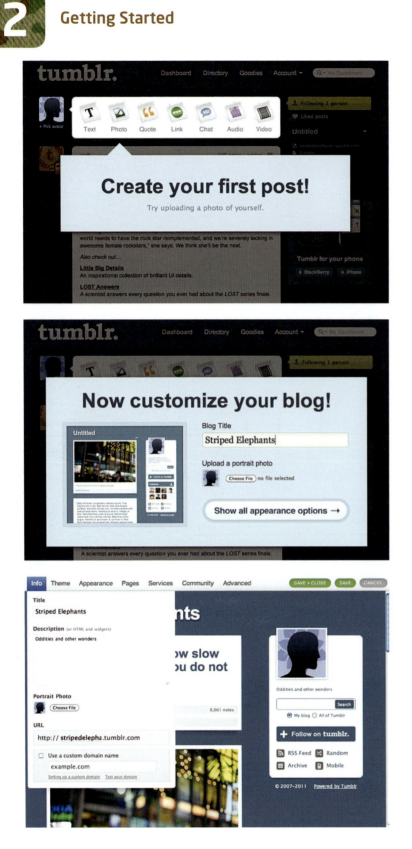

You can add links to additional social media services to appear on your page.

When done customizing your blog, proceed to the Dashboard to share with the world your first post, photo, link, or whatever else is on your mind.

You're blogging!

And we're in business.

One clever feature in Tumblr allows you to either upload an image from your computer . . .

. . . or take a photo with your webcam and use it instantly.

All of your posts show up in the Dashboard together with a thumbnail of your image, where you have an option to edit or delete them.

To preview your posts on the blog page, click the link to your page in the right column.

Why Themes Are Important

The world of websites is rife with noise and duplication. That's why you want to carefully consider the appearance and usability of your blog, and the way your readers will be able to interact with it. Most hosting platforms offer unique "themes" that give a site its own look and feel. If you look at enough blogs, you become familiar with certain types of themes that appear again and again.

Now, there's a plethora of choices, and many themes are free. Over the past several years, there's been an explosion of design for blogs, offering literally thousands of designs with which to dress your blog. Blogging software such as WordPress allows you to change these themes with a few clicks, transforming the entire site to a completely different look in just a minute or two.

Both free and paid themes are widely available. Not only does changing the theme alter the layout and style of your blog, but also themes can give you a flexible format that allows your users to enjoy your blog on mobile devices, tablets, and desktops alike. If you don't pay close attention to the structure of your blog, its design and usability, you'll be leaving money on the table.

The fastest-growing segment of your audience is smartphone users, and according to the latest data from 2012, Pew Internet found that 17 percent of smartphone users prefer to access the web on their mobile devices (www.pewinternet.org/Reports/2012/Cell-Internet-Use-2012.aspx). It's growing quickly, with 55 percent of all Internet users now able to go online with their phones, up from 31 percent in April 2009.

Pew found that many of those users are accessing websites on their phones because the smartphone is their sole device for accessing the Internet. One reason accessing websites on smartphones is becoming more appealing is because of the proliferation of much faster cellular data networks, such as LTE, giving mobile users speeds that are as fast as the broadband they became accustomed to at home.

That's where choosing a theme that's equally good on mobile platforms and desktops is essential.

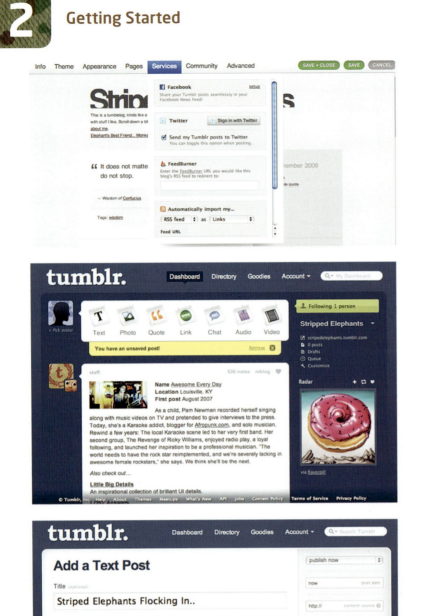

They're called "responsive" themes, where graphics are automatically sized for a mobile screen, and graphics, text, and links all work together harmoniously, as if they were custom-designed for mobile. We advise you not to choose a theme for your blog unless it's responsive. That way, you'll be certain that you'll be able to reach this burgeoning group of readers who want to access your site only with mobile devices.

Beyond mobile devices, your choice of theme is crucial to the type of content you plan to display on your blog. There are themes specifically created to display portfolios of artists and photographers. Other themes are targeted toward news sites that display multiple top stories at the same time. There are purist themes that use minimal design and put the focus entirely on text and graphics. And then there are moving, sliding carousel themes that display as much content as possible, trying to attract the most attention possible before the reader decides to click away to another site.

Perhaps you're not interested in design, and would like to go with a basic theme. It depends on your personal preference, but it's important to express yourself with not only your content but also the way it's presented. Not choosing a fancy theme is also a design choice, and can still be credible and successful. A notable example of that is John Gruber's *Daring Fireball* (http://daringfireball.net/), a site where opinions, concepts, and information rule, all playing out in off-white text over a drab gray background.

Buying Themes

When you first start with your blog, try the free, default themes that are available for your platform. For instance, WordPress has a workable group of themes you can install right away that might be appropriate for your purposes. In addition, there are countless designs available online that are completely free for you to use. Best of all, almost all designs allow you to try them on for size before you commit to them, giving you a live preview of what your blog will look like before you install a different theme.

When we were searching for the ideal themes for our various WordPress blogs, we were happy with some of the free WordPress-designed themes. They carry the additional advantage of almost-certain compatibility when WordPress updates its software. However, we're constantly tempted by some of the beautiful designs of some of the new themes, available for a fee, usually between $25 and $75, if you're using the theme for your own site and not selling it to a client.

As you browse around the Internet for various themes, note how some of them are so sophisticated that they rival the old overcomplicated Flash-based sites from days of yore. Many of them are truly unique. And that brings up another plus for buying a theme rather than using one that's free: relatively few other bloggers are willing to pay for that particular design, giving you near-exclusivity of the design. It's like buying a designer evening gown or tuxedo when you go to accept your statuette at the Webby Awards ceremony, where you'll be assured that no one else will be wearing the same thing.

Sometimes you can go overboard with a store-bought theme, where plug-ins are bundled with the theme, and the theme can't work without those plug-ins. The danger there is sometimes the plug-ins are developed by different people from those

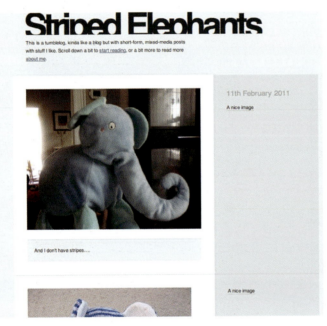

who created the theme, and if you encounter a problem with a plug-in when you're using a new theme, the theme developer might point to the plug-in designer, and vice versa, leaving you in the lurch. Another thing to watch out for is adding too many plug-ins to an already complicated theme, which could slow down your site, even if you're using a dedicated server.

Should You Hire a Web Designer?

Once you've decided on a theme, next it's time to slightly tweak it so it doesn't look like a cookie-cutter site. The first step is creating a new logo. This is where a designer is useful but not absolutely necessary. While discussion of logo design is beyond the scope of this book, remember: the simpler the better. A logo should look good on paper, on the screen, and on a business card.

If you decide to go the DIY (do-it-yourself) route, congratulations. Learning by doing is rewarding, and there are plenty of resources to help you edit HTML and CSS style sheets to tweak your site to perfection. If you do need a web designer, look for one locally and try to meet face-to-face first. Many web designers will appear out of the woodwork when you start looking, and the cheapest service is almost never the best.

Running Your Own Server

Running your own web server is outside the scope of this book, but let's comment a bit on a few best practices when it comes to serious blogging.

Your dedicated host will show you how to point your site's name to your server. Think of this service, called a domain name server, as sort of a road sign for visitors. When a user types in "knittingfun.com," for example, a DNS points that user to your server. Without a domain name, the only way for users to find your site would be to type in an IP address, a set of four numbers with periods in between (such as 192.168.1.1) that identify your computer on the web.

In general, once your blog has started to gain traction we would recommend running your own copy of WordPress on a dedicated server. If you're unsure as to how to proceed, visit WordPress.org, the download site for the actual WordPress program, or visit Square-Space.com where you can build a fairly robust website with multiple features without knowing much about running your own server.

Still stumped? Ask a computer-savvy friend to help or contact us directly. We're here to help.

Tools of the Trade

By now you have the basic concept of your blog put together. You've planned exactly what you're going to do, and filled yourself with ambition and hope. It's time to get together the tools and skills you'll need to make this a successful venture. It's not necessary for you to be a master of every one of the tools and techniques involved in blogging, but you do need to put together enough skills and equipment to get the job done well enough. Working with your new bloggers toolkit might feel awkward at first, but after you've worked with the various hardware and software for a while, your skill level improves. Since you'll be using these tools every day, you'll steadily increase your knowledge and familiarity with each, until finally you've reached a level of proficiency.

A Computer and an Internet Connection

Certainly, you already have some way to get onto the Internet. As with any computerized pursuit, the faster your computer, the more work you'll be able to get done in a given time. However, you'd be surprised how little computing power is actually necessary for writing blog posts. While you can blog on a smartphone, you'll probably be a lot more comfortable using a relatively fast PC or Mac.

Think about what kind of coverage you'll be doing with your blog. If you plan to attend lots of trade shows, live-blog at Apple keynotes, or write posts on the run, you'll need a fast laptop to handle photos, and wireless Internet access (which is getting faster and cheaper by the day) to get your posts online from the field. You might be able to get your connectivity on by using your cellphone as a modem, otherwise known as "tethering." By the time you read this, tethering might be the best, cheapest way to connect your laptop to the Internet. Or you might opt for blogging directly from your smartphone, which is made easy by apps from WordPress and Tumblr that give you the same text creation and graphics-insertion functions on a mobile platform that you'd have on a laptop.

You'll need extra batteries to power all your stuff, or if you're using a MacBook, you'll need an external battery or two to keep things humming.

If you have an iPad or one of the other tablets flooding the market these days, they're getting to be popular tools for field blogging, too. There's also Automattic's WordPress app for the iPad (http://bit.ly/1cROkWp) that's so sophisticated you might prefer using it over the desktop version. You're better off with one of the models equipped for cellular broadband data, though, since Wi-Fi coverage is not always around when you need it, especially in crowded trade show conditions. Bandwidth is scarce at well-attended trade shows such as the Consumer Electronics Show (CES), where all networks—cellular and Wi-Fi—are often so overused, you won't be able to connect to anything.

If your proposed blog won't be covering gadgetry or breaking news, consider settling for the PC or Mac you're using now. Unless you're planning to do some heavy HD video editing, you're probably okay with your current computer (within reason, and you know who you are). If you're thinking of doing lots of image editing or photo manipulation, think about getting a larger monitor before buying a new PC—a big screen has been proven to enhance productivity, and we've found a pair of 30-inch monitors to be a significant advantage when using Photoshop, writing blog posts, watching news feeds, and communicating with colleagues at the same time.

Minimum: That old laptop you're still using will probably work.

Mid-Range: A dedicated laptop like a MacBook Pro with enough chops for graphic and video work.

Ideal: Desktop workstation with lots of RAM and disk space for graphics and video production, two 30-inch displays, complemented by a thin, light laptop with long battery life and cellular broadband connectivity for the road.

An RSS Reader

If you read blogs, you'll probably need a newsreader. A newsreader pulls in data from an RSS feed and displays it separate from the original site. Newsreaders, for example, do not show the original layout of the site from which the information is sourced. This is an important distinction: people who use RSS readers may never visit a site they read in their newsreader.

This movement of blogs to newsreaders changed blogging considerably. For the first time, the content on a page could exist as a standalone entity, devoid of advertising, images, and other clutter. Blog posts had to drag the reader from a newsreader to the website and create a fan where there was once a passive consumer. Many bloggers see the divorce of content from website to be a bad thing. After all, it reduces pageviews and potential ad revenue. However, with the right content, you can force the reader to put the two back together again, creating a unique opportunity to turn a mass of "grazers" into an audience. Now applications like Flipboard are replacing newsreaders by turning blog posts into magazine articles with high production values and high-resolution images. But, in the end, we're still using Winer's original technology.

Sadly, Google just closed its reader and new services like Flipboard and Digg Reader have come to fill the vacuum. See a more-detailed discussion about RSS readers in Chapter 5, where we offer tips about picking an RSS reader and building your own feed of sites.

As it stands, anywhere you can see your favorite blog content quickly and easily works just fine for story discovery. For example, I have a list of bookmarks called Morning that opens all of my favorite sites in one window. A quick perusal of these usually sets me off on the right track.

Connectivity

In this game, the speed of your computer is less important than the speed and reliability of your Internet connection. Sending your text and small graphics to your web host probably won't require much bandwidth, but when you're looking for stories all over the Internet, reading RSS feeds, and quickly bouncing back and forth between different websites, a fast Internet connection will be a vital component of your success. Don't skimp on your Internet speed, or else your research efforts will feel like they're being impeded by a ball and chain.

Minimum/Mid-range: At least a DSL or cable broadband connection.

Ideal: Verizon FiOS fiber optic connection, or a faster cable broadband connection such as Roadrunner Ultimate at 100 Mb per second or Google's gigabit broadband if you're lucky enough to live in a city that provides it.

Image Editing Software

You might be able to get away with using other bloggers' or websites' graphics, or better yet, find appropriate graphics that you can legally use via Creative Commons, which we'll explain later in this book, but it's inevitable that you'll need to modify some of those for your own site. But beware of copyright violations (we'll talk more about this in the Ethics chapter)—many times you can get permission to use a unique pic with a quick email. Short of that, you can grab pictures from other websites and blogs and turn them into your own with your own specific style, and if it's different enough from the original, you're probably safe from copyright concerns. How do you do this? If you're short of funds, there are a variety of free online image editors such as the Photoshop-like and free Pixlr (get it at http://pixlr.com/), the excellent and free cross-platform image editor Gimp, and dozens of others that are fully capable of image resizing, sharpening, color correction, and a lot more.

If you can somehow get your hands on a copy of Adobe Photoshop, that's the gold standard of image editors, which many think is the best software package ever written. We agree. Available for both Mac and PC, it's now available by subscription for $19.99 per month, but student discounts can bring that price down significantly. You can try it out for a month by downloading it from the Adobe website, giving you a good idea of whether it's something you'd be interested in using.

There is a learning curve to Photoshop, but to learn its most powerful features doesn't take long at all. There are scores of Photoshop tutorials available online that can show you every tip and trick imaginable. What can it do for you that other image editors—such as Adobe's dumbed-down Photoshop Elements—can't? One of our favorites is its "Smart Sharpen" capability, turning fuzzy-looking pictures into professional graphics. More recent versions of Photoshop (starting with Photoshop CS5) have a nearly miraculous capability called Content-Aware Fill, where you can select an area, hit the Delete button, and make that area magically disappear. The newest version of the software, Photoshop CC, can also magically eliminate many types of lens blur. Features such as these might make it worth it for you to consider investing in Adobe Photoshop, particularly if your chosen blog will be one that deals with lots of products, graphically enhanced stories, or anything else that might benefit from pictures.

Minimum: Online image editor; there are plenty of good ones.

Mid-range: Paint.net, a free image editor for Windows, or Pixelmator, an inexpensive editor for Mac.

Ideal: Adobe Photoshop CS5 or newer.

Digital Camera

Speaking of pictures, you'll often need to create some of your own for your blog. If your chosen topic has to do with any products or devices, a decent camera is a necessity.

Your photos of your hands holding those products will serve as proof that you actually tested them.

When we first started blogging, we tried to make do with low-cost point-and-shoot cameras. It took a lot of extra work to get professional-looking pictures with these cameras. While they're steadily improving, their low-light performance is still no match for even a low-end digital single lens reflex (DSLR) camera, which has a much larger sensor and can give you noticeably better pictures without needing to use a flash. Invest in a good DSLR, and the photography and product shots on your blog will give you a distinct advantage.

When shopping for a suitable camera for your blogging adventures, pay more attention to low-light performance than pixel size. Image stabilization is also an advantage, allowing you to take pictures in lower light and still hold the camera still enough to prevent image blur. For blogging, it's convenient to have video capability and still-picture capability on the same camera. That'll lighten your load, accomplishing two functions with one device, and most cameras are now equipped with both video and still capability.

Smartphones are improving so much that you can get away with using one for your images, but don't expect miracles. You might be tempted to use a smartphone for photos or video, and some of the more advanced smartphone cameras will work for a few simple shots. In a few years, smartphones will probably be perfectly fine for blogging use under almost any circumstance. But compared with a DSLR, an iPhone's or high-end Android phone's pictures aren't nearly as good, but then, you might not have your bulky DSLR with you all the time.

Look at the difference between a product shot with DSLR compared with an iPhone camera. Notice the "bokeh" (blurred background, pronounced boh-KAY) of the DSLR's shot, adding extra dimension. With its aperture fully open, a DSLR's 50 mm lens results in a shallow depth of field, throwing the background out of focus while keeping the foreground sharp. It has an almost 3D look compared with the iPhone's results.

DSLR

iPhone

Minimum: Point-and-shoot camera you are familiar with and enjoy using, or a smartphone camera/camcorder.

Mid-range: An entry-level DSLR such as the Canon Rebel series or Nikon D5200.

Ideal: Nikon D800, Canon EOS 5D Mark III, or one of the micro four-thirds cameras from Olympus, Panasonic, or others.

Camcorder

If you have a relatively modern point-and-shoot camera, you already have the minimum video capability for grabbing quick video clips on the run. The latest cameras often have high-definition video capability, and some even allow you to immediately place that video onto YouTube. Then you can go to your computer and quickly create a blog post, embedding the video within it for easy one-click playback.

In a pinch, video from a smartphone will suffice, and as this technology improves, that will probably be your main means of video capture and upload. If your video activities consist mostly of you talking to the camera, a webcam might do the trick, and if you're looking for faithful reproduction of every zit and ingrown hair on your face, there are now high-definition webcams available for recording your rants of wisdom. For this purpose, we've had great success with the Microsoft LifeCam Cinema webcam, and the webcam built into the MacBook Pro or just about any laptop.

You want to concentrate on quality with everything you do, but with video, concern yourself mostly with the content you'll be showing. In many cases, timeliness of your video upload is more important than its technical quality (within reason—make sure the video is at least watchable). In fact, a study from Rice University concluded that if you're interested in whatever it is you're watching, you're less likely to notice the difference in video quality.[2]

We'll have more tips for effectively shooting and editing video in the next chapter, but before you concern yourself with that, assess the value of shooting video when you need to and uploading that video from anywhere. The best candidate for that might be a smartphone with video capability, as long as there's enough bandwidth available to upload its video.

If you want to go to great lengths to create professional-quality video, you'd be surprised what a great job cameras that cost as little as $500 can do when shooting video. Key features to look for in high-quality shooting include image stabilization, the widest-angle lens you can find, and enhanced low-light shooting capability. Whatever camera you choose, make sure it uses flash memory cards to store the footage. That will make it easier for you to transfer your footage to your computer and ultimately upload it to YouTube or Vimeo for use on your website.

Making matters even easier would be a laptop with a slot for the same type of flash memory cards used by your camera and camcorder, allowing you to take the card out of your camera, place it in your laptop, and immediately begin editing or uploading that video. Or consider using a point-and-shoot camera with video capability that can also upload stills and video to YouTube.

An often-overlooked way to enhance the quality of your video is to accompany it with high-quality audio. If you're planning to feature lots of video on your site, consider getting a wireless mic to capture audio, and immediately you'll separate yourself from most of the amateurs. Another way to set yourself apart from novices is to use a tripod as often as possible.

If video will be a serious focus for your blog, consider procuring lights specifically suited for video, and video editing software. You can use iMovie, the excellent video software included with every Mac, or the less capable Windows Live Movie Maker that's free to download for any PC. You can even use the built-in video editing capabilities of YouTube, which can give you simple cuts, dissolves, text overlays, and more. But if you're serious about your video, look into using Final Cut Pro for the Mac or Adobe Premiere Pro for the PC.

Minimum: Cellphone with video capture capability, or a point-and-shoot camera with video; some even include video editing software.

Mid-range: A pocket cam with, ideally, an external microphone jack.

Ideal: Dedicated HD camcorder with effective image stabilization, a tripod, lighting, and good microphones.

Collaboration Tools

If you're working with other writers, efficient communication is crucial. All the blogs we've worked with have used two methods of instant messaging—one for a group and another for individuals to communicate with each other one-on-one. In the blog world, instant messaging software such as AIM and Google Talk (now transitioning into the all-purpose Google Hangouts) is the most prevalent way of communicating one-on-one. It's efficient because you and all of your co-writers can instantly chat with each other, but can wait to respond to each other when it's convenient for you. For the group to communicate, we've had great success with an application called Campfire by 37 Signals, a chat room where everyone working on your blog can communicate and collaborate with each other at the same time. You could also use a secret Facebook group, which functions as a powerful message board and communications system that lets you upload files and pin posts.

Another excellent new way to work together on documents and files is by using Dropbox or Google Drive, cloud-based file hosting services that work on Windows, Mac, and Linux. They make collaboration easy. Both Google Drive and Dropbox show up as an icon on your desktop, and when you click the icon, you see the local version of your documents that are also stored online in the cloud. Open one of those documents, and you automatically check it out as soon as you change anything in it and save those changes. Its checked-out status is then designated by a red "X" on the online document icon. As soon as you close the document, Dropbox or Google Drive synchronizes the changes you've made with the online version. That's cool, because it keeps you and your collaborators from overwriting each other's changes. We used Dropbox for our collaboration in writing this book, and it works beautifully. Best of all, you can use the service free as long as you don't have more than 2 GB of files online (and you can get more free storage if you get others to sign up for the service).

An older yet still common method of collaboration is using Microsoft Word's "Track Changes" feature. This doesn't happen in real time like the other methods we've mentioned, but it's well-suited for feature writing, where an author is working with an editor. The editor can make changes in the document, and all of those edits are visible later, letting the author either accept or reject each change. It also lets you highlight words or phrases, and then add your notes and suggestions, which appear in a bubble next to the text. Track Changes has been a common collaboration tool for journalists for many years, and still has relevance today.

Minimum: Instant messaging such as AIM, MSN Messenger, Google Hangouts, or the text chat feature in Skype.

Ideal: A chat room such as Campfire with all participants online. Additionally, everyone is linked with instant messaging, and all have each other's phone numbers handy for those times when only texting or talking with each other will do.

Audio Recording

Consider telling your stories with your voice. Podcasting is less complicated than shooting video, and it's a way to reach your readers when they're driving in their cars or exercising. Audio recording gear is surprisingly affordable, and software is easily installed on smartphones, or even included on many. For $100 or less, you can get a tremendously sophisticated audio recording device, to which you can attach good microphones for professional-quality recordings. Open-source audio editing packages such as the free Audacity for Windows, Mac OS X, and Linux are readily available, or you can get more sophisticated with sound effects and your own original music. And you could use the free Skype software for online interviews that are easily recorded with apps such as the free Skype Recorder (www.extralabs.net/skype-recorder.htm).

Minimum: Dictation recorders can get the job done on the cheap, or you could use an audio recording app on your smartphone. Don't forget Skype for easily recorded interviews.

Mid-range: A recording device such as stereo or surround recorders from Roland or Samson.

Ideal: High-end recording devices might be overkill. For instance, Samson's Zoom H4N4 with its XLR inputs for professional microphones might not result in noticeably better sound in your final output than one of the mid-range recorders that give you "good enough" quality. If your material will be broadcast or podcast and you have the cash, look for a dedicated uncompressed audio recorder such as the Samson Zoom H2 with high-quality built-in mics and external mic inputs.

Typing and Voice Recognition Tools

The best way to instantly speed up your work, especially if you're not a good typist, is to use the PC-based Nuance Dragon NaturallySpeaking (or the similar Dragon Dictate for Mac OS X, also from Nuance) speech recognition software. Even if you type as quickly as 100 words per minute, you can probably talk a lot faster than that. The latest version 12.5 of NaturallySpeaking is so accurate that it's uncanny. Be sure to get a good USB headset mic to use with NaturallySpeaking, and you can write, edit, and then post your articles twice as fast as your slow-typing competitors.

Further speeding up typing are macro applications. Using your choice of hot keys, you can quickly type often-used words or phrases with just a few keystrokes. You'd be surprised how many phrases you repeatedly use every day, and these can be typed instantly with a macro program. Our favorite for PC is called KeyText, a $29.95 software utility that types any words or phrases when you strike your favorite hotkey combination, and can run programs daily at a designated time. This one's saved us hours of typing. For Mac, similar time-savers are QuicKeys ($59.95) or TextExpander ($34.95), letting you type a few keystrokes and then quickly pouring out boilerplate text onto your page.

Minimum: A macro program to automatically type frequently written words and phrases. Try TextExpander for OS X or KeyText for Windows.

Ideal: A text macro program, used along with the $99 Nuance NaturallySpeaking software (or Dragon Dictate for Mac OS X), which we've found to be faster than typing, and makes our writing more conversational.

Bloggers "Go Bag"

If you're planning to cover events, get yourself a comfortable backpack or briefcase into which you can stuff all your essential blogging tools. In addition to your laptop, camera, note-taking device, and audio recorder, you'll carry all of your common-sense items, including extra batteries for everything with replaceable batteries, chargers for all of your gadgets, and battery-based field chargers for those times when there aren't electrical outlets available. In case PR people aren't handing out press kits on thumb drives or discs, carry your own USB thumb drive with at least 4 GB of capacity so you can exchange photos or info with PR or your blogging comrades, or grab screenshots from demo computers when you need them. Always carry an extra USB cable. And one other item we wish everyone would carry and use copiously: Altoids, or some other "curiously strong" breath-freshening accoutrements.

Minimum: A notepad and pen, or borrow one from someone. Short of that, you'll need a good memory.

Ideal: Pack everything into your "go bag" you could ever possibly need for any blog post you might dream up in the field, balanced by the inescapable fact that you will be the one carrying all that stuff. Don't forget to wear comfortable shoes.

Forgetful? Create a go-bag checklist to refer to when you're packing. Charlie likes to use iOS to-do app Clear for his go-bag checklist.

Notes

1. http://most-expensive.net/domain-name
2. http://scienceblog.com/37469/video-quality-less-important-when-youre-enjoying-what-youre-watching/

Target Practice
Essential Blogging Skills

Now that you've gathered all the tools you need and established a place where you can start out your world-changing website, you might be wondering, "Hey, that's just a lot of equipment, code, and hardware. What soft skills do I need?" Writing talent, finesse, and the quirkiness of just being human are all-important factors that will determine whether a blog will be successful, and you need them all to succeed.

First, realize that you're taking on a large commitment. Who's going to do all this stuff? Unless you can hire a staff of dozens of people, each specializing in a particular area of expertise, you'll need to be versatile. Each of the subtopics of this chapter are the bedrock of entire careers, encompassing tremendous craftsmanship and decades of practice to fully master. However, if you can become conversant in this core group of skills, you'll be off to a great start.

Web marketers say this all the time, but you are your own brand. You are aiming to be a trusted source on fishing or dancing or onion rings. Think of this as writing a nonfiction book—for years you will be consumed by one topic. It will define you. When you are done, you will be the guy or girl who wrote the definitive book on your topic. It will define you as a brand. Just as Mentos is the freshmaker, you will be the onion ring expert.

Enhance Your Writing by Reading

The first step toward becoming a good writer is reading. William Faulkner, one of our favorite writers, said, "Read everything—trash, classics, good and bad, and see how they do it. Just like a carpenter who works as an apprentice and studies the master. Read! You'll absorb it. Then write. If it is good, you'll find out."

Begin your day by scanning your news sources (we'll show you how to gather those later in the book) and assessing the "big" stories of the day you'd like to write about. We'd also recommend keeping a list of writing topics for slow days. Read everything you can find on your chosen topic. Read forums, read news stories, read Google News alerts. Read. Your goal is to gather the ingredients for your posts. Do not spend more than an hour on this process. Don't waste time. Blogging requires an economy of movement akin to athletics. You'll find yourself sucked into multiple sources, stories, and other minutiae. Your goal is to produce, not consume.

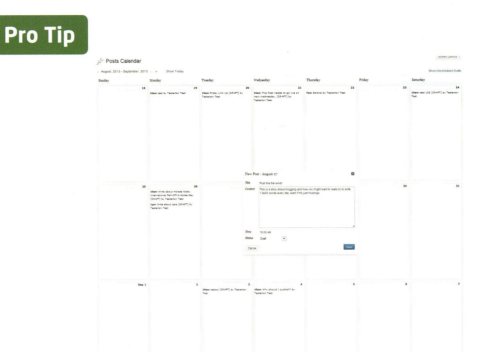

Pro Tip

WordPress has a plug-in that is a handy editorial calendar. Try it here: http://wordpress.org/plugins/editorial-calendar. However you do it, keep a written record of what you're planning to write about that day.

Unless your topic is fast-moving like technology or politics, you will be able to find just enough to write about in the hour you dedicate to research daily. **Bloggers take small stories and magnify them with research, opinion, and humor.** Take this mission to heart. No matter what your topic you will find something to write about.

Our best advice is to open a list of stories you will later address, or create a to-do list using a separate program. We use RememberTheMilk.com, but feel free to create a method that works for you. Perhaps you just want to open a text file that you constantly update or you open all of your chosen files in tabs on your desktop. Or you could place your post ideas on a calendar.

Current news stories can also be jumping-off points for your own commentary and reporting. Just because blogging seems like a reactive medium doesn't mean it has to be. Create your own topics of conversation. Some of the best bloggers "riff" on current events, adding humor and their own slant to the story. Take *BikeSnob* (aka Eben Weiss), at bikesnobnyc.blogspot.com. Rather than write about the potentially esoteric world of bikes and bike racing, he turns that world on its head. By adding humor and hyperbole to a self-serious topic, he makes it approachable.

Writing

To blog, you need to know how to write. You're going to be writing a blog. People tell us writing is hard. But don't let what happened to you in English class affect you at all. If you've excelled in the literary arts, lucky you. But blog writing is a lot different from writing term papers. You might have choked in creative writing class, but never mind that. You might be able to pump out AP-style copy on a deadline for a daily paper. But that won't make you a great blogger. Now that you're on your own, with the wonderful freedom that blogging brings, let your voice emerge.

The blogger motto is primarily "First Thought, Best Thought." Like Kerouac before you, allow the words to flow. There is no writer's block in blogging. If anything, the process of daily writing will assuage any writer's block you already have. Writing begets writing—and the more you write, well, the better you write.

To be fair, we're probably oversimplifying this, but there's a reason: Blogging is about writing *a lot*. It's also about producing videos, podcasts, and images. **It's about making things quickly and making them great.**

You'll need mastery of the rules of grammar (either by ear or rote), a knack for scintillating prose, a good-sized vocabulary, powers of observation, insight no one has thought of yet, work ethic, and a dash of friendly humor here and there. Do you have anything to say? Make it coherent, clear, concise, and accessible, and readers will come back for more.

Bloggers are journalists, but writing a blog post is not the same as conventional journalism. The best bloggers craft their text to be tight and scannable. Bullet points, pithy headings, punchy paragraphs, and short summaries rule. Readers might skip your post if confronted by a wall of text, so keep those paragraphs short, add headings, pull quotes (there are plug-ins for those, too), boldface first-words in paragraphs, in-line pictures or icons—anything to break it up and facilitate browsing and grazing.

Don't get in a rut, though, always writing lists or using the same phrases. Switch it up. Do a Q & A, poll your readers, write info-packed captions on a slideshow of pictures. Write a haiku. Surprise them! Maybe even write something crazy or weird, if your blog style permits. Predictability is death for you. The only thing predictable about your posts will be their unpredictability.

When you write, "listen" to the words as they flow onto the page. Does this sound right? Is there a rhythm to it? Listen to your prose in your head, and you'll soon get a sense of what sounds right and what just ties the reader into a Gordian knot. Or even read it aloud, which will also help you proofread. Think accessibility, entertainment value, and understandability. These are the factors that will make your writing fun. Unlike the stuffy world of academia, with blog writing there's no premium placed on making your writing *less* understandable.

"Perfection is the enemy of greatness," said R&B musician Janelle Monáe, and we agree. As a blogger with limited resources, there is no way all of your work will be perfect. You will be the source of typos, grammar mistakes, factual errors, and other annoyances

War Story

Will the readers notice if you're repetitive? Yes, some will. You'd be surprised. One day when Charlie was writing for *Gizmodo*, he decided to reuse a catchy phrase he had included in a post two years earlier, concerning a gadget whose chief function was deodorizing the air. Away he went with "Does your abode smell like the shithouse door on a tuna boat?" Who would remember that from two years earlier? Much to his chagrin, not ten minutes after he had published the post, a reader complained that he'd already experienced that putrid imagery written by Charlie, proving it with a link to a post from two years before.

that, in the end, will train you to be a better writer. After a few critical comments questioning the value of your content and your plethora of boo-boos, you'll quickly learn to proofread your own work.

Great writing goes beyond just the possession of a sharply honed skill set. The best writers pour personality onto the page, making you feel the way they feel. Tell a good story, make them laugh with you, become angry with you, cry with you. Attack their senses with descriptions of sounds, smells, tastes, sights, and true feelings. Fill your paragraphs with emotion, and touch a part of your readers that makes them feel that way, too.

Now, let's start writing.

The 1,000 Words Rule

When you begin you must write a minimum of 1,000 words a day.

Every new endeavor requires a period of ascetic dedication. Some bloggers make this their ceiling, but many make it their floor. Either way, you must produce on a daily basis. How do you do this? You can crank out, perhaps, three posts of a few hundred words each in the morning and three in the evening. Or you can write one big post. Either way, do the word count. Why is this important? Because if you have a goal, you can meet it. After his heart attack, blogging great Om Malik set this number for himself to ensure he produced quality content in a timely manner and did not kill himself in the process. Sadly, Om's heart attack was brought on by the blogging lifestyle, as well as too much booze, cigars, family history, and bad luck. It took a massive change in his everyday life to reorient him toward a saner blogging schedule, and he found this 1,000-word limit invaluable.

This word count is not impossible. It's about two pages of standard paper a day. At first, do not surpass this word count. This is an endurance race, not a sprint. The recommended dosage of 1,000 words a day is doable by the average writer, is a concrete number for you to strive toward, and is about as much as your audience can read in a day. Do not do less, either. This is a regimen. You need to get used to producing this much content quickly and without complaint. If you use one of our favorite speech recognition tools we told you about in the previous chapter, you'll be pounding out words without pounding on the keyboard. In fact, you'll find that by speaking your posts you often write *more* than you originally intended.

This also brings up an important point: Writing for blogs is conversational. Some of the best bloggers write like they're telling a story. For example, Eben Oliver Weiss, author of *BikeSnobNYC*, does two pertinent things when he creates a blog post: He first offers a bit of information about an important aspect of biking lore or current bike news, and then blends that news into a tightly spun yarn connecting the news to his unstated

War Story

When John started working at *Gizmodo* he had to write twenty-eight posts a day. If that sounds like Grandpa complaining he had to walk uphill both ways in the snow to school, so be it. But it was awful. He wrote ten posts in the morning, hit a few more by 3 p.m., and then wrote from 6 p.m. until midnight. This kind of regimen–as far from the 1,000 piffle we're proposing–was damaging and insane. Try it at your peril.

mission: to poke holes in the smug superiority of biking experts. It's a noble goal, and he's been rewarded with a book deal and great popularity.

The hardest part of this 1,000-word regimen is accepting that your audience may not appear magically out of thin air as you write. Luring readers to your writer's online lair will be addressed later in the book, but rest assured the 1,000-word regimen will give vibrancy and life to your blog. A blog that has not been updated for days is a sick blog. A blog that has not been updated for a month is a dead blog. If you do not produce 1,000 words a day, no matter what, you're risking running out of momentum far too early.

Some bloggers do considerably less than 1,000 words a day and some do more. For example, John Gruber at *DaringFireball* posts small "nugget" posts and then creates long, well-written essays on technology every week or so. Like the prize in a box of Cracker Jacks, Gruber's long posts are a reward to his readers and a joy to read. Why not do the same? Post lots of nuggets—100 words each—and one or two huge posts every few days. Or you can publish one large post every day. Either way, you're going to gain an audience if you give them something they want. **Just remember our motto: ABP—Always Be Posting.**

Now for the bad news: You will burn out. When this happens, take a break. Always take weekends off (or a couple of days side-by-side during the week if you're writing weekend-centric stuff). But take time for yourself.

To recap, keep writing. Write 1,000 words a day. Do this every weekday and leave the blog alone on weekends. Or, if there is no one in your niche writing on the weekends, that might be an opportunity for you. Either way, give yourself a regular weekly break.

The Bloggers Survival Kit: Essential Skills for Getting through the Day

Interviewing

If you can't make the 1,000-word minimum, why not have your subjects write the words for you? Interviews are a convenient way to meet high-ranking officials in your blogging world. Interview great thinkers in your niche. Introduce yourself, ask them if you can send them a few questions, and then prepare a list of five simple things you'd like them to tell you, and by extension, your readers.

Interviewing is different from a conversation, where instead of a 50/50 effort, it's supposed to be the person you're interviewing doing most of the talking. However, the two forms of social discourse have one key skill: listening. Even if you're nervous, don't obsess about your next question. Listen, *really listen* to what your interviewee is saying. Then ask about something your interview subject just said. This seems like an obvious and stupid suggestion, but it's astonishing how many people forget this easy rule.

Be curious about everything. Think about what your readers would want to know. It doesn't hurt to have a list of questions written down that you want to be sure to address during your interview, but you don't want to just read those questions off like a list to your interviewee.

When possible, an interview should be a conversation. Go down strange corridors with your subject and be prepared for silence. In a lull, do not speak. Let your interviewee speak. There is no reason to step on a thought—don't try to imitate the combative pundits fighting on a cable-TV gabfest, interrupting each other before any complete thoughts can be expressed.

Pro Tip — For the Record

You might want to record your most important interviews on an audio recorder or an app on your smartphone. Even though it adds extra work to your production workflow because of the need to listen and transcribe the recordings, you're better off recording your most important interviews. It gives you confidence that your quotes are accurate. If you get into legal trouble with an interview subject, a recording can serve as proof the person actually said the quotes you included in your article. Transcribing does take time, but it's much easier when you use a speech recognition program to repeat the conversation as you listen to it—it's an efficient way to transcribe quotes in near-real time.

Always have two methods of recording going at once. You may not use your backup recording, but it's important to have it if something goes south.

Note-Taking

You learned how to take notes in school, didn't you? Well, if you didn't, get good at taking notes now and you won't have to record audio and video of everything you see and hear. The advantage of notes over recordings: speed. You won't have to listen to that recording, playing everything you already heard once. Learn to write down the key points, and you're golden, saving time and writing your post like a ninja.

Quickly note the salient facts, pithy quotes, and your impressions of the demonstration you're attending or the person you're interviewing, and be sure to develop the skill of listening while you write. It's not as easy as it looks. If you're attending a press event, be sure to grab a press kit as soon as you can, and peek inside to see (or ask) if all the specs and facts you'll need are listed. That saves you a serious amount of note-taking.

Unless you know shorthand—which is extremely handy when you want to take accurate notes—we've found the most time-saving note-taking technique is a hybrid method using a recording and your note-taking skills. Have your audio recorder running within glancing distance throughout any interviews and info exchanges, and note the recorder's exact counter time when you hear key pieces of information. Next to where you've written the counter number, note the topic, and you can always go back later and get exact quotes and info as needed. Then you're free to write down your impressions, observations, and feelings about what's happening.

Text Editing

As a writer, you must also be an editor. As you've probably already noticed, spell check isn't going to cut it. For instance, we're reminded of a cover letter written by a hapless job applicant, starting off with the astonishing mistake, "Dear Sir or Madman." The word "madman" was spelled perfectly. Thanks, spell check!

Editing your own writing is the most difficult proofreading you'll ever do, though. You still remember most of what you wrote, and will have a tendency to overlook incorrect words and grammar. That's because there's a weird tendency to skip over certain words you've just written, not really reading the whole thing. It's the mental shorthand that makes us more efficient readers, but this time, switch into another gear—the one where you're an anal-retentive and persnickety grammar Nazi. Better for you to perform that role now, because certain readers will be eager to humiliate you later, making themselves feel superior.

As the wise Japanese saying goes, you're "too close to the lighthouse." So figuratively stand back and get some perspective. Wait an hour or so (if you have that kind of time), and you can approach your work with a more critical eye. Don't have that much time? Reading your writing aloud often reveals errors. Some writers read their work backwards, and that helps them see errors they didn't notice before. Read it from bottom to top, go to another computer, and if you must, print it to give you another angle. Cleanse your writer's palate by reading something else for a while, and then revisit. Edit! Those mistakes you catch will keep you from sabotaging your credibility.

If you're working with other bloggers or have a literate friend nearby, get another pair of eyes to read your work. They'll see things you took for granted. They'll be unfamiliar with whatever it is you just wrote. They'll make you slap your forehead, wondering, "Why didn't I see that?" If your helpful proofreader doesn't understand something you've written, assume a large percentage of your readers won't understand it, either. Fix it!

Proofread everything you write, fact-check everything, edit for clarity, add new facts, and continue to polish until time's up. If you're like us and most writers, you'll feel like the editing is never done, always finding ways to improve your writing. In fact, it feels like articles that we've written are never quite done—like many a lost football game, it's just that time ran out. So, edit your article to the point where it's good enough, and then let go.

Layout

As we mentioned before, you should know at least the rudiments of HTML. Being able to <b>old (or bold's muscular cousin, <strong>), <i>talicize, and <u>nderscore is the very least you should know how to do. Many content management systems (CMSes) also have special layout features. For example, some systems allow you to upload an image and set its position, left, right, or center. If it's set to left or right it will flow text around an image floating to the left or right.

The **class** attribute in HTML is how most WordPress themes handle image position (<img src="x.jpg" class="right">). You absolutely must become familiar with your own CMS's layout functions.

We also recommend using the "more" tag often. The "more" tag, usually represented by <!-more-> in WordPress, adds a pagebreak. This moves the rest of the content after a **Read More** link, allowing you to move most of your content off the front page. Why?

The obvious reason is to gain pageviews. But there are other, less mercenary reasons to clean up your front page. By placing a single paragraph on the front page, you train yourself in pyramidal writing and you force each of your introductory sentences to be a little bit of literary gold. By pushing only a bit of the story to the top, you are forced to think about which stories will please your readers the most and which parts of the story are most important. This also prevents huge blocks of text from cluttering up the front page. It allows your readers to browse effortlessly and find what they want, instead of clicking away from your site.

There are a few bloggers who leave their entire posts on the front page, but in many instances, these writers post so rarely that it oftentimes looks better if there is more fresh text on the front page. Generally, however, if you stick to our 1,000-word-per-day challenge, you'll have plenty of new stories to fill up your front page.

Blog Photography Tips
Photography

If you're just starting out, the important thing is to take lots of pictures—more than you think you'll need to be sure there's a good one in there somewhere—and then transfer those digital photos to your computer. Then study your results. Learn by trial and error, visit websites that specialize in photo tips, and talk with others who have learned about photography.

You've probably already at least dabbled in photography, but taking photos of products and using them in a blog will prove to be a different undertaking from snapping photos of your pals with your point-and-shoot or smartphone camera. The key to great photography is practice. Look for opportunities to take pictures, and think of photography as an art form. Constantly strive to improve your photographic knowledge and skill, and that extra work will pay off big in making your blog look a lot more professional.

You don't have to be a magazine-level photographer, but a few basic camera skills would be helpful. For starters, learn to properly focus and expose a picture, import it into your computer, and modify it for use on your website (see the section on Photoshop ahead). If you're writing about products, it would help to learn basic product photography, proving to your readers that you actually got your hands on the products about which you're writing. Get the best camera you can possibly afford, and learn how to use it, and you'll be glad you did.

Whenever you can, use natural light. Even the best-quality flash units usually cast an unnatural glare on your subject. If you must use a flash, you'll get the best results with a separate flash head with a diffuser on board, giving you more natural-looking lighting. Whatever you're using, learn to get the most out of your equipment. Before going out on an important story, test and practice with any new equipment you've added to your photography kit, and make sure you can use these new devices quickly and efficiently. Practice by taking dozens of pictures, and then scrutinizing your results. Any deficiencies will be immediately evident.

Adobe Photoshop

We mention Adobe Photoshop again here because it's the preferred image editing software, and perhaps the best piece of software ever written. See if you can get your hands on a copy of Photoshop, and we're talking about the main Photoshop CC application. We're not talking about Photoshop Elements, which is not even in the same league.

You don't need to learn every one of Photoshop's thousands of magic tricks if you want to be a good photo editor for your blog. However, you should be able to properly crop and resize a picture, adjust its exposure, contrast, and colors, sharpen it using Photoshop's unparalleled "smart sharpen" capability, and cut out objects and people, combining them with others. For instance, it's often helpful to be able to combine a logo with a person, or two products together.

If you can't afford (or somehow find) a copy of Photoshop or don't want to spend the time learning it, lesser applications, some of which are browser-based and readily available online, can perform many of these same functions. Whichever software you use, a few skills will go a long way toward enhancing any online endeavor. Any further sophistication can give you an extra edge, and you'll know how to rescue some of your personal photos, too.

As we mentioned before, we also recommend a program called Pixelmator for OS X. Pixelmator is a simple, complete image editor that runs on Macs and costs about $60. It has most of the features included in Photoshop except a few specialty commands used by professional photographers and graphic designers. An app like Pixelmator (or the free Paint. net on Windows) is excellent for bloggers performing daily graphics tasks.

Generally, your images should be exactly as wide as your blog column—usually between 520 and 640 pixels—and smaller images should be 250 to 350 pixels on the top side if they are "flowed" into the text. For example, you would have something like this if you have a big, bold picture:

Large images that span from one side of the column to another have tremendous appeal. If the product is the star, and you have gorgeous pics available, flaunt it! Splay one of them across the top of your post. Many readers are interested in the pics more than your text, especially when your subject is something they've never seen before, such as this laptop, whose maker claims that it is the world's thinnest.

Samsung's Laptop Is Lighter, Thinner Than a MacBook Air [GALLERY]

by Charlie White
202

Before you rush out and buy that ultrathin MacBook Air, take a look at the Samsung Series 9 Notebook that will begin gracing store shelves starting Thursday.

You might remember this wispy little black number from CES 2011, where we briefly mentioned the Samsung Series 9 amid a flurry of product rollouts. Exciting? Yes, but talk is cheap, and now Samsung delivers this 13.3-inch laptop that's lighter, thinner and packs a more up-to-date processor than a MacBook Air.

Origin EON17-S Gaming Notebook Ships Overclocked, Running At A Mind-Blowing, Lap-Burning 4.5GHz

by **Matt Burns** on April 25, 2011 [Edit]   1 Comment 24 retweet   f Share 5

Never mind Alienware's upcoming overclocked M18x, the Origin EON is shipping today and can be configured with a variety of overclocked Sand Bridge Intel Core i5 and Core i7 CPUs. The mad computer builds at Origin will even overclock and warranty the systems up to 4.5GHz. Your credit card limit is really the only barrier between you and a mobile powerhouse as the system can be configured with 2GB Nvidia GTX 485M GPU, 32GB dual-channel RAM, 480GB OCZ SSD, and the aforementioned CPUs. Even an optional $40 wooden shipping crate is available. The EON17-S can be ordered right now with shipping estimated for the middle of May.

Read The Rest ▷

Smaller pics have their place, too. You can arrange them like this, with text flowing around the image:

Smaller images often encourage "clicks"—folks want to see what they're looking at in a bit more detail. So if your CMS supports two views—an excerpt and a full view that appears when you click Read More—you should upload two versions of an image. The first version should be about 640 pixels wide and appear *after* they click through, and the second, smaller image should appear on the front page.

Don't Forget the Retina Displays

Now that most new smartphones have higher-resolution displays, you'll want to create graphics that take advantage of all that resolution. Graphics expert Aaron Chu, a web engineer at Huge in Brooklyn, says those high-resolution smartphones and iPhone Retina displays have at least twice the resolution of their predecessors. "WordPress users can certainly develop their own Javascript-based solution to implement responsive images, but there are also many WordPress plug-ins that allow users to optimize their images," he said. Which plug-in would he recommend? "Out of the many plug-ins, I would recommend Picturefill. WordPress has it as a direct port from Scott Jehl's original Picturefill."

Videography

You might've noticed video taking over the world lately. That's no exception with blogs, and you can give yourself a competitive edge by getting good at video shooting and editing. Mastering the medium of Internet video is not the same as becoming a polished broadcast TV producer, director, or editor. Rather than cinema-style visual effects and smooth voice-overs and sound effects, Internet video needs to feel real and immediate. On top of that, it needs to stand out from the crowd, and if you're lucky, your concept could be original enough that the video could become viral, spreading across the world like wildfire.

Aiding and abetting the twenty-first-century guerrilla video producer are smartphones and tiny cams, both so portable they can easily fit in a pocket, ready for you to whip them out at a second's notice to shoot HD video, which you can then quickly place on YouTube for worldwide viewing.

Blogging Video Tips

When to Use Video

Some stories are tailor-made for video, while others don't require it at all. It's up to you to determine when video is the only way to cover a story. When movement is central to your story, that's when it's time to whip out the camcorder. For example, remote-controlled helicopters, a new puppy, a dance technique, or a fashion show all cry out for video coverage. *Do not be afraid to shoot video.* You can always edit it later, and even if it seems boring at first, a little background music and some clever cutting can create compelling content.

When should you shoot video?

- **If you have the time.** Blogging is time-consuming, but video editing is *even more* time-consuming. If you're simply embedding video as you shot it, it won't take long to produce, but if you're getting into clever editing and quick cuts, it could take hours (or even days) to create a minute of finished footage.
- **If you're showing how to do something.** Demonstrations require video. You can show off a new device or piece of fashion, as well, using video. It's much better than describing it. Run a cooking blog? Take a video of yourself cooking and show the finished product. A bike blog? Show a few repair techniques.

War Story — Making A Viral Video

Charlie once had four GPS units on hand, and wanted to do something goofy with them. First, he set up his camcorder on a tripod on the backseat floorboard of his car. Then, he stuck all the GPS units to the car's windshield, flipped them on, entered a destination into all of them, and then started disobeying every command. They all erupted in a maelstrom of commands, bleating out "recalculating!" "Make a U-turn, if possible!" and so forth, all talking at once. He named the video "GPS Gang Bang"[1] placed it on YouTube, and 2.8 million views later, figured that counted as a viral video. By the way, we think the title helped, too. Think up something like that, and people will notice.

- **If your topic is so complicated** that only a moving demo will do. This is similar to the previous reason but a bit more important. Perhaps you can't *write* what you want to show. You'll *need* to shoot video.
- **If you're talking with a charismatic person.** If you have the opportunity to meet amazing people, take advantage of that fact. If they're beautiful (on the inside or outside), video will bring out their humanity.
- **If you're writing about an unusual experience.** Say you somehow finagle a ride with the Blue Angels aboard an F/A-18 Hornet fighter jet. Words won't describe what that's like, nor will still photos.
- **If your topic is sexy.** Literally and figuratively, sex sells.
- **If there are animals involved.** People love animals. Enough said.
- **If you're attending a historic event.** Enough said.

Ten Tips: How to Shoot Video

Shooting video is not as easy as it looks, and even though most people have tried their hand at being a videographer, few are proficient at it. If you can keep in mind a few basic concepts, your shooting will instantly improve. Follow these ten tips, and you'll set your videos apart from the crowd:

Tip 1: Get in close. The classic beginner mistake is to shoot a wide shot of a scene, forgetting that video is an inherently close-up medium. For instance, the beginner videographer will shoot a head-to-toe shot of a mom pushing a stroller. The professional gets in close on the baby's face, framing the mother's adoring face looking on in the background. Get in close, where the emotions happen.

Tip 2: Notice the background. In the heat of shooting, you're concentrating on your subjects, which happen to be in the foreground. You're listening to what they're saying, and watching what they're doing. Only when you bring the footage back for editing do you notice that distracting or unattractive background you overlooked. We've worked with pro TV directors who seem to pay more attention to the background than the foreground, but strike a happy medium here. Find (or add) pleasing colors for a background. Don't place your subjects close to a brick wall, looking like they're ready for the firing squad. Watch out for trees or potted plants positioned behind your subject, which might look like they're growing out of your video star's head.

Tip 3: Steady as she goes. Whether you're using a cellphone or a sophisticated video camera, find a way to mount it on a tripod, and short of that, hold your breath and lean against a wall to stabilize your shot.

Tip 4: Let there be light. Get as much light on the subject as possible. The more light, the better your scenes will look, so carry a battery-operated light, set up lights whenever possible, or shoot in brightly lit areas.

Tip 5: Don't forget the sound. If you can afford it, clip a wireless mic onto whoever is speaking, and at the same time, capture the sounds of everything that's happening in the scene with the mic that's on your camera. You can mix the sounds together later, and it makes a huge difference.

Tip 6: Don't move too much. Before you reach for that zoom control, think about why you're doing it. Do you really need to get a closer look at your subject? Or are you just playing around with that zoom because you can? Careful—your constant zooming in and out could get you accused of "tromboning." If you can't think of a really good reason to zoom or pan, don't. Keep in mind that directors such as Spielberg and Hitchcock have shot entire feature films without zooming one single time. If you must pan (moving from side-to-side; moving up or down is called a "tilt"), move slower than your instincts tell you to. Almost every beginner video has a pan that is so fast that it elicits laughter among the initiated.

Tip 7: Give them some headroom. Don't cut off your subjects' heads when framing them in your viewfinder. But don't give them too much headroom, either, or you'll end up with your subject appearing to be sitting in a hole with tons of space over his or her head. A telltale sign of a pro shooter's work is the amount of headroom allowed.

Tip 8: Don't shoot a puppet show. If you're shooting an interview, use a two-shot from the front sparingly. Concentrate on people's faces, shot from as close to head-on as you can get. A shot of two people talking to each other, shot in profile, doesn't resonate emotionally. We want faces. If it's an interview situation, tell the interview subject not to look at the camera, but to look at the interviewer. Then position your camera almost behind the interviewer so you can see as much of the interviewee's face as possible. After the interview's over, you can get the interviewer to re-ask the questions, and then you can fake it later, joining questions and answers together when you edit.

Tip 9: Shoot more than you think you'll need. The pros call this "coverage," where you're providing a variety of angles that can be used when you edit. For some reason, most people don't feel like they need as much footage when they're shooting as they actually end up needing when they're editing. When you're shooting a flower, for instance, stay on that shot about five seconds longer than you think you'll need. That way, you'll have more options in the edit session. Allow yourself as many options as you have time to shoot. As my wise grandma used to say, "Better to have it and not need it than need it and not have it."

Tip 10: Shoot for the edit. If you're creating a video that's more than just one shot, think about how you'll edit while you're shooting. For instance, if your subject is talking about swimming, make the effort to get some shots (called "b-roll") of people swimming, or better yet, the subject swimming. And keep Tip 9 in mind for this one, too: Shoot a lot. Every edit session we've ever done over thirty years of broadcast experience has moments of serendipity, where we think of something we hadn't planned. And that's usually the best part of the final product. Allow for these insights. Give yourself options.

Video Formats and Video Editing

Your choices of video formats are easier now than they were a few years ago. Your chosen camera will probably have a lot to do with whatever it is you have on hand, and chances are if you have a point-and-shoot still camera, you have video capability right there. The best news is that almost all video shooting equipment created in the past couple of years is digital and tapeless, and will be relatively simple to transfer from camera to computer for editing and ultimately upload to the web.

When you're done with the shooting, you'll need to learn how to narrow down all that footage into a consumable package of around a minute or two. Editing is relatively easy, too, where basic editing software is included with Macs and PCs. There are now excellent video editing packages available as apps for smartphones. You can even do video editing online, and quickly place those clips on YouTube. Just remember to keep it short and real.

Sometimes your situation will allow you only to shoot a quick video on a smartphone camcorder, and then immediately send it up to the web. But when you have more time, you could use a higher-quality camcorder that's inside your point-and-shoot camera, or even use a dedicated video camcorder for your shooting. An advantage of that camcorder capability of your smartphone or point-and-shoot camera is that you're more likely to have that device with you in any given situation. As the old adage goes, the best camera in the world is the one you have with you.

Once you get your video back to your computer, you can massage even mediocre footage into something that's a lot better. You'd be surprised how complicated even the simplest video productions can get when you're editing. After a while, you'll be using advanced editing techniques, such as splitting the audio and the video, allowing you to show someone talking, then while that person's still talking, cutting away to video of whatever it is that person's talking about. Soon you'll be correcting colors, adding way too many tacky transitions (don't do that), and inserting infographics into your video footage (yes, do that).

That sounds like a lot to learn, but don't worry. Even though the degree of sophistication you can bring to your video editing is nearly unlimited, we've found that video to be posted on YouTube, Vimeo, and other video-hosting websites works best if it's simple. In our experience, we've tried bringing in sophisticated video editing, chromakeys (where a green or blue background screen is replaced by other video or images, like on weather broadcasts), lots of graphics, and multiscreen effects, and those videos didn't do as well with the blog audience as a simple one- or two-shot video based on a kooky concept. Remember, ideas are more important than technique when it comes to shooting video for the web.

Quick Looks vs. Video Reviews

When you get a new product to review, or if you've heard someone say something news-worthy and you've captured it on video, a quick look might be your best bet. When time is critical and you don't want to be scooped by your competitors, simply put together a few video shots that cover the essence of the story, and send them up to the web so you can post them on your blog as soon as possible. However, if you're covering a complicated topic, or if you're reviewing a more complex product where you'd like to explain most of its features and give the readers an in-depth look at its capabilities, edit together a video review that tells the whole story.

Video Interviews

For quick interviews, an informal style where you're holding the camera pointed at your interview subject is probably the easiest and quickest way to go. For more important interviews, shoot with two camcorders, one framed on your face and the other on your interviewee's face, with you and your subject shot with a minimum of profile. That means, head-on, full face, from the front. This is a little more complicated, because you probably need to have two people running those cameras while you do the interview.

Because of video conferencing software such as Google Hangouts and Skype, online videos are getting easier to shoot. Now you can invite multiple interview subjects to join you on a Google Hangout On Air (www.google.com/+/learnmore/hangouts/onair.html), each of you using a webcam, and everything's broadcast publically and automatically recorded on your Google account. If you want to get even more sophisticated, you can use a technique called the "double-ender." That's where you and your interview subject can separately record your individual webcam videos, and you can combine the two shots later when you edit your video together.

Of course, these brief instructions are oversimplified, but you'd be surprised how much better your videos will look if you follow each instruction carefully. There are entire books and gigantic websites dedicated to effectively shooting and editing video, so be sure to frequent those; follow our basic suggestions here, add your own original ideas, and you'll learn as you go.

Podcasting

Podcasting—namely, recording an audio-only program for distribution alongside (or in place of) your written content—is an effective way to gain readers. Most bloggers simply need a laptop with a built-in microphone and an audio editing program like GarageBand or Audacity to build a podcast. You can then upload the finished product to SoundCloud or Libsyn, two podcast distribution services, and embed it in a post on your site. Heck, if you do a podcast we'll even waive the 1,000-word rule for that day.

Here are a few tips for creating a cool podcast.

Use an External Microphone—We like Blue Microphones' Yeti or Spark Digital because it offers excellent sound quality at an affordable price. You should also invest in a microphone wind screen to keep you from "popping your Ps" when you talk into the microphone. Look online for inexpensive screens. You can use your laptop's internal mic but you'll be surprised how great your projects can sound with a good external mic.

Add a Little Theme Music—Go to FreeMusicArchive.org to find a theme song. These songs are free to use for non-commercial purposes, but you should always credit the creator of the music. Use about twenty seconds of the music as you intro your show and close with the same snippet. This adds a bit of personality to your work.

Get Some Guests—The best way to record guests on your podcast is to record a Skype call using Call Recorder for OS X or the Evaer Skype Recorder program for Windows. Call your subject, set up a few guidelines, and just chat.

Get on iTunes—Every podcast distribution system offers an RSS feed of your podcasts. Visit http://support.apple.com/kb/HT1819 on the Apple website to learn how to add your podcast to the iTunes mix. This allows people to search and find your podcast.

Make It Short—As exciting as we all think we are, no one has time for long podcasts. There are some exceptions, but we like to end our podcasts at between fifteen and thirty minutes. There is no reason to stretch things out unless you have an amazing topic or guest. Ignore this advice if you want, but remember that people are rarely patient when it comes to boring podcasts.

Publish at the Same Time Every Week—The best podcasts are published at the same time and same day every week. Why? People love the comfort of knowing that your podcast will pop up on a certain day. They will begin to tune in and hunger for new episodes. There's a reason, after all, that AMC doesn't show *Mad Men* at odd times during the week. By broadcasting on a certain day, you create a habit and a buzz.

Note

1. www.youtube.com/watch?v=_isVdeRwnus

Hello, World

This chapter is about launching your blog. Why are we putting this here instead of after all of the other skills necessary to run a blog? Because your launch is something you'll need to think about long before you're ready to put up your first post. **Like a restaurant holding a splashy debut, how you present yourself to the world is sometimes more important than your first few blog posts.**

In this chapter we discuss creating a biography, creating a set of introductory posts, and understanding blog marketing. These are the first steps on a long journey and probably the most important.

Introducing Yourself

First, define yourself. If you've decided on a niche topic, you need to define the characteristics that make you the best person for that job. Why are you the best yarn blogger out there? What makes you special enough to write about Hello Kitty all day? Is it ten years of fandom? The ability to knit a skullcap in three minutes? If someone wanted to contact you for a short biography, what would it contain?

Remember: Once you become a blogger on a certain topic, you become a *de facto* expert. You need to back this up in your bio. Your readers will initially come to you for a few simple reasons. These include, but are not limited to, your experience in the field, your skill at describing the vagaries of that field, and your readability.

Face it: most "enthusiast" websites, while thorough, are baffling. Tech websites, until the rise of sites such as *Gizmodo* and *CrunchGear*, were almost unreadable. They were usually forums full of technophiles yelling at each other over minutiae and scaring away "n00bs" in an effort to look plugged-in and cool. However, blogging plugs *everyone* in, noob or old, young or geriatric, die-hard fan or dilettante. Your goal is to offer the reader a window into a specialized world that is at once simple and complex.

Turn no one away. Remember that today's baffled forum readers are your future blog fans. There is a lot to be said for a solid curatorial instinct.

Your goal in this chapter is to prepare a one-minute introduction. This introduction allows you to define yourself as a writer in one minute or less by explaining:

1. Who you are
2. What you do
3. Why what you do is important

Think of your bio as something a reporter or reader will use to guide his research. You need to seem like someone worth reading and talking to. Let's, then, begin with a bio. Here's John's:

> I live in Brooklyn, NY, and write about technology, security, gadget, gear, wristwatches, and the Internet. After spending four years as an IT programmer, I switched gears and became a full-time journalist. My work has appeared in *The New York Time*s, *Laptop*, *PC Upgrade*, *Surge*, *Gizmodo*, *Men's Health*, *InSync*, *Linux Journal*, *Popular Science*, and *Sync*, and I've written a book called *Black Hat: Misfits, Criminals, and Scammers in the Internet Age*.
>
> I am currently East Coast editor of TechCrunch.com, and I run the BWL family of blogs, SlushPile.net and WristWatchReview.com. I also run the HourTime Podcast with Ariel Adams.

Note these lines:

> I live in Brooklyn, NY, and write about technology, security, gadget, gear, wristwatches, and the Internet.

and

> After spending four years as an IT programmer, I switched gears and became a full-time journalist.

These lines define you to readers. The first describes what you write about, the second why you're uniquely qualified to write about that topic. For example, you could say:

> Joe lives in the Great North Woods and writes about cooking and kitchen gear. He worked as a cook for a spell in New York, London, and Beijing and then settled down with his wife and family and now runs a restaurant in Rutland, Vermont. This is his blog about running a Thai/Swedish Fusion restaurant in granola country.

Or

> Sally writes about Manga and Anime. She lives in Tokyo and has been an avid reader of the form for twenty of her twenty-nine years.

Or

> Joe is a mechanic by day and gamer by night. He loves racing games—every single one of them, from *Pole Position* to *Gran Turismo*—and will rap you on the head with a ratchet if you make fun of *Gran Trak 10*.

As you see, these are a mix of mirth and cold hard fact. Your niche should flow directly into your bio and explain why, exactly, you are the man or woman for the job.

Here's a quick work-sheet to help you build your bio.

Make a set of lists, each one noting three pertinent aspects of your CV.

Work/Educational Experience

A list of pertinent jobs/degrees

Play Experience

A list of pertinent hobbies

Location History

Something to give you character and encourage local news to pick up your story

Notable Facts

Things about you no one knows, also pertinent to the mission

Pick the most interesting to use in the first sentence of your bio (for a blog about werewolves: "Frank **has been working as a costume designer** for four years in **Portland** and loves werewolf movies"), the second most interesting things in the second sentence ("**Since studying drama at Carnegie Mellon**, birthplace to Sam Romero's first movies, and **catching the horror bug**, he has **been collecting werewolf memorabilia and costume components**"). The third sentence sums up the blog ("This blog is about his unnatural obsession with the hairy and scary").

Crafting a good bio is the first step in defining yourself as a blogger. Think of this biography as the first thing people will see when they search for your niche on Google. You are the face of this topic.

Producing Intro Posts

Before you launch your blog, you should create a group of sample posts. Make the blog look like an ongoing concern, populated with numerous stories. Many of these can be evergreen, meaning they need not be immediately newsy. Evergreen posts are sort of "freebies," features that live outside of the normal news cycle. As in our werewolf example, a few evergreen posts would include:

Top 10 Werewolf Movies
Scariest Werewolf Snouts
How Did They Film Teen Wolf?
Rrrawr: What the Stars Would Look Like as Werewolves

Create a list of five of these and prepare them before launch. Your first post, however, should introduce yourself and your mission. It should describe your mission.

Here's a sample we did when John launched *CrunchGear*:

```
Hello, and welcome to the latest CrunchNetwork blog, CrunchGear.com,
a daily journal of all things gadget-tastic. Our goal is to take a
long, hard look at the daily gadget grind and separate the wheat—the
gear we will actually buy and that will actually reach our shores—
from the chaff. Every day we hope to bring a digest of the hottest
tech stories and intelligent and informed commentary on the industry
as a whole.
   No greasy kid stuff here—this is all meat. We have a great boss
(Mr. Arrington—heckuva guy), a great team and a great mission—to bring
you the next-generation tech that will keep you connected, enter-
tained, and educated. We have a great global audience—you—and you're
the folks to whom we're going to deliver our daily missives from the
heart of gadgetopia.
   We have one request: if you work at a tech company, please add us to
your PR list ASAP. If you are releasing a product, email us a high-res
image of the device and a spec sheet at the very instant you launch.
Our press release and tips email is tips at crunchgear dot com. If
you're a super-secret spy in the house of tech, please send tips and
rumors to the same address.
   That said, let's get started. If there's something you'd like to see
or just feel lonely, drop us a line or AIM me.
   Here we go. Let's have some fun.
```

Take a look at the structure we used for this post. It is fairly basic, consisting of:

Intro—What's going on here?
Bio—Who is running this joint?
What?—What's going on at this site? How often will you post? How quickly will things be updated?
Why?—Why should you return?
Closer—Something fun and personal. This is your letter to the world.

When you start your blog, publish four or five new posts from your evergreen pile and then post your intro. The evergreen content we discussed earlier will make a great bit of "padding" for readers to enjoy while they're getting used to your style and schedule.

Writing Your Contact Page

Short and sweet is key for the "Contact Us" page of your blog. Always have a tips@[your domain] email address available to readers, and you can also include pertinent contact details for PR professionals and general website questions. If you don't want to craft an entirely new "contact" page, simply cut and paste your intro post onto this page.

Building a Social Media Presence

Now that you've got your first few posts up, you have to tell the world what you hath wrought. Social media should not be your only means of spreading the news about your new site. You can't just Tweet yourself into existence. Social media is a means to an end.

Social media has become a powerful engine for promoting your blog. In fact, if you're not tweeting and posting on Facebook about your content, you don't exist on today's Internet. It's that important. If you haven't already, you should make it one of your main missions to build up your Twitter following, beef up your friend count on Facebook, and add people to your LinkedIn network.

In this section, we will show you how we've done these difficult feats on *TechCrunch* and *Mashable*. We'll describe the tools we use to maintain our presences on those social media platforms. Most importantly, we'll give you tips for leveraging social media to address your audience, promote your content, and make people feel good about you and your blog.

Twitter

This microblogging platform has become ubiquitous among journalists, denizens of the Internet, and anyone who wants to find out what's happening in the world as quickly as possible.

Before you get started, learn the basic rules of Twitter. The platform works in specific ways that are not immediately evident. For example, when you're replying to an individual, start with that person's Twitter handle, like so: "@charlie_white, I agree with you 100% on that." By designating that person's handle, that tweet won't be seen on the feed of everyone who's following you on Twitter, but can be seen by the person you're addressing it to. If you want everyone to see your reply to that person, place one character before the @ symbol, such as a period, like this: ".@charlie_white, I agree with you 100% on that." Then it will be seen by all your followers.

When someone addresses you by your Twitter handle, you can see the message in the "Connect" section of the Twitter site on the web, Tweetdeck, other Twitter software, or one of the many Twitter mobile apps. If you address a Twitter message to two people (such as @charlie_white @johnbiggs), it's like setting up a conversation between the three of you. Keep in mind that those tweets are semi-private—if someone visits your individual Twitter account, all those tweets will be visible. But they won't be automatically sent to the main Twitter feed of everyone following you on Twitter. These are the most basic rules of the road with Twitter. Online, you can get exquisitely detailed information and advice about Twitter, and we advise you to do so before you dive in.

Once you have the rules down, keep in mind that this is *social* media, so be social. Reply to tweets that interest you, especially when you have something to add. When you initiate your own tweets, tweet about not only your own content—you don't want to become known as just a promoter of yourself—but also other articles and posts you find fascinating. If you have a sudden flash of insight, tweet it. Just like in the world of interpersonal relationships, on Twitter, to make friends you have to *be* a friend.

Join the conversation. If everyone is talking about, say, the Super Bowl, find out what the hashtag for the Super Bowl is (for instance, #superbowl2014), tweet something interesting or insightful about the Super Bowl, and include that hashtag. Reply to other's comments about the Super Bowl. Get involved, and you will be noticed. The more involved you are, the higher you'll see your follower count go.

By the way, hashtags used to be placed on every tweet, but lately they've become more specialized, useful only in a situation where there is a particular event going on, and you want to tweet about that specific event. In some ways, hashtags are redundant, because you can still search tweets and find your keywords without using hashtags. In the modern world of Twitter, hashtags are most useful when referring to an ongoing and specific event.

Sometimes, you'll be tempted to write a story on your blog, but it might be better suited to the 140 characters of a Tweet. If you don't have anything more than 140 characters to say about a topic, go ahead and tweet about it. Such a pithy and compact missive might be exactly what you need to make your point and show people that you're insightful and interesting—and worth following.

We'll have more about promoting your site using Twitter in Chapter 8.

- **Google Hangouts**—Google's Hangouts (formerly called Chat) application is gaining traction as well. It's increasingly popular with those who use Gmail. *Mashable* uses it all the time, and gets a lot of good use out of its "off the record" feature where there's less risk in typing passwords and sensitive information to each other because they're not logged and potentially accessible to hackers.

- **Facebook page**—A Facebook page is different from an individual account. It lets you do more sophisticated advertising for posts, and gives your blog a presence on Facebook that is separate from your personal account. Feel free to start a Facebook page for your blog, but don't worry about updating it at first. Without more of an audience, a Facebook page can be pretty barren. For now, you can paste links of your best stories into your personal Facebook feed (you do have a Facebook account, don't you? No? Get one, now). As your blog gains popularity, Facebook will become a powerful promotion tool. Then, you can also use it for instant messaging—Facebook's on-board chat tool is gaining a lot of traction lately. Once you begin to get more people liking your Facebook page, you might want to consider boosting posts by advertising. We'll address strategies for Facebook promotion of your posts and advertising posts on Facebook later in this book.

- **LinkedIn account**—LinkedIn is not as strong for promoting your blog as Facebook or Twitter, but it's excellent for promoting yourself. If you're not already on LinkedIn, we'd suggest you open an account and start linking with people you know. Build up your profile so all can see what you've accomplished, while promoting your blog at the same time. Once you develop a network of those both inside and outside the blogosphere, you'll be surprised how often people contact you with job offers, useful information, and serious networking opportunities.

Crystal Ponti, whose successful MommiFried blog (http://mommifried.com/) is among the best "mommy blogs" we've seen, uses LinkedIn to her advantage. She suggests that you "create a killer profile that includes who you are, what you've done and where you've done it. Make sure you include your blog as part of your resume, with an active link." She discourages linking with every single person who contacts you. "Consider each connection a link in a very long chain," she said. "Weak links do nothing to support or enhance your network or professional opportunities." Armed with a strong network, then you can post updates on LinkedIn that will help to promote your blog. Once you've assembled a network of people you actually know, Ponti suggests, "post regular updates including a mix of your own work (blog posts) and also third-party content that your specific network will find relevant and useful." She also recommends joining groups and participating in discussions, and adds, "when possible, reference material that you've produced."

Here are some other accounts you'll need at first:

- **YouTube account**—This is the simplest and easiest way to make your videos instantly available. The only caveat is that you cannot under any circumstances upload video that could be misconstrued as infringing on anyone's copyright. Doing this could result in your account being closed, and as a result, you'll lose control of your videos. If possible, keep copies of all videos you upload on your own machine. Another advantage of YouTube is that you can upload HD video, and unlike other video sites such as Vimeo, you can enjoy unlimited pageviews free of charge. Best of all, if one of your videos gets popular, YouTube will start putting ads at the beginning and superimposed over that video, and you get to share the profits.

- **Google Analytics**—This is a free web-based application that shows your site's traffic, visitor engagement, and lets you know where your visitors are coming from. This is an invaluable tool that will let you watch your traffic grow. Go to google.com/analytics and follow the instructions for adding analytics to your account.

Here are a couple of accounts you *won't* need at first:

- Any other analytics provider—Until your traffic hits quadruple-digit visits daily, you probably don't need more complex analytics tools. Keep it simple at first.

- Any other image or video hosting service—Host images on your own server. Do not host images on any other system simply because of the current vagaries of the market. You want control over your content. If an image hosting service shuts down you may be stuck with a set of empty pages and little to show for your work.

- Any other social networks—Do you focus on design or fashion? You'd better have a Pinterest account. This service is designed with specific goals in mind, and you should use them accordingly. For example, Ariel Adams's *A Blog to Watch* features a Pinterest page and ways to pin pictures of famous and expensive watches to Pinterest. This is intrinsically important to him. It may not be that important to someone writing about, say, entrepreneurs.

Dangers of Social Media

Don't let Twitter be a part of your 1,000 words a day. Social media is, in a word, addictive. Hanging out on Facebook all day does not a blogger make. It may be fun to connect with friends and potential readers on social media services, but what you're really doing is procrastinating. No good work is ever done on social networks. They are tools for expanding your reach and presence. They shouldn't be your primary medium of communication.

Social media is secondary to your goal as a blogger. We've seen too many people sucked into mundane conversations on Facebook while avoiding real work. To some social media is a calling. To you it's something to do when you have a few minutes.

Three Rules for Spreading the Word

Be nice but human. Your feed is your public face. Be nice but human. Endlessly perky quotes and "Go get 'em" commentary is grating. Be human. Talk about issues. Ask questions. Discuss news. But try to be nice.

Don't flood the feed. We'd recommend creating a separate account for only your blog posts—try Twitterfeed.com to connect your blog's RSS feed to Twitter. This will Tweet your stories automatically to an account dedicated to your site. Your personal feed should contain select stories with a bit of commentary to make them interesting. For example, John's feed, @johnbiggs, consists of dumb jokes and banter with some posts thrown in. The @techcrunch feed consists only of posts.

Don't feed the trolls. Some social media users will hassle you, complain about you, and say you're doing something wrong. Ignore them. Connecting with a troll is exactly what they're looking for. Interaction should be respectful and if it isn't, drop the call.

What to Write About

Now that you know how much you need to be posting, let's discuss *what* you need to be posting. There are millions of blogs now in existence, so your mission will be to convince your readers to bypass most of those other blogs and come directly to yours. Why would they do that? Because they can get original content from you, in your own voice, and in your own style, which they will *like*. Your original content is something that's sitting on your blog—something they can't get anywhere else. It's your job to consistently deliver that new stuff every day.

Therein lies the problem, dear blogger. There is only a limited amount of new stuff every day, and most of your competitors probably know about the most exciting items, too. That's why you're going to have to make the news *new*. Make it yours and add your perspective, getting to the heart of what's really going on, not only on the surface but underneath, around, and through every topic you tackle.

Here's a little secret: **Most bloggers are finding news items on the web, and then rewriting those stories with their own byline at the top.** That has worked just fine for the past half of a decade, but things are changing. What you might call "paraphrasing" is what's known as "content creation" in some circles and "lazy blogging" in others. To be clear, it's still a valid strategy, but it's not an ideal one.

This is where you need to go further than simply paraphrasing news, not just rewriting stories but finding more, fresh information, and adding your own opinions to the mix. If the story of the day is a major rally on Wall Street or a revolutionary change at a famous restaurant, figure out what you can do to gather just a bit more than your competitors. Compare and contrast the various points of the story with other concepts or products that have come before, and explain what's really new about it, and what's just a rehash of other stories you've reported. Link to those earlier stories you've written, which is as good for enhancing your pageview numbers as it is for adding context to your story.

This is not to say there isn't room for "straight" industry news. Straight news—the act of reporting a few simple facts—can be valuable to readers of certain blogs. A blog about publishing would be remiss in ignoring the big book deal of the day, and a blog about bikes would be useless if it didn't at least include the latest news from Cannondale and Specialized.

There is a huge misconception about blogs: You see it at least once a week, where people who have just started reading blogs make comments such as, "Why do you insert your opinion into this news?" and "This is biased!" Another expectation is that you report the news objectively. So why not be a "just the facts, ma'am" reporter when you're telling us the story? We'll tell you why—because the list of objective facts can be told only once, and that list is probably already being recounted dozens of times. **Commentary is great when it's backed up by a steady stream of fact.** Yes, you'll need to state at least *some* of those facts quickly and concisely (and link to all the details for the benefit of your more curious readers), but you'll need to differentiate yourself by going a few steps further.

Journalism as we know it is changing, but that doesn't mean the old methods are no longer viable. Online journalism, as opposed to mainstream "old-fashioned" journalism, is characterized by a few defining and important factors:

- **Lack of access**—Most posts *are* built on other posts. This means that you may not have access to the original source, and therefore are depending on hearsay or "reliable sources." Sadly, these reliable sources are actually shrinking, giving rise to unreliable stories based on, ironically, blog posts and tweets.
- **Quick and dirty**—In the "old days," newspapers ran through a full gamut of fact checking and copy editing systems put in place to ensure that the publishers didn't get sued. These failsafe measures are gone. You, if you're a lone blogger, will not have a "word nerd" sitting in a room sipping coffee and reading your pages. Instead, you will have angry readers who complain about every typo. Be aware of this and proofread. Read, re-read, and re-re-read every story you write before publishing. Make it quick and *clean*.
- **Readability**—New journalism requires readability. This can mean the posts are short and quick, or the posts are long and full of detail and opinion. Either way, there is some research required to gather the "nut" of the story, and the shell is formed of your own opinions or experience.

Old and New

This is not to say the traditional "news pyramid" is dead. The news pyramid consists of a few basic rules that state, in short, that the five Ws—who, what, where, when, and why—appear in the "lede," or first paragraph (this newsroom slang is spelled "lede" to avoid conflict with another publishing term, "leading," or the distance between lines of type) and the most important detail appears in a "nut graf" in the second or third paragraph position. Just in case you're not hip to this newsy *patois*, remember that newspaper editors usually use the word "hed" for headline and "graf" for paragraph, along with the aforementioned "lede."

For example:

HED:
    AT&T and RIM Release the Blackberry Torch, a Social Media Phone Running OS 6
LEDE:
    Today in New York, RIM released the Blackberry Torch for AT&T's network, a new smartphone with touchscreen and keyboard.
NUT:
    The phone marks RIM's first foray into social media with the addition of OS 6, a new operating system that adds RSS and Twitter functionality.

Here you see three important bits of information, the hed, the lede, and the nut graf, arrayed in easy-to-read order. The following is an actual report on Lincoln's death written in 1865. It is one of the earliest examples of the *inverted pyramid* style:

```
This evening at about 9:30 p.m. at Ford's Theatre, the President, while
sitting in his private box with Mrs. Lincoln, Mrs. Harris and Major
Rathburn, was shot by an assassin, who suddenly entered the box and
approached behind the President.
   The assassin then leaped upon the stage, brandishing a large dagger
or knife, and made his escape in the rear of the theatre.
   The pistol ball entered the back of the President's head and pen-
etrated nearly through the head. The wound is mortal.
   The President has been insensible ever since it was inflicted, and is
now dying.
   About the same hour an assassin, whether the same or not, entered
Mr. Seward's apartment and under pretense of having a prescription was
shown to the Secretary's sick chamber. The assassin immediately rushed
to the bed and inflicted two or three stabs on the chest and two on the
face. It is hoped the wounds may not be mortal. My apprehension is that
they will prove fatal.
   The nurse alarmed Mr. Frederick Seward, who was in an adjoining
room, and he hastened to the door of his father's room, when he met
the assassin, who inflicted upon him one or more dangerous wounds. The
recovery of Frederick Seward is doubtful.
   It is not probable that the President will live through the night.
   General Grant and his wife were advertised to be at the theatre . . .
```

To be clear we're not trying to make you an AP reporter (but that is a noble goal to which to strive). But when you pay attention to the stylistic techniques used for more than a century by reporters around the world, you become a better writer.

Rules are made to be broken. Straight news is often boring and does not grab readers. However, before you find your voice, we'd advise you to let straight news be your guide until you feel confident enough to try your hand at more adventuresome writing.

Need to Know

After that first paragraph of the inverted pyramid style, the rest is, in many cases, detail, seen as marginal but equally valid. Bang out the first paragraph as accurately as possible and then work magic with the rest of the story. Add context that only you know. Add your opinion, stating your position on the story's place in the great river of content flowing through this strange world of your niche. Bring the story into context in the grand scheme of things. Why is this news important? Why should your readers care?

The job of a successful blogger is to convey the facts about a story, and start a conversation. You can get your readers fired up—maybe even start an argument—simply by writing. This is not merely inciting a mob, though. Readers will see right through some cheap-shot post designed just to lure comments at the bottom of the page. Readers will, however, react to a well-reasoned stand you take on a particular topic.

That's why you need to take special care not to write a bunch of hurried nonsense. Readers will cry out that you need to "do your research," and many will become so frustrated with your lack of knowledge about a topic that they'll never come back. So, yes, you need to know all the available facts of a particular story, giving you a basis upon which to state your opinions. In turn, that entices your readers to state their opinions, and boom! You've started a mega-conversation.

What is news? Does it have to be new? That depends entirely on how you're going to write your blog post. For instance, if the latest iPhone was introduced yesterday morning and you write a blog post today acting like no one's heard about it yet, you won't capture the interest of many readers, especially gadget aficionados. However, if you write that post a day after the iPhone's introduction telling people why they don't need this new iPhone, explaining why they won't miss anything if they keep their old one, and give them some perspective about how unimportant its new features are and why there are plenty of other phones that can do the same thing, you have yourself a "Day Two" story.

Many will say bloggers aren't journalists. In fact, one prominent writer, Chris Hedges, calls the entire industry a sham:

> It has been replaced by Internet creations that mimic journalism. Good reporters, like good copy editors or good photographers, who must be paid and trained for years while they learn the trade, are becoming as rare as blacksmiths. Stories on popular sites are judged not by the traditional standards of journalism but by how many hits they receive, how much Internet traffic they generate, and how much advertising they can attract. News is irrelevant. Facts mean little. Reporting is largely nonexistent.[1]

Hedges, as magnificent as he is at his job, is simply wrong. The "training" he's talking about happens in blogging. His complaint smacks of elitism. His argument—that journalists need long years of training—sounds like an older journalist complaining that the reporters at a community newspaper (with its wispy coverage of parades and school boards) aren't doing real "reporting."

And it's important to note that advertising pays his salary. In short, the next Chris Hedges or Walter Cronkite or E.B. White will come from the realm of blogging, a place where advertising can still pay salaries and the practice of journalism as an art is still prized.

Bloggers are practicing journalism just as ballet dancers are practicing dance. There are many disciplines inside the umbrella of each defined activity. It's our mission to teach you how to be a good blogger, not a newspaper-era reporter. The expectations, the context, and the readership are different for both, and the distinction is real. But the mission is the same: to inform and entertain.

We must also make a distinction between blogging for fun and blogging for profit. While we don't like to come down on either side of the "What is blogging?" debate, our goal is to make you a readable and successful blogger, not someone who is good at writing about stuff that interests you and you alone. Your goal is to gather readers by covering a niche. You can do it for free or you can do it professionally, but you must do it with a mindset of maximizing reader utility.

How to Decide What Matters to Your Readers

Try to think about why your readers should give a damn about what you're writing, and try to picture them asking, "Why should I care?" Tell them why they should care. However, all the logic, reason, and cleverness in the world won't make a bit of difference if the topics you're choosing don't matter to your readers.

Try to picture your readers in your mind's eye. Remember they don't have the dedication to a topic you do, but they might understand it more deeply and completely than you. Be prepared to defend your work in the public sphere, and more importantly, be aware that there are some readers who just won't be placated.

Sometimes, it's not that hard. If you have good news sense, what interests you will interest your readers. But that's not always the case. When you're first starting out, it's going to be tricky to figure out exactly what your readers want. But as you go along, pay close attention to which stories give you the most traffic, and then you'll get a better sense of your readers' interests.

Finding News

Before you write anything, you're going to need to find out what's going on. There are so many websites blasting out news every day, you might think it's impossible to gather it all in one place, make sense of it, and sort through what's news and what isn't. Thankfully, that's gotten a whole lot easier than you might think. There are specific tools created for just this purpose, and you'll need to use them every day, making sure you're aware of what's happening in the real world, giving you a solid foundation upon which to write your own original material.

RSS

You might already be using an RSS reader, but if you're not, let us fill you in: RSS stands for Really Simple Syndication, and it's an essential tool for bloggers. An RSS reader allows you to create your own personal collection of news sources that you can quickly dive into, alleviating the need for hunting and clicking through hundreds of websites. Best of all, you can sort the various news items from your chosen sources according to when they were published, letting you see only the freshest news. When you first use an RSS reader, you quickly realize you've lashed yourself onto a tool that turns you into a superhuman newshound. This tool is so important for blogging that if you're not using an RSS reader, you're at a tremendous disadvantage.

There are a variety of RSS readers available, and most are free. Most RSS readers let you easily identify and then sort through stories you're interested in covering. Most let you place a star on the stories you deem worthy of further investigation, and then later you can list only the starred stories you've culled from the herd.

We mourn the loss of Google Reader, summarily discontinued by the search giant with no reason given, but celebrate the crowd of newsreaders that arose in its absence. One of our favorite survivors that sprang up just in time for Google Reader's demise is Digg Reader, built by the same group that brought us the once-powerful (and now faded but still alive) source of crowd news-picking wisdom, Digg.

The Digg Reader gives you a rough approximation of the features of Google Reader, and lets you import all your settings from Google Reader, too. Sign up for an account, and you can access Digg Reader and your settings anywhere, and you can mark your favorite stories to read later. There are iOS and Android apps for Digg Reader, giving you the same features you get on the browser version. The service even shows you which stories in your feeds are most popular on Digg, but that's of limited usefulness at this writing. Even so, it's a useful RSS reader, and includes the most powerful features for our purposes.

That's just the beginning of the RSS reader story, though. Since Google Reader disappeared, dozens of replacements have appeared, and many that already existed have been improved. They are sprouting so quickly and gaining so many new features that it's beyond the scope of this book to evaluate all of the components of this fast-moving train of development and innovation. We advise you to search for the latest reviews and opinions about the readers, and pick the one that best fits your style.

One key point: Don't miss out on RSS readers and get all your news from Twitter. While Twitter can give you the news quickest, RSS feeds accelerate your overall news-gathering power, showing you more stories in less time than any other tool.

How to Select Sites for RSS

Regardless of which RSS reader you choose, the most important task you'll first need to do is select the sites you'll visit every day when you're looking for news. You probably already have a good idea of which sites are the market leaders in your chosen topic area. Place those sites in your newsreader (or in newsreader parlance, *subscribe* to the sites). You'll soon discover that the blogosphere is aptly named, where there is an interconnected web of sites covering the same topic. These will be your competitors, and this is the environment against which you'll differentiate your own blog.

A superficial roundup of top sites is not going to be enough, though. Your search for the ideal sources has just begun. You'll need to go way beyond just using the same sources your competitors do. Search your topic, and find your own group of sources you like, probing deep within your area of expertise for blogs that might be less well known but on their way up. Sometimes offbeat sources can provide you with powerful and original news tips that haven't been beaten to death on all the other blogs yet.

Begin by figuring out which blogs are your favorites. Then follow those blogs to see which sources they link to. Then follow the sites those sites link to. Repeat *ad infinitum*. Are you writing about interior decoration? You'll need to read tech blogs to see what the latest TVs are. Are you writing about food? You'd better be subscribing to liquor and cigar blogs as well. Create a constellation of information on which you can depend daily.

You can also ask friends and co-workers which news sources they tend to use and enjoy. By hand-picking news sources and adding them to your newsreader list, you'll find that you have quite a collection of blogs and websites from which to gather your news.

Looking for the best sources will be an ongoing project for you. We've noticed that the best bloggers are constantly refining and adding new sources to their lists of sites. Building a strong list of sites for your RSS feed will be an illuminating quest. It will give you a feel for the lay of the land, determining who the big dogs are and who the followers are. As you build your RSS subscription list to its peak of refinement, keep it confidential, especially from your competitors. That's proprietary information—guard it with your life.

The sites where we've worked consider their lists of sites trade secrets, constantly refining them to a keen edge.

Our absolute favorite news sources are industry websites like Eurekalert and blogs that cover specific topics. If you read other blogs, all you're going to be doing is reading the same stories over and over again. If you read industry sources you will learn something new every time.

Hopefully, one day soon, all those sites you're evaluating will be adding *your* site to *their* lists! By the way, your lists can be freely exchanged between your colleagues, exported from RSS readers in the OPML (Outline Processor Markup Language) file format.[2]

Building Your RSS Feed

Let's put this site hunt into action. How do you build your own OPML file? There are many ways to use an RSS reader, but we've developed a method that enhances its efficiency, grouping sites in a hierarchy where we can grab the top stories quickly and then go more in-depth after we've covered the most important stories of the day.

For this method to work well, you need to first become intimately familiar with the best sources for your topic area. Let's start with those two or three sites you've chosen for your RSS feed as market leaders, those that consistently break news first and cover your topic in the most comprehensive way.

In your RSS reader, subscribe to those top sites, and then create a new folder, which most RSS readers will let you do (and if yours doesn't, find another one). Name that folder something meaningful like Top Sites (Charlie named his Engagzmodo, after his top sites for tech), drag your chosen sites into the folder, and you're ready to go.

Now, when you start your workday, you can simply select that top folder with your two hottest sites, and on the right side of your RSS reader you'll immediately see the top twenty or thirty stories the two sites have published since you finished working the day before. It's fast—this will give you a quick look at any breaking stories, especially if you've picked sites that stay on top of the news every minute.

Every RSS reader has a way to bookmark stories for later reading (Digg Reader calls it "saving" stories), so select stories you deem post-worthy, and then after you've finished your preliminary story search, you can quickly bring forth a list of your chosen items with a single click.

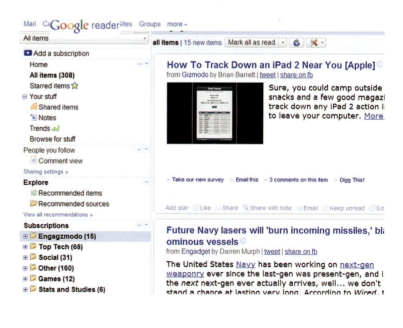

Once you've determined those top two or three sites, then find and subscribe to the next-best twenty-five sites that have proven to be good sources of stories and news. Create a separate folder for them, and that will be your second group of news stories to scan each morning.

After you've created those two top tiers, create a third tier of the next fifty most reliable and credible sites, and then a bottom tier with all the rest, placing each of those groups into its own folders as well. Any time you want to know what the absolute latest stories are, click on All Items, and at the top of the list will be the newest stories of all the sites in your RSS feed.

Twitter

Don't just stick with Google when you're searching for the latest happenings, because Twitter often gives you more immediate and targeted results. The microblogging service has gone way beyond people just using 140 characters to tell us what they had for breakfast. Now it's a gigantic forum where people point to hot stories, and it's all-searchable. It's a powerful, real-time link-fest that lets you put your fingers on the pulse of the populace. Yes, here's a near-perfect tool for the up-to-the-minute blogger.

The way to get the most out of Twitter as a blogger is a two-pronged attack. First, you must follow the right people. However, that's easier said than done, and Twitter experts say that curating the list of people you follow on Twitter is something you should always be working on and evolving. According to Stephanie Haberman, social media producer at NBC News, it's an ongoing process of trial and error. "I will follow someone, and if I don't like their stuff, I will unfollow them," she told us. She's been doing this for years, so she has one of the sharpest lists of newsmakers to follow in the business. Armed with that highly evolved list, Stephanie parlayed her expertise as a news finder at *Mashable* into a big-time job at NBC News.

How did she build that list? She said, "I curate it over time based on my interests, what's going on in the world, and how my subjects' personal news feeds have evolved." She reads lots of news, and carefully observes who's reporting on it. She said, "If I'm reading a story that I'm really interested in, or if I'm reading about a news event I'm interested in, I will look up that reporter and see if they are on Twitter." Constantly adding to and subtracting from her list results in an up-to-the-minute group of reporters who feed her the most important stories, all in real time.

The best way to find stories on Twitter is to use Twitter Advanced Search, located at search.twitter.com/advanced. It's a surprisingly powerful tool for sifting through Twitter's enormous haystack of information, helping you find that needle of info you seek. Haberman said, "It's incredibly underutilized. If you go into Twitter Advanced Search you can search for absolutely anything." She likes the flexibility of Advanced Search, and especially its extensive filters. She said, "Instead of just putting in a term, you can search for 'all these words,' 'this exact word,' 'this phrase,' 'these hashtags,' 'this language,' 'from these accounts,' and 'near this place.' I use 'near this place' all the time. I use it with disasters, tornadoes, trying to find not just journalists who are tweeting about things but *people* who are tweeting about them from that location."

That powerful "near this place" filter could also be useful for, say, a sports blogger who's covering the trade of a beloved player. For example, let's say Green

Bay Packers quarterback Aaron Rodgers was traded to the Minnesota Vikings. In that nightmare scenario, you'd find a huge contrast in fan sentiment by searching for tweets about Aaron Rodgers within 50 miles of Green Bay, and then comparing that to the tweets about Rodgers within 50 miles of Minneapolis. Twitter Advanced Search even lets you find tweets with a positive or negative attitude. Imagine the results you'd find. Sounds like the makings of a good blog post, doesn't it?

Twitter is getting to be so ubiquitous that now news breaks first on it. Set yourself up to find out what's going on from people within your blogging topic by creating a Twitter list. This works like an RSS feed, except it's even more immediate. Besides her main feed, Haberman has two lists that come in handy. She said, "I have one list that I keep just for fun—it's sports people. I have another that I keep of newsmakers." That 500-name list is a subset of the 2,500 people she follows. "I know 500 sounds like a lot, but it can be local people from one area or local people from another area." She's following newsmakers, rather than news outlets. Haberman points out the weakness of following just news outlets when a big story hits: "If you create a media list like that, you're going to see a lot of the same tweets over and over again."

Here's how to create a list on Twitter that you can use just as you would an RSS feed, keeping track of breaking news from sources you trust. To create a list, first use Twitter Advanced Search to find industry luminaries, pundits, and experts in your chosen field who are using Twitter. You can combine them all in an easily scannable list right there on your home page at Twitter.com. You know, on your Twitter account. You do have a Twitter account, don't you? If not, sign up for one now—it's free.

Under the Settings and help gear icon, click on Lists, and then select Create List.

Name your list, and decide if you'd like for it to be public or private. In this case, click Private, because you don't want your blogging competitors to see your list of sources, a proprietary asset you'll want to guard carefully.

Name your list, and then start populating it with publications, websites,

73

influential people and experts you've found. You might be surprised at how many publications are tweeting links to every one of their articles, every day. You can search for companies and people to add to your list, or you can add people from any profile page.

In this example, we'd like to add popular tech site *Engadget* to our list, so we've searched *Engadget* from the Twitter home page, gone to *Engadget*'s profile page, clicked the "user actions" drop-down list to the left of "Follow," and then clicked "Add or remove from lists.?

That brings up the "your lists" box, where we select our new list, *Bloggers Boot Camp*. *Engadget* will take its place among our other sources we selected.

To use our new list, simply go back to your Twitter home page, click the "Me" tab, click Lists, and select the list you just made. Behold, a custom queue of sizzling stories, selected specifically by you according to your area of interest. Of course, your list is only as powerful as the sources you've added, so dedicate some time curating and refining your list, and it will repay you many times over. Use your list wisely, and soon people will be adding you to their Twitter lists. As you probably already realize, Twitter is also a powerful way to promote your own stories, and we're going to show you how to use this microblogging powerhouse to its fullest extent later in this book.

LinkedIn

One of our favorite sources of information is LinkedIn Groups. Many professionals form ad hoc groups on line—UAV manufacturers, journalists, interior decorators—and post news and job listings. These groups allow you to gather sources straight from the industry you're interested in and see what they like to read about. Think of it as a cheat sheet for your niche.

Go to www.linkedin.com/myGroups to start adding groups to your account. Do searches for interesting topics and add them. Some groups require a moderator to approve you, but that's usually not a problem. In a few seconds you can gain some fascinating insight on your niche.

Aggregators Such as Google News

A good starting point for big stories is to visit the huge aggregators of the news of the day, including such names as Google and Yahoo. You can search for your preferred topic area, or you can subscribe to the RSS feeds of these giants, narrowing it down to your area of interest. For instance, you can sign up for the RSS feed of technology and science news with Google, and read the results in your RSS reader every day, along with your other news sources. Or you can sign up with Google Alerts, where you'll receive free email updates of relevant Google results matching your topic or keywords.

When we're looking for a list of raw press releases, one of our most useful services is BusinessWire.com. If you sign up for the free PressPass News, you can designate which areas you'd like to hear about. Then, you'll receive a list of press releases specifically tailored for your subjects of interest. Of course, the press releases are just a bunch of corporate-speak, but it's a starting point for information and the PR agents responsible are usually listed.

Google Trends

Another efficient way to put your fingers on the pulse of the Internet is to check Google Trends. Check Google Trends regularly, and it will give you powerful guidance about what people are searching for on the world's largest search engine. If you want to give your readers what they want, look on the Google Trends list of Hot Searches, and you'll find what they're looking for. Whenever we see a hot search term that is within our topic area, we'll write a post about it that usually performs well. That possibility is a good reason to make it a habit to check Google Trends at the beginning of every day and often throughout the day.

More Sources: Press Releases from PR People

A large percentage of original news is first generated in press releases, written by public relations (PR) professionals hired by all kinds of companies and individuals, large and small. After you've made numerous contacts in your chosen field, you'll be receiving a lot more press releases than you'd like. But at first, you won't be receiving *any*. You'll need to start somewhere, so look on websites to find press contacts. Almost every company has a press area—go there and make your first contact with that organization's press personnel. Send them a brief email, introducing yourself and asking them to include you on their list of contacts to receive their latest press releases. They're almost always happy to comply with your request, and before you know it, you'll be receiving plenty of first-hand (yet often overblown, propagandistic, boring, and hyperbolic) information about your chosen companies.

You'll discover the people in the world of public relations are outgoing and gregarious, more than happy to include you on their email lists. As you receive responses from press people and otherwise unravel which public relations and marketing people are associated with which companies, place them in your contacts list (you do have a My Contacts section in your email software, don't you?), and don't forget to associate the name of any PR person with the company he or she is working for. Be sure to use contacts software that's always available to you on your computer and cellphone, and that's easily searchable and quickly updated. For that, we like to use the Contacts area of Gmail because it's so easily searchable and ubiquitously available on all network-connected computers and smartphones. As you continue building these press contacts, that database will grow into one of your most valuable assets. By the way, because this info is so valuable, be sure to back up any cloud-based databases onto a storage medium you can hold in your hands.

Finding those press contacts by searching websites is a first step, but there are easier ways to find press releases, which usually include contact information at the end of the document. There is a bountiful barrage of press releases blasted out onto the web every day. You can find them on services such as *PR Newswire* and *Business Wire*, which will let you sign up for daily listings of press releases in your chosen field, delivered free to your email address. Once you start the torrent of press releases flowing your way, you might be wishing you didn't have so many coming in every day. However, those press releases will help you get in touch with the people who are making the news, and often a quick phone call or email can uncover additional information and get your questions answered immediately. This is where the news starts, not where it ends.

Conferences/Trade Shows

One of the best sources of original stories is a trade show or industry conference. This is the most target-rich environment in the world for bloggers, because it's filled with manufacturers, product managers, inventors, analysts, and entrepreneurs. Pursuing these sources are droves of fellow journalists and bloggers like you, all interested in gathering original information from those who are responsible for the products and services they write about every day.

Larger events such as the Consumer Electronics Show (CES) are so big that if your beat is consumer electronics, your cup runneth over. Held in Las Vegas each January, CES attracts so many thousands of companies and hundreds of thousands of attendees that it's almost to the point of being impossible to cover. There are lots of trade shows like that. At such a large event, you'll need to narrow it down, identifying the companies you're most interested in covering before the show starts. That list will be subject to many changes, of course, but at least you'll have a starting point. Pay close attention to the pre-show buzz (use your newfound Twitter search skills), and you'll get a good idea of which companies will be most worthy of your attention. At the same time, stay alert for surprises.

Then there are smaller shows like JCK, a jewelry show in Las Vegas. Or various home and fabric shows in New York and Europe. Or mobile phone shows in Orlando and Barcelona. Or auto shows in most major cities. The list is long and exhausting, but be sure to assess which events will make the most sense for you as a writer. Attending these shows is expensive and time-consuming, and if you aren't making your living blogging yet, you might have to take time off from work. Choose wisely before buying a ticket to Outer Nowheresville to cover the Eastern Seaboard's Mid-Sized Quilting and Canning Festival when the main Quilting and Canning event in Las Vegas could be a better bargain and much better source of news and information.

How do you decide what's worth visiting? Here's where your earlier legwork of building a network of PR representatives can pay off. Pay attention to early press releases before a key trade show, and if something looks like a big story that will interest your readers, make an appointment with the company to meet at the show. There is no substitute for the firsthand experience, personal conversations, and hands-on evaluation of new products that you'll get on the trade show floor. Better yet, you can meet with companies or newsmakers in meeting rooms that are either attached to the trade show or off-site in hotel suites. This is where you get a chance to find out a lot more about the products you're writing about. But be careful about accepting off-site appointments, which can waste a lot of precious time if there is no new product or exciting story to cover.

At smaller trade shows, you can often find topics for posts that no one has thought about before. These smaller get-togethers are either stand-alone events or organized around the same time as major trade shows as a subset of what's happening on the gigantic show floor. We've noticed that the major challenge of these smaller events is to discern which products are new, and which ones have already been available for a while. It's also a challenge to figure out when many of the products and prototypes on display will actually become available to consumers. Vaporware abounds. Be careful. Too often, it's a little game that exhibitors play with press people and bloggers, trying to convince them that a product is real when it's not, or that a product is new when it's years old. It's your job to know when something is new, but there are so many products available that it's impossible to keep up with it all. Ask a lot of questions.

Should you ask for press passes to these events? Sure, if you are well-established. Smaller blogs are now part of the news cycle, and these events need as much exposure as possible. This doesn't mean you'll always get a press pass, but it never hurts to ask.

Before you go to a trade show, be sure to have high-quality business cards on hand, prominently displaying your blog logo, your name, email address, and phone number (although many bloggers like to leave off the phone number these days, keeping junk calls to a minimum). Part of your mission at a trade show or conference is to collect as many business cards as possible, and to pass out as many of your own at the same time. If you're not working for a company that supplies business cards, get your own. We found the best deal for business cards at Vistaprint.com or MooCards.com, but don't go for the free business cards that have a printer's logo on the back—that will reflect poorly on your professionalism. However, for very little money, you can get yourself hundreds of business cards that look first-rate. We'd suggest using quality 100-lb. paper with a glossy front and matte back, giving your logo graphics a supersharp presentation. And the contrast in texture between the front and the back makes them easier to grab quickly.

Dinners and Events

As you get to know more PR people and company officials, you'll be invited to special press dinners as well as various events featuring music and alcohol. This is fertile ground for rooting out vital background information. Sometimes, if you're lucky, you'll hear hints about upcoming products or services that might fascinate your readers. These hybrid and sometimes intimate gatherings are a combination of social occasion and business meeting, but they can serve the purpose of bonding between you and the company you cover (but don't get too close—remember, you're a watchdog, not a lapdog). Pay close attention to off-the-record opinions, statements, or information. Even though you can't write about them right away, some of the most valuable things you'll hear are off the record, giving you an idea of what the company has in mind, and what direction it's headed. Be sure to honor any off-the-record information, and that will help you build trust with those people who might give you a scoop later.

To be clear, there is no such thing as "off the record," although the tradition of taking information and not writing about it, or printing it without clear attribution, has existed for most of the past fifty years. Anything anyone says to a reporter is fair game, especially in the world of blogging. However, if you abuse the privilege offered you by trusting sources, you may find yourself cast out of the inner circle and in hot water. If you agree not to write about something, stick to your promise. Tell the truth. Journalism is a gentleman's—or gentlewoman's—agreement to tell the truth, not only in your writings but also in your dealings with your sources. You need to gain their trust. Abuse that at your peril.

Other more elaborate events are frequently called "parties," but that's a misnomer. While these get-togethers also can offer a good opportunity to get to know company officials and socialize with some of your colleagues, they're frequently a waste of time. Many of the fanciest events hosted by large companies are done to thumb the corporate

Companies will try almost anything to get you off the show floor, away from their competitors, and in front of their products. Once at a trade show, a company offered to whisk Charlie from Las Vegas to San Francisco in a corporate jet, show him its product, and return him to the convention center two hours later. That sounded like so much fun, but Charlie refused–it's *Mashable*'s official policy not to accept such extravagances from sources.

nose at the competition, and massage the egos of the company's top officials. "We're big, and we can spend a lot of money on this kind of junk," is the statement made by these evening events held at expensive venues. Carefully consider whether it's worth your time to become a theatrical extra in these corporate dramas.

Tipsters

When you're first starting out, you won't be getting a torrent of tips in your inbox. But if you prominently display a link for tipsters, as your site grows, you'll notice a trickle of information starting to find its way into your email. The challenge with these tips is separating fact from fiction. For every one tip showing you spy shots of the next iPhone, there are hundreds of others of lesser import. Whenever you receive a tip that looks like it could contain a kernel of truth, investigate it thoroughly, ask a lot of questions, and probe as deeply as you can, and you might be lucky enough to come up with the scoop of the year.

Tread carefully here, though, because many tips are just rumor, hearsay, or gainsaying against competitors. If you find yourself getting numerous usable tips every day, congratulations—you've made it to the top of the blog world. In our experience with *Gizmodo*, a good percentage of our biggest and most original stories came from insider tips. With *Mashable*, for some reason our tipbox usually contained a much higher percentage of useless pitches, but there was still the occasional gold nugget. However, your goal is to get as many tips as possible, even if a large percentage of them breathlessly tell you, "The Apple Store is down!" Always encourage your readers to send you tips, and as your blog grows in size and stature, you might be lucky enough to receive some firsthand, valuable information.

Dealing with PR People

It's inevitable: you're cruising along, publishing content, getting popular, and suddenly fawning PR people want to bend your ear about a new product or service. They want to send free stuff your way; they want you to write about their clients. Once you've reached this pinnacle, be intensely wary.

You're not friends with these companies—you're more of a friendly watchdog, keeping an eye on them for your readers. So no, the PR people are not really your friends, but they're not your adversaries, either. They need you to write about the company they're working for, but you also need them to get you the information and let you talk with the company's newsmakers. There is a unique relationship between journalists and PR people, with the PR person's boss-company sometimes hiding behind those representatives, and with you always standing up for your readers.

This strange relationship takes a little getting used to. It feels like all of the PR people love you, and they might, but in reality, they're afraid of you. They're afraid of what you might write. They know you can give them the most valuable thing they seek, a positive review on your website or blog. To them, you are what they call "uncontrolled media," as opposed to an advertisement they completely control. The gold that you can dole out to them is a well-reasoned and fair review that shows their product in a positive light. But if you negatively review their product, that could mean curtains for their prospects of selling many of them. In that transaction, they lose, but your readers win: You've warned your readers of a crappy product or service, saving them from worlds of grief. Nice.

Underneath this delicate relationship with companies and their PR agents, it's your job to build your personal credibility so your readers will trust you and believe what you write. A friendly rapport with PR representatives will help you get the facts you need in a timely way. But it can also go overboard, where you become such close friends with the PR person that you feel like you're jeopardizing a personal relationship by writing anything negative about the company. Keep your distance. As long as you remember you're experiencing these products and presentations for the benefit of your readers, you'll be fine.

Review Units

There is a school of thought that says when a product has already been reviewed by numerous blogs, there is no point in your reviewing it too. However, if you've been developing a relationship of trust with your readers, they will probably want to read about your opinion of said gadget, product, or service. That review won't be redundant if you weave your own personal experience, perceptions, opinions, and perspective.

Is It Worth It to Review?

Even though a specific review might constitute a lot of work for you, and might not seem to get more pageviews than simple posts, doing reviews adds prestige to your site, keeps readers returning for more, and shows that you're a writer with your hands on the hottest products. You learn a lot more about the products when you use them yourself. You'll know what you're talking about. That will come in handy, especially when you want to compare that item to its competitors.

You can't review everything, but think of it this way: You don't *need* to review *everything*. If you go to a dance and say you're not going to dance at all unless you can dance with every guy or gal in the room, you won't be dancing much. Forget that! Review every worthy product or service you can find, and your readers will thank you for it. You'll be more knowledgeable, and so will they.

How to Snag Review Units

Of course you'd like to review stuff, but how on earth do you get your hands on products or services without buying them yourself? Welcome to the review unit, the press sample, the freebies that make it so you can do original research and report to your readers about your firsthand experiences. As you establish contact with various press representatives, they'll start to offer you review units of new products. If they don't, ask. Be assertive. As your site grows and gains readership and credibility, it will be easier to convince companies to part with review samples. Especially at first, it helps to assure the company you'll be fair with reviews, emphasize the growing number of readers to your site, and promise to return review units promptly.

Review It or Not—Pan It or Skip It?

Sometimes you'll receive products that are of questionable value. Then you're left with a quandary: Should you bash this product to hell, giving it a horribly negative review? The plus side of that scenario is that you'll be warning readers to save their money and time, a valuable service that could increase your blog's value. On the other hand, there is that old adage about how "any press is good press," meaning that even *mentioning* this product will be its own type of promotion, a good argument against reviewing it at all.

In our experience, this has been a tricky call to make. Generally, if a product is so ubiquitous, highly anticipated, and well known that most people have heard of it or its brand name, it's a good idea for you to relish the fact that you've gotten your hands on one, and honestly and fairly criticize or praise it. But if it's some cheap gadget that few people care about, what is the point of holding it up and smashing it to pieces like a piñata? Negative reviews can be fun to read (and write), so you don't want to eliminate them entirely, but you also don't want *all* of your reviews to be negative, unless that's the particular kind of site you're planning.

Should I Return Review Units?

We cover this extensively in the Ethics chapter, but the rule of thumb is the more stuff you return to PR people in a timely manner, the better your chance of receiving more review units. **Blogging isn't a way to get free junk. Sometimes getting a beer koozie or a USB key is a nice side effect of being a blogger, but it should not be your primary mission to get as much swag as possible.**

Further News Gathering

Don't depend just on the computer and the Internet to find news. Most of the bloggers and journalists you're competing against are finding *all* their stories on the web, so a smart way to beat them is to go out there in the real world and find some news. If you write about products, for example, look for things people are doing with those products. If you write about parenting, talk with parents and parenting experts, observe parenting techniques in public, draw from your own parenting experience, and write about those. Firsthand experience is often unique and valuable, and stories come from the most unlikely of places. So go out, find news, and incorporate your personal experiences into your writing.

Ten Questions to Ask before Posting

This is the one skill that you *must* get right. If you miss it, you'll fail. After all, if you consistently choose stories none of your site's visitors are interested in reading, they're not likely to return for more. Before you decide to write a story, think about this: Why are my readers coming to my site? They're probably looking for variety, novelty, and entertainment in their lives. They want to be engaged. So you need to be sure that every post you write has entertainment value. That doesn't mean you have to be a comedian. It simply means you need to tickle that novelty-and-variety jones almost every reader has. This story-selection process is complicated and changes from day to day, but we're here to help. We've boiled down your selection of stories to a list of questions you need to ask yourself before you give it the go-ahead for publication.

1. Is It New?

There's good reason why it's called "news." Your readers will be expecting the latest products, services, and occurrences. If you're in the tech world, posting about an old product that you characterize as new will hurt your credibility, showing readers that you don't know what's old and what's new. Check carefully to see if the product is indeed brand-new, and this is not as easy as it seems, because as we've warned, PR people and over-eager companies often try to characterize older products as new.

```
Example: "Ray Dolby, Father of Modern Noise Reduction, Dead At 80"
   Ray Dolby, creator of the Dolby noise-reduction system that revolutionized
recording, died on September 12, 2013. (http://techcrunch.com/2013/09/17/
ray-dolby-father-of-modern-noise-reduction-dead-at-80/)
```

2. Is There Something Fascinating and Different about It?

People are drawn to novel situations and products, and if you've never seen anything like the item you're considering, that might be a good enough reason to post it. Talk about why it's groundbreaking, what's new about it, and what you think about its implications for the future.

```
Example: "Your Board Game Is in My Video Game: Tangible Play Mixes the
Real and Virtual"
   What do you get when you put a pair of board gaming geeks who have worked
at NVIDIA, Google, LucasArts, and Ubisoft together in the same room?
(http://techcrunch.com/2013/09/10/your-board-game-is-in-my-video-
game-tangible-play-mixes-the-real-and-virtual/)
```

3. Does Anybody Really Care about This?

When you ask the question, "Why should I care?" do you have a good answer? Many skeptical readers are thinking that phrase to themselves as they read every one of your blog posts: "Why should I care? Why should I care?" After scanning the day's possibilities, always ask yourself that, too. If you can't come up with an answer, move along—there's nothing to see here.

```
Example: "Bing Refresh Brings a New Logo, More 'At a Glance' Info with
Cards and Info from Your Friends"
   Microsoft's search engine continues to push the rock up a hillside as
it chases Google, and some new Bing features add or enhance its search in
very familiar ways. (www.engadget.com/2013/09/17/bing-logo-refresh-new-
features/)
```

4. Is There Something Hilarious, Quirky, or Unbelievable about It?

Some story topics are wonderful sight gags, with built-in humor that will make readers laugh as you tell them the story or show them the picture. Sometimes few words are needed for these humorous and crazy stories.

```
Example: "Hilarious iPhone 5S Launch Parody Touches on Truth"
   As buzz reaches a fever pitch over the iPhone 5S launch just a few
days away, Matthias and J-Fred might have stumbled upon some truth in
this parody video. (www.charliewhite.net/2013/09/iphone-5s-launch/)
```

5. Have You Had Personal Experience with It?

Here's your chance to relate your own unique experiences. This is the gold that you have to mine—your own observations, judgments, and firsthand opinions about your topic. Elevate yourself above the crowd that's busy rewriting press releases and scribbling their secondhand accounts, and talk about what you've learned, firsthand, about your chosen topic. Maximize your personal experiences with the field you're writing about, and you'll be a much better blogger.

```
Example: "iOS 7 Makes My iPhone 5 Feel Brand New [REVIEW]"
   Even if you aren't buying a new iPhone this week, you'll feel
like you did if you upgrade to iOS 7. (www.charliewhite.net/2013/09/
ios-7-review/)
```

6. Is There a Good Graphic or Photo Available?

Sometimes even a so-so story will be a winner if you've found an interesting graphic. Most readers are skimmers, and a compelling photo will draw their eyes into the story and get them instantly involved, where a blurry shot or tiny icon-sized graphic might not draw in their attention enough. Besides the headline, the quality of the graphic is one of the main factors in drawing readers into your work. And we've noticed that a big graphic is more likely to attract the interest of users of discovery engine StumbleUpon, who are more likely to be lured into your post—and ultimately click that "Thumbs Up" button—if there's a compelling pic at the top of your post.

```
Example: "Smartphones Leave Yesterday's Supercomputers in the Dust
[INFOGRAPHIC]"
   Do you have any idea how powerful that smartphone in your pocket is? (www.char
liewhite.net/2013/09/smartphones-vs-supercomputers/)
```

7. Is Everybody Else in the World Covering It?

When a major story hits (such as the release of the next iPhone), everyone will be writing about it, and if you're writing about gadgets, you will, too. But if there is a minor gadget or story topic that everyone seems to be writing about, and you don't really have anything extra to add to the conversation, skip it. However, don't let what other blogs are covering dictate what you'll cover. Keep in mind that your readers aren't scanning hundreds of blogs like you do. See the situation from your readers' point of view—do they want to hear what *you* have to say about this product? If you're a good blogger, the answer is probably yes.

```
Example: "The NSA Can Read Some Encrypted Tor Traffic"
  Security expert Robert Graham has done a bit of research and posts
that the encryption standard used by earlier versions of the "secure"
Tor protocol is most probably insecure and readable by the NSA. (http://
techcrunch.com/2013/09/07/the-nsa-can-read-some-encrypted-tor-
traffic/)
```

8. Is It a World's First or Record-Breaking?

People are delighted by something they haven't seen before, and finding something that's the world's first, fastest, craziest, tallest, oldest, smallest, etc. might be interesting enough to capture a crowd of readers. Just think, something that's the best in the world! How can they resist?

```
Example: "Sharp Unveils World's First THX-Certified Ultra HDTV"
  Ultra HDTV is getting more affordable, and Sharp did its part on
Wednesday by unveiling a THX-certified 70-inch ultra-HD television for
$8,000. (http://mashable.com/2013/06/26/sharp-ultra-hdtv/)
```

9. Is It a Hot Topic of Considerable Controversy That Will Lure Comments from Readers?

Sometimes people are itching to comment about something that's going on in the news. Give them a chance to comment on that topic in your blog, too. Be sure that the current event that's causing such controversy is related to your blog's mission, but if the story is, for example, a massive terrorist attack or natural disaster, there's probably a way you can figure out an angle that would fit with your blog. (Find the hot topics of the moment by using the Google Trends site we mentioned earlier in this chapter: www.google.com/trends/hottrends.)

```
Example: "NSA Project XKeyscore Collects Nearly Everything You Do on
the Internet"
  Further leaks have revealed an NSA project called XKeyscore that, with
a few keystrokes, can give a data analyst access to nearly everything a
user does on the Internet—from chat sessions to email to browsing habits.
(http://techcrunch.com/2013/07/31/nsa-project-x-keyscore-collects-
nearly-everything-you-do-on-the-internet/)
```

10. Do You Have a Unique Opinion or Spin on the Topic?

If an item you're considering writing about has the potential to function as a springboard for you to go off on a rant about a related topic, this might be your chance. After all, your unique interpretations of topics are what will make your blog unique and keep those readers coming back to you day after day. Maybe there's a great unanswered question you've pondered, and you're ready to reveal your grand answer. Post it.

```
Example: "Are iPhone 5S, iPhone 5C Worth the Upgrade?"
   Apple rolled out the iPhone 5S and iPhone 5C on Tuesday, and there were
few surprises (www.charliewhite.net/2013/09/iphone-5s/)
```

Notes

1. www.truthdig.com/report/item/huffingtons_plunder_20110221
2. http://en.wikipedia.org/wiki/OPML

How to Write a Blog Post

Now that we've addressed *what* you'll write about, let's talk about *how* to write for blogs.

You're about to dive into a whole new way of writing, creating stories that are certainly "journalism," but with added peculiarities and immediacy that are nothing like the newspapering of the past. You're trying to set yourself apart from the crowd, to attract readers who might feel jaded by your particular choice of material. The key is to entertain and inform those visitors so much that they'll want to come back again and again.

You've got to keep your audience engaged, and remember that you're not making your pronouncements from some ivory tower, but you're starting a conversation. That's one of the main differences between this new type of journalism and the old-school newspapers and magazines, which publish letters their readers wrote, but only at the whim and convenience of their editors. Now, your readers can type back at you immediately, often with no censorship and complete anonymity, depending on how you choose to handle your comments.

While you might not want to constantly ask questions of your readers, with controversial topics, you can spark the discussion by asserting your own point of view. With most stories, you can inject your opinion, which can be bolstered by adding a few key facts. Don't be afraid to speak out—your unique opinions will ultimately be what differentiates your blog from all the others. Accompany your posts with strong opinions, and you'll bond tightly with some of your readers. But others will vehemently disagree with you. That's not necessarily a bad thing, either, because sometimes readers are entertained by a writer with whom they constantly disagree.

With breaking news stories, in the interest of speed, you might find yourself quickly writing the story and giving it to the readers straight, without injecting your own opinion. For example, if Jay-Z and Kanye West just got into a fistfight on national television, you might want to do your readers the service of giving them a "just the facts, ma'am" look at what's just happened. With those kinds of stories, you want to break the news as quickly as possible; there will be plenty of time for blow-by-blow analysis later. A simple headline like "BREAKING—Kanye Punches Jay-Z" is often more than enough for an important piece of news. It gives your readers exactly what they need. Do this sparingly, however. It's akin to the boy who cried wolf—if everything is breaking, nothing is.

With any topic, bring your own perspective to the conversation. Many times you'll be getting your facts from other sources, and that's when you have to make a special effort to refrain from copying the work of your sources, unless directly quoting them. In addition, beyond the plagiaristic verbatim lifting of sentences from other news sources, you need to constantly strive to place your own spin or analysis into any story.

While you're reading a source's story, think of your own ideas and angles for the story, rather than copying your source's original ideas. Many a failed blog was brought down by simple paraphrasing of all the other posts written that day on that specific story. Don't simply rewrite. Own the story with your own perspective, comparing it to what you've seen before, explaining why this matters, and drawing readers into it. That will make it your own. That's what makes this your blog, your story, and your work. That's one thing that will keep readers coming back for more.

Pro Tip

Your story needs context to stand out from the crowd. For example, if the Tesla Model S electric car just got the best safety rating ever from the National Highway Traffic Safety Administration (NHTSA), every car site will be reporting that as quickly as possible. If you add the fact that a few months earlier, the Tesla Model S also received the highest rating ever from *Consumer Reports*, and point out that Tesla CEO Elon Musk mentioned a week earlier that later this decade the company will introduce mass-market electric cars that will cost half the Model S's steep $70K+ price, you've put the NHTSA rating into perspective. Your readers might not know this additional information. Now you've given them insight they wouldn't have found elsewhere. They'll thank you for that by returning to your site the next time a hot story breaks.

When Should You Post?

As we mentioned before, your goal is ABP—Always Be Posting. However, you may find that blowing out all your posts at once in the morning is counterproductive. If you write on a slow-moving topic, post slowly. Write your 1,000 words in multiple posts and slowly post them over the course of a day. How?

Most content management systems allow for "scheduled" posts. The key here is to post once every few hours to give your readers something to read during the course of a day. Try to post as much as possible early. For example, if you already have three posts on your site at 9 a.m., other sleepyhead sites are more likely to link to you when they get up later in the day, finding your fresh slate of stories glistening there in the noonday sun. This is why Charlie would get up every morning at 6 a.m. to start his day with *Gizmodo*, finding the stories first and then enjoying the link love from the late-sleeping me-too bloggers. Experts say people read blogs the most in the morning, with the hour between 10 a.m. and 11 a.m. at the peak. But since you're blogging worldwide, it's always between 10 a.m. and 11 a.m. somewhere, so know where your readers are before you start trying to time the blog-reading market.

You should be posting every day, but don't post all at once. If you are posting ten stories a day, we'd recommend dropping them out once an hour. Many larger blogs will post every ten to fifteen minutes, although there is no hard evidence that slow or fast posting will change traffic overall. However, it does offer a sense of routine and rhythm to a blog, and by spacing out posts you encourage the reader to graze throughout the day rather than only during a set period.

This is not an attempt to solicit pageviews. It is an attempt to secure *an audience*. Consider your posts as a sort of delicacy to be savored by your readers during the course of a day. If you lay out this smorgasbord all at once, your readers will overdose. At all the large blogs where we've worked, our teams posted more than fifty items per day on a good day; if we posted all of those between 9:30 and 9:45 in the morning, we'd basically train our readers to visit our sites once a day to pick up all our stories, leaving the sites dead for the rest of the day. Scheduling posts is a great way to maintain space between posts, just like you want to maintain an assured stopping distance between cars in traffic. A few feet—or hours—keeps things from backing up and crashing. It also keeps your posts from competing against themselves so much.

The blog is an animated medium. It has a life cycle and a pace. The best blogs have a pulse, a sense that they're constantly being updated. The worst blog is updated once a week or less, with no rhythm or regularity to the posting. Blogs are popular because they are always fresh. Some bloggers can get away with one big post a day, but if you want to keep your interest high and the site moving, we'd recommend a few posts, one every three hours or so. This is not an exact science, but generally it is something to consider.

Now, without further ado . . .

Deadly Headline Kills 200,000 Innocent Readers

Gotcha. It worked, didn't it? We'd like to flatter ourselves into thinking that readers will pore over our every word. In reality, the most widely read words you'll ever write are headlines (or "heds" in old newspaper talk). Many readers are scanners, not taking in everything you've written in depth, but skimming over headlines and their accompanying graphics. Many of your prospective readers are seeing your story for the first time on an RSS reader, or in a link on Twitter or Facebook. That's why you must think of how every headline will look on Twitter, or on someone's Facebook newsfeed. It must be tightly written. If you don't get this headline-writing task right, no one will ever know if your posts are well written or not. How will they know? Just as the old carnival barkers said, "You've got to get them into the tent."

Blog readers read quickly. They have no interest in your finely crafted fifth paragraph if your first graf is sufficient for their information-gathering needs. Feel honored if they care enough to read all the way down to the end of a story. One of our favorite writers, Farhad Manjoo, did an informal study for website *Slate*, and discovered that most visitors read about 60 percent of each story. But almost all read the heds, and 10 percent *never* scroll (www.slate.com/articles/technology/technology/2013/06/how_people_read_online_why_you_won_t_finish_this_article.html). The headline, in many cases, is the big opener that encourages them to stay for at least part of the main attraction.

Headlines are gold. Without a good headline, no one will read your story. Headlines must be concise, interesting, and *almost* tell the story, or if you are taking a contrary position on a popular news story, express your opinion cleanly and succinctly. In fact, some of the best headlines are those that ignore the conventional storyline—"Dog Bites Man"—and instead focus on an aspect of the story that will be of interest to your readers—"Are Shi Tzus Dangerous?"

Use action words in your headlines, and give your readers good reasons to read your posts without revealing everything. Lure them in, make them curious, startle them, or outrage them, but just get them into that tent. How is this done? Write your headline first, leveraging its most intriguing point, before you write the story. You can revise it after you write your post, if you learn new facts in the meantime or think of something better.

What was it that made you decide to pick this topic? Encapsulate that into a punchy headline. Entertain your readers with your headline, while at the same time giving them a good sense of what the story is about.

When writing heds, keep them as short as possible, while still including enough info to entice the reader. And keep it simple. Don't write a bunch of jargon or use obscure acronyms in your headlines, because not everyone knows what all those initials stand for. But be careful because readers aren't dumb. If you keep posting the same gimmicky headlines—lists, questions, and the like—they will move on.

War Story

Remember, you want to lead the reader into your story, not *mislead*. For instance, some readers will laugh when they find out your headline "Friend Count Linked to the Size of a Certain Body Part?" (an actual hed written by Charlie) is referring to almond-shaped portions of the brain called the amygdalae, not that other body part you're thinking about. Others will feel tricked and cheated, and will complain about it in the comments. Using misleading terms as a joke places this headline right on the edge of acceptability, but when your credibility is at stake, misleading headlines are best saved for April Fools' Day.

Question

Is God Dead? Remember that title from the cover of *Time* magazine in 1966?[1] A question can have tremendous allure, especially if it's one that readers have been asking themselves. Question marks at the end of titles also serve as an indicator that the accompanying story is a rumor or not completely understood yet.

Secrets

The Secret to Living Forever. You would read that post, wouldn't you? That's why readers read, isn't it—to discover secrets, to uncover things they didn't know? Establish yourself as a reliable source of those secrets, and the readers will keep coming back for more.

Numbers

Affordable Supersonic Mini-Jet Zips along at 2,000 MPH. Use a number in your headline if it's something unusual, something never done before, a key fact of your story, or a breakthrough. In this case, even fighter jets rarely travel at 2,000 mph, so, yes, that's compelling.

Weird or Unusual

A headline stating **Dog Bites Man** is not that unusual, but **Man Bites Dog** is. Your readers are looking for the unusual, the novel, and the strange. Something completely unheard of might be just what you need to get them to click through and read the entire story. Connect it to a question and ask **What Do You Get When You Mix Pecans and Beer? The Best Cheese in the World.**

Amazing

Household Robot Cooks Breakfast, Cleans Up. If it made your jaw drop when you first heard about it, it will probably do the same to your readers if you express that in the headline. They're sitting there, dying to be amazed, and it's your job to fulfill that wish.

Finally

Finally, Electric Car Drives Coast-to-Coast without Recharging. Is your story about something everyone has been waiting for? People are looking for relief, they're tired of waiting, and they will be more than happy to read about how the wait is over, at long last.

Lists

Top 10 Ways to Kill Your Landlord. Top 10 lists are so pervasive on the web that you'd think they've been overused. You'd be right, but the venerable list shows no signs of abating. Heck, the site *Cracked* publishes lists almost exclusively. Lists are popular because it's easy to read these bite-sized morsels, they're usually accompanied by pictures, and they usually revolve around a fun topic. Make your headline signal how fun its topic is, and your list is well on its way to success.

Shock

The iPhone Sucks. Half your readers will love you, the other half will hate you, but they'll all be compelled to read whatever prose you place underneath an outrageous and controversial headline. Use sparingly.

Rumor

Rumor: Warp Drive to Debut in 2020? You can lead with a rumor as long as you preface it with an explanation. When you've heard a rumor you trust, feel free to publish it. Just be careful to couch it in terms that carefully explain the sourcing and the potential validity. At *Mashable*, we put a [REPORT] at the end of hed to make it clear the story's not a confirmed fact.

The Straight Story

Scranton-Area Teachers Walk Out of Union Talks. There is something to be said about straight news headlines. Not everything has to be an absolute gimmick. Telling the story clearly in the headline and then expanding it in text is always a winner when nothing else fits. Not every headline has to be a gotcha.

To Capitalize or Not to Capitalize

We're used to seeing capitalized headlines in newspapers and magazines. Generally, we would recommend capitalization of the first letter of each word, unless it's an article (a, an, the) or coordinating conjunction (and, but, or, nor, for) that's not the first word of the title. There are some esoteric beliefs that Google reads capitalized headlines as different content than body text and treats it accordingly, although in many cases that is no longer true. According to UK style, only the first word of a headline is capitalized. Outside of the UK and Europe, capitalized heds seem to be falling out of favor. In a *Conductor* study of reader preferences of headlines, 64 percent preferred sentence case (www.conductor.com/news/5-data-insights-headlines-readers-click). However, never write a HEADLINE IN ALL CAPS. It is considered junk by Google and makes you look like you're screaming in text.

Lead with Your Ledes, Don't Bury Them

Get to the point, fast. When you're starting up your story, make it punchy. What you're trying to avoid here is burying the lead (or, in newspaper talk, "lede"). That means in the first sentence, or at most, in the second sentence, plainly tell your readers what the story is about, drawing them in with a good reason or two why they should care.

News stories consist of a lede, a nut graf (the important statement you are trying to make), and research. In general, the lede brings the reader into the story and the nut graf tells them why they came. The research is an added bonus (although many stories are far too long and boring to be considered a bonus).

What you don't want to do: "throat clearing," where you dance around the subject and don't really say anything about the topic until many sentences, or heaven forbid, paragraphs later. **Don't bury the lede, or you'll soon be burying your blog.**

This is not to say your first paragraph can't be playful. For example, you could write:

Remember when Coca-Cola released New Coke? The uproar? The anger? Well, the company's done it again.

It's called Coca-Cola Throwback, a new beverage that contains 100% real organic sugar instead of corn syrup. And trust me: There will be no riots in the streets over this new addition to the Coca-Cola family.

Your nut is actually the second graf, but the first graf, in this case the lede, was something to catch your reader's attention. It gives them something to think about—perhaps reminisce about. Then you can move right into the meat of the story in the nut. A lede should be a few dozen words, at most, and express everything you're trying to say in encapsulated form.

Use Perfect Grammar or Your Credibility Is Shot

Even if your story selection is the world's best and your headlines the grabbiest, your readers' respect for you and your writing plummet when you make a grammatical error. As soon as your readers think you're uneducated, they'll start suspecting that your research methods, your judgment, and your basic level of intelligence suck, too.

This is not to say you can't make typos—go ahead! You can always fix them. But if you're not comfortable with a certain construction or turn of phrase, avoid it. Simplify your writing to prevent potential problems.

If you decided to become a writer, yet still aren't familiar with basic rules of grammar, you've got some work to do. Of course, we know that most of the readers of this book are well versed in the eccentricities of English grammar, but if you don't fall into this group, it's time to study up and hone your grammatical accuracy to perfection.

This is especially true if you're writing in English as a second language. We've seen countless excellent posts butchered by poor translations. If you're writing in English, write in an English that a native speaker would find concise and dry rather than imprecise and floridly bad.

How do you study grammar? One way to hone your grammatical skills is to read a lot, learning by observation. Or you could visit one of the dozens of websites that specialize in grammar and common usage mistakes. Or you could get Strunk and White's *The Elements of Style*, laying it all out for you in one terse treatise. There's a multitude of books written about grammar, but for the sake of a quick lesson, we'll school you on the grammatical, style, and usage crimes you're most likely to commit. Keep in mind that many of the following examples are opinions John and Charlie have honed over the years of writing books, magazine and website articles, and blog posts—your site or editors might have a slightly different approach.

Top Fifty Grammar, Usage, and Style Goofs

1. **It's/Its:** This is by far the most prevalent grammatical error on the Internet. Just keep in mind that the word "it's" is a contraction of the words "it" and "is." What you're saying is a shortened form of "it is." The possessive form of "its" doesn't work like other possessives in the English language, because it needs no apostrophe. For example: *It's a shame that the English language must be mangled by those who haven't mastered its subtleties.* By the way, whenever a word is plural, don't go putting an apostrophe before the s. We're reminded of a sign at a gas station that read, "Drink's, 50 cent." Of course, no reader of this book has ever been guilty of such a grammatical crime.

2. **There/Their/They're:** "Their" is a possessive of "they," "they're" is the contraction of "they are," and "there" is the opposite of "here."

   For example:
   They're lying there, checking their email.
   By the way, this brings to mind the terms lie and lay: You lie around, you lay yourself down to sleep, you're not an easy lay. Hens lay, you lie!

3. **Lose/Loose:** People constantly misuse these words. We're still trying to figure out why, because it's so easy to understand that loose describes something that's not tight, while to lose means to misplace something.

   For example:
   As he ran, his phone worked its way loose from his belt, causing him to lose it.

4. **Your/You're/You:** This one's easy. "Your" is the possessive of "you," and "you're" is just an easy way to say "you are."

   For example:
   You're certainly taking your time, aren't you?
   By the way, increasingly, we're seeing the word "you" used instead of your, but we suspect that's usually a typo.

5. **Pronoun and antecedent agreement:** "Each person must remember their own name." No. "Each person must remember his own name," or write around it if you want to be gender-neutral: People must remember their own names. Or if you must, write "his or her."

6. **For free:** The word "for" is not necessary. "Get out of jail free."

7. **As:** We can't understand how the word "as" has crept into writing like this, but it has: "He can walk long distances, as he is a nomad." ". . . then look no further, as we've found 10 . . ." Use a dash if you have to, but don't misuse the word "as."

8. **Out there:** This is almost always unnecessary. It separates writer from reader. Products are not "out there." Out where? For example, "There are thousands of cellphones out there." "For all you readers out there . . ." Draw them in—don't place them "out there."

9. **Over at:** "The writers over at *Boing Boing* found an entertaining video." Unnecessary words. It's electronic, they're not "over at" anything or anywhere. And you need only one directional, not two of them up in here.

10. **Reach out:** Strangely enough, this cliché phrase began its touchy-feely life in a television commercial for AT&T. "Reach out and touch someone." That was the slogan. Now it's grown into an all-consuming monster. It's dragged out every time we want to say we contacted someone. I think it's important to be specific about how you contacted someone. Say emailed, or called, or talked with someone. How did you "reach out?" Was the guy drowning and you reached out to pull him onto the dock? Even if you have to say "contacted someone," it's better than "reaching out." You're not reaching out to anything—this is all electronic. No reaching.

11. **Clichés:** Grails, antes, touch base, loop in—the first time someone used these, it was probably clever. Now it's tired business speak. No grails, and don't raise any more antes.

12. **Towards:** It's toward. It's forward. Not towards, not forwards (unless you're writing in British English).

13. **The word "that" can often be omitted:**—for example, "There's not much that its code-free apps can't do." We use the word "that" in sentences so often that it's something that we think that we might want to stop. Stop that. Try dropping the word "that," and you'll notice that your sentences are tighter. We mean you'll notice your sentences are tighter.

14. **Company/their:** A company is singular. People in a company are "they," but the company is an "it."

15. **"Should" instead of "if":** "Should you find yourself without water or power . . ." We're not sure where this one came from, but it's popping up too often. The correct form using "should" would be "If you should find yourself . . ."

16. **Awesome:** This used to be a wonderful word. Now, it's been overused and it's lost all its power. I would suggest using it only in its proper context, such as times when you're referring to explosions, hurricanes, things that are gigantic, unbelievable, one-of-a-kind, and rare.

17. **Amazing:** This word is elbowing in to take the place of "awesome." Use it sparingly.

18. **Use a semicolon** if the second part of your sentence can stand by itself but is still related to the first part: "Basic apps are free; more advanced options start at $39 per month."

19. **An ellipsis** needs an extra dot (with a total of four) if it's the end of a sentence. . . . And be careful with the ellipses overall—they're on the verge of overuse.

20. **Impact as a verb:** "How has Google impacted your life?" Although some grammar mavens will disagree with us on this one, "impact" is not a verb unless you're talking about an asteroid impacting the earth, or a wisdom tooth being impacted. You could have an impact on something, but you can't impact it.

21. **Very:** Write very, very, very powerfully and you won't need to lean on this crutch.

22. **We want to hear your thoughts:** We've never heard a thought before. We would rather use the word "opinion" for thought, anyway. Or perhaps say, "Let us know what you think." Thoughts? Don't ask for them. No one is going to write down thoughts. They're thinking them, not writing them.

23. **Premiere vs. premier:** Charlie messed this one up on a TV graphic once, and that's how he learned it. A premiere is an event when something new is presented. Premier is something at the top of its class, the best, or a person who is in charge of a government. Adobe Premiere is a software application. It is the premier video editing application.

24. **No period** at the end of a phrase that isn't a complete sentence and isn't followed by another sentence (think: bullet-pointed lists)

25. **Passed away, passed:** "Passed away" softens death and sounds folksy. Funeral directors say it a lot. But it doesn't sound professional for writers. People die. Deal with it. They are dead. Someone has died. "Passed away" has religious connotations, and it's amateurish. "Passed" is even worse, sounding like something your great-grandmother would have said. I don't even like to use the term "RIP," which also has religious connotations and is archaic, but it's good for SEO.

26. **People that, those that:** This should be "people who," or "those who." People are referred to as "who," not "that." People are humans, not things.

27. **Throat clearing:** When emailing or writing anything, you have only about a dozen words to grab a reader's attention. Use them wisely. Get to the point in the first paragraph, as quickly as possible. People are busy, and you can't squander your only chance to lure them in.

28. **In order to:** There's rarely a case when you need to use this phrase. Just leave out the words "in order" and just say "to." In order to make the most of your writing, stop using the inefficient and flabby phrase, "in order to." It's similar to that other hitchhiker of a word, "that." Try getting rid of "in order to" and "that," and notice how much tighter your sentence sounds.

29. **Whenever you talk about a couple of things**, don't forget the word "couple" has a trusty companion, the word "of." Sure, people like to talk about having a couple beers, things that happened a couple months ago, giving a couple examples—but I think it's a bit too folksy for pro writing.

30. **Passive voice:** Make your writing more rigid by losing that passive voice. "The world was in disarray, so changes were made." Changes were made? No. "World War III changed the world." BOOM!

31. **New words:** These two relatively new words haven't gotten their usage nailed down yet: ereader and checkin. Make those electronic books easier to read about by referring to them as e-readers. And please, make your favorite thing to do on Foursquare sound like something beyond a description of barnyard animals, and call it a check-in.

32. **Junkies:** The era of calling people "junkies" if they like to do something is over. If you've ever seen, known, or heard about what junkies are really like, you won't want

to call someone that, or refer to yourself as such, either. Better to use the words aficionado, fan, lover, or even fanatic if you must, but junkies are sad and ill and need our help.

33. **Real time:** When you talk about real time, leave out the hyphen. If the words "real time" modify another word, put in the hyphen. (Correct: in real time, real-time acceptance.)

34. **Wide variety:** A variety is already wide enough without adding the word wide. Ask yourself whether there is such a thing as a narrow variety.

35. **Tweeted out:** It's stylish to talk about "tweeting out" and "sharing out" things, but is the word "out" really necessary in this context? Is it possible to "tweet in" something?

36. **Called out:** Unless you're writing extremely informally, the phrase "called out" is not exactly a professional term to use if, say, a company has criticized another company. Nor does it need a hyphen in this context: "Being called-out for his policies by the public."

37. **Retina:** Apple's high-resolution displays are Retina displays, not Retina Displays or retina displays.

38. **Dollars dollars:** When you have a dollar sign next to a word, you don't need to have the word dollar written after it: "$13 billion dollars" is incorrect. All you need is $13 billion. And love. Love is all you need.

39. **Crowdsourced, not crowd-sourced.**

40. **"Like" instead of "such as":** If something is like something else, then you're not referring to that thing. You're referring to something else—for example: "Bands like the Beatles were big in the '60s." A band like the Beatles would be the Rolling Stones, not the Beatles. The correct usage here would be, "Bands such as the Beatles were big in the '60s."

41. **Teen slang:** While we're on the subject of the word "like," a word we hippies were so fond of using in the '60s and which has grown to the teen-slang monster it is today: like, stop, like, using it in that context. You know?

42. **"My personal favorite":** No need to write the word "personal" here; tighten it up. Just write "my favorite." Same with the word "personally."

43. **How many?** "A number of" or "numerous" tells you nothing. What's that number? Is it a secret? Just write "several," or "a few" for rough estimates—or better yet, get the actual number.

44. **Begs the question:** Writers get this wrong almost every time it's used. The phrase "begs the question" seems to say that it practically begs for a question to be asked. But the term "begs the question" actually means using an unproved point to prove itself. For example, "You shouldn't beg the question because begging the question is something you shouldn't do." That's begging the question.

45. **Cellphone:** one word

46. **Borrow:** "Can you borrow me a dollar?" This might be a Midwestern thing, something we were surprised to hear someone say. But we put it in here for laughs and to make you feel superior for not saying it.

47. **But:** Starting a sentence or paragraph with "but" is not a good idea, in the opinion of some grammar sticklers. But we think it's okay, and this is our book—it says right there on the cover. So that's our opinion. But we could be wrong.

48. **Email:** This word has no hyphen—it's just "email."

49. **Any more/anymore:** Here's how to use these words: "I don't buy books anymore because I don't need any more books."

50. **Only time will tell:** Charlie once worked at a TV station where the news director said he would fire anyone who used the term "only time will tell" at the end of a story. That was unforgettable, and maybe the guy had a point. The news team had just gone through four newscasts in a row where reporters ended their stories with those words. The phrase was never spoken again within those walls. Will we actually use this phrase again? Only time will tell. Uh, no, we won't.

Choosing Details

People talk about paying attention to details, but what they really mean is paying attention to the *right* details. Invariably, you'll find yourself writing a blog post about a concept, product, or service that's complicated. In the political world there might be a detailed proposal that you'd like to critique. Or in the technology world, there could be a new digital camera that was just rolled out, with a feature list as long as your arm.

Will you write about every one of those new features? No, please don't. Pick the most important details, and write about those. For instance, in that digital camera example, write about the one thing that makes this camera better than its predecessor. Is it the camera's ability to shoot image-stabilized HD video as well as pro-quality stills? Write about that, rather than waxing poetic about megapixels, ISO numbers, and a long list of shooting modes included in the camera's interminable menus.

Find the meat of the story, write about it, put it into context, and nail it. Few readers will remember a flurry of details, but more will remember a single point you made. Tell them why that new feature that you singled out is so important; tell them something they didn't already know. Some of your readers will be interested in the minutiae—provide them with a link to a list of the product specifications. That should satisfy the small percentage of people who want to know every detail.

Include "telling detail," a finer point that could potentially explain a situation in a more poetic and lucid way than your own explanation. If a politician kept fiddling with her hair during a debate, write that instead of saying, "She was nervous." If a musician flipped off the crowd and threw a water bottle at his roadies, write that instead of "He looked angry." Blogging is a visual medium, and the text should reflect that vibrancy and immediacy.

Another consideration when you're trying to decide what to write about and what to leave out: Take a look at the picture you've selected to go along with your post. If, for example, you can plainly see that the camera you're writing about is available in four different colors, you need not mention that in the text. The same goes for food, cars, people—anything visual. Why show it once and say it twice? Economy of language is key.

Some topics simply cry out for detail, and that's when you can artfully include numerous specifications in your post. There is a way to do this, but you must be clever about it. For example, you can use some of the camera's attributes as modifiers, like so: "This 12-megapixel sharpshooter gets you up close with its macro lens." While it's best to avoid long lists of specs, if you must include them, compare them with other competing products for context.

Repeating Yourself Again and Again, Using Unneeded, Unnecessary, and Uncalled-For Words and Phrases and Expressions and Stuff

Avoid constructing a twenty-word sentence when four words will do. Think more like Mickey Spillane, with his arresting four-word sentence, "He punched him, hard." Think about Ernest Hemingway's six-word short story: "For sale: Baby shoes, never worn." Be yourself when you write, shedding that college-level formality you used when writing those oh-so-important term papers. This means you can toss out all those wordy and useless phrases you have swimming around in your brain. We'll give you a little preview. This is by no means an exhaustive list, but it contains the ones that bother us the most:

This point in time
A number of
I myself
Close proximity
Personally, I think . . .
Hot water heater
Each and every
That being said
The fact of the matter is . . .
Essentially

Developing Your Writer's Voice

Once you've gotten comfortable with grammar, vocabulary, word usage, and all those other nitpicky details, toss it all out the window and be yourself. By now, that should all be automatic. The most important thing you need to do as a blogger is to develop your own voice, and the way to do that is toss the caution and let your readers get to know you.

Will you be friendly? Angry? Rant-prone? Authoritative? An expert? Reader-dependent? Whiny? Asking a lot of questions like we are right now? Look at your posts and see if there's a thread connecting them all. Do they sound alike? Can readers tell you wrote it because of the style? Then you, sir/madam, have a voice. Do your humble authors have distinctive voices? Can you tell which of us wrote this paragraph? Go ahead, guess.

Be warned: Your voice may move into your everyday writing, something that could hinder you if your day job involves more formal forms of communication. While we've never met a person whose writing hasn't been improved by regular blogging, we have noticed a change in tone and detail when it comes to more advanced projects. Take this book, for example: We wrote it like we would write a blog post, peppered with whimsy and in a conversational style. However, if we had to go to work tomorrow and write documentation for a computer system or a digital camera, we'd be concerned the blogging style may emerge. Writing for blogs is different from writing for, say, a law office. Be aware of the effects blogging may have on your outlook and voice.

Think of it this way: You wouldn't go up to your best pal and start phrasing things differently, picking out unusual words, and distracting your friend with flowery phrases from somewhere way beyond left field. Of course not. You'll get to the point of what you're saying, speaking clearly in a friendly tone, and injecting everything you say with . . . the essence of you. That's what you need to do with your writing. Relax, be yourself, find your personal essence, and put it down on the page.

An easy way to accomplish this exercise is to imagine one particular person you're writing for, and then dash out your post while keeping that person in mind, telling the story exactly the way you would if the two of you were face to face. Just like you would with your best friend, don't be afraid to take risks, veer over to that quirky angle, inject humor, and generally play around with your message. But if you're not funny, or quirky, or never generally play around with anything, don't start doing it now. Just be yourself.

How to Keep Your Readers Engaged

You picked your blog's topic already, right? That doesn't mean you have to write only about an extremely narrow subject. Part of what will entertain your readers is the element of surprise, where you write occasional posts that are entirely off topic, but are certainly something your readers have never seen. Don't be afraid to diversify. Keep your mind open to novelty, and your readers will thank you for it. You might choose to place this sort of novelty on your blog at random, or you could reserve a day and time for your quirkiness—for example, "Freaky Friday's craziest video," or "Kooky Pic of the Day." Tie these themed ideas into your topic, and they're even better. Keeping your posts unpredictable plays into the main reason your readers are visiting your blog: for entertainment.

You can also write outside of your comfort zone to gain a new readership. For example, we often recommend writing about topics outside of your realm of experience, but on topics that will appeal to other bloggers you admire. One blogger we spoke with writes primarily about parenting the over-twenty-one set—boomerang kids—but she wrote a handful of posts about "technology and the older parent" to catch the attention of a few of the tech blogs.

This is not "writing to suit." Instead, it is more like writing to get a bit more attention and to cross over into other audiences. If you write primarily about cars, why not write about a bike that features some special Porsche technology? If you write about beekeeping, why not interview a scientist about ecological issues facing not just bees but birds, trees, and even humans? You're trying to gather new readers by working outside of your comfort zone.

Scannability

Make your writing more accessible by inserting scannable elements such as boldface subheads, or short beginning sentences for each paragraph that are highlighted in boldface. See that subhead above this paragraph? That's making this text more scannable. These elements encourage your site visitors to read your post, luring them with easily accessible, bite-sized pieces rather than the gigantic wall of solid text.

At the very least, follow our earlier suggestion of keeping your paragraphs from running on too long, further discouraging your readers to dive in. When your paragraphs get longer than four or five lines, that's pushing the edge of too much text in one place for a blog. Many of your readers will scan just the subheads if you do give them these boldface steppingstones, but that's better than having them skip reading the page altogether.

Blogging Traps

When you begin blogging, all is lilacs and peppermints. However, after a few weeks or months, you may find your resolve and attitude wavering and waning. Don't worry; it happens to everybody. Maintain your 1,000-word minimum and watch out for these blogging traps.

The Cynicism Trap

There is a period in blogging when nothing you do is any good and you will become mean. Commenters will know you're not writing well, and they'll call you on it. You'll also notice that nothing is any good and that everything you write about is, in a word, stupid. You've hit the cynicism cycle, but if you're careful you can escape it fairly quickly.

Writers, when given the opportunity to express their opinions to a real audience, will eventually gravitate to a period of wild cynicism. We've seen it happen time and time again: Let's say you're a new blogger who gains some readers and becomes an expert in a field. Instead of looking at things with fresh eyes, you'd rather that your chosen topic be shut down altogether. You've started to believe there's nothing new under the sun for you to write about. You'll be so enamored with the process that you'll forget the ground rules. Stop, take a deep breath, and start writing "straight" news. Don't inject your wisecracks or cynicism into the news and slowly dig yourself out of the cynicism trap.

This is only one of the traps bloggers will face, but it is the most insidious and the most damaging. If unchecked, the cynicism trap could become your entire MO, thereby reducing the value of your opinion. Watch for untoward anger toward your subject, and slow it down before it runs away with you.

The Swearing Trap

Go ahead and swear, but watch out: You're writing for a big audience. If you assume your audience is comfortable with your language, so be it. We're not here to stop you. As a rule of thumb, however, treat swearing the same way you'd treat lawn fertilizer—a little can help a sentence pop, a lot can burn out your whole post. Our stance is there should be no profanity in straight news reporting, and as much as you see fit in more opinion-orientated pieces. As blogs mature, this is changing. For instance, when we first started writing for *Gizmodo*, we both liberally used vulgarities, even in headlines. As the years went by, a quiet plea to omit them in headlines emerged from the ivory tower of management. Now, the site is nowhere near as profane as it once was. That's because excess profanity can chase away a mainstream audience. Now, we don't choose to swear a lot when we write about tech, damn it, but politics could drive you toward uttering a blue word or two. It's your choice, but remember that not all vulgarities and oaths are created equal. You might be able to get away with a saucy vulgarity sometimes, but be careful with the F word, and unless you're a skinhead or crazy, never use racial or sexist slurs. Your commenters will let you know if you've gone too far.

The Context Trap

In most blog posts, context is king. You may have followed a story from beginning to end, but that doesn't mean a new reader has followed you on that journey. Remember that nothing is ever self-evident. Assume that your readers are familiar with what you've written about in the past, but always offer a way for newer visitors to further research the topic at hand if they are unfamiliar with all of the details. How? You can simply write something like "If you'll recall, XYZ Corp. was involved in shady dealings (detailed here) in the cat food trade, resulting in an ASPCA investigation." The words "detailed here" will link back to a previous story about the topic you—or someone else—wrote. You can also link to resources like dictionaries or Wikipedia or you can add a few links at the bottom of the story pointing to previous stories in the same thread. For example, perhaps you're writing about the building of a new dam on a nearby river. You can link to the first story written—the proposal for the dam passing at City Hall—and then the subsequent debate and discussion. This is called a "tick-tock," and newspapers used to create these stories at the end of a news cycle, recounting everything that happened from the beginning. This is rarely productive, however, and as you can imagine, it's far easier to use hyperlinks to build a timeline for your reader to follow along in history. And, if you hyperlink to stories you've written on your own blog, it's a great way to enhance your pageview statistics.

You should also use tags and categories to create archives of data for your readers. For example, *CrunchGear* used to have a set of tag pages—words that WordPress recognizes as tags—to organize posts on a particular topic. If you visit crunchgear.com/tag/ipad, you will find a list of all iPad-related posts we've ever written. Consult your blogging platform's instructions for handling tags and use them to add context to your stories within the text.

The "Not Today" Trap

Blogging is like any sustained, regular activity: You get better with practice and you get worse with inattention. If you put something off today, you'll probably put it off tomorrow and tomorrow and tomorrow. Like working out and flossing, blogging should become a habit before it becomes your job. Remember: a dead blog is worse than no blog at all.

Types of Posts
Short Post

This is where blogs started. A writer would roam the web, find interesting links, hopefully add a comment or two, and publish it in a time-based layout starting with the latest posts at the top. It was a web log of what the author had seen that day, or that hour, similar to the way Twitter is used today. A short blog post is probably going to be the mainstay of your site, where you find a story, post a picture of it, briefly tell the readers the gist of the story, add a pithy comment or some context of your own, and you're done. Write it tight. No need to be overly verbose—just make your point, perhaps link to another story within your blog that you've written on a similar topic, and then show them the link where you found the story, letting them peruse all the details for themselves.

Reviews

If your blog is about products or services, here's where you show your stuff. The presence of reviews on your site can accomplish a lot, such as protecting your readers from slipshod products, alerting them to spectacular values and showing them aspects of a product no one else has noticed yet. Beyond that, a good review satisfies your readers' basic curiosity about a product. When you're reviewing products, the objective is to call 'em as you see 'em, just like an impartial umpire at a baseball game. Prove yourself to be a trustworthy guide to your topic. Along the way, you'll learn a lot about your chosen field, getting your hands on the products that define your blog's essence. Reviews can be simple and short when you're covering a minor product, or can be thousands of words long if you're covering a complicated and important item.

If you're writing a technology blog or something that involves a highly technical review, we recommend creating a boilerplate header for reviews. For example, *TechCrunch* usually uses a bulleted list of pertinent features and then a basic pros/cons list. Then we have a "short version" of the review to sum up our opinions.

Using that macro software for Mac we told you about in Chapter 2 called QuicKeys (or KeyText for Windows), we paste this boilerplate into every review. It saves time. Instead of entering the code for those lists, we simply type "revhed" and the following HTML appears in our posts.

```
<strong>Features:</strong>
<ul>
<li></li>
<li></li>
<li></li>
<li></li>
<li></li>
</ul>
<strong>Pros:</strong>
<ul>
<li></li>
<li></li>
<li></li>
</ul>
<strong>Cons:</strong>
<ul>
<li></li>
<li></li>
<li></li>
</ul>
```

These sorts of macro systems are excellent if you type the same things over and over again and are available on both Macs and PCs. Develop your own "look and feel" for reviews for your blog, such as various icons for pros and cons, or your own rating system.

Features

A "feature" is a longer story about a specific subject or news item. It can be a profile—a discussion of a person or item—in context or it can tell a longer story. Feel free to split longer features up into multiple posts.

You're close to your subject, studying it every day and discovering all the details surrounding it. Give your readers perspective by writing in-depth features about your chosen topic. As you work on your blog each day, develop a running list of features that you'd be interested in learning more about. If there is a local event that fits into your category, attend that, take lots of pictures, and turn it into a feature. Identify relationships between subjects that you routinely cover, and write an exposé. Think about trends, undercurrents, and potentially explosive controversies within your chosen field, and then call some experts, interview people, and turn that kernel of an idea into a full-blown feature. A few good features add a lot of credibility.

There's an old adage that often rings true: **posts bring pageviews, but features bring readers.** Some of the most important features you write might not get tremendous waves of pageviews, but regular readers will appreciate the more in-depth articles. That appreciation can spread to multitudes of other readers through word of mouth or linking on social networks. Think long-term. That could likely be responsible for a slow groundswell of growth that will eventually make your blog consistently successful.

Lists

There's good reason why lists of items are so popular on the web. Their ordinal nature implies judgment, where you've placed all of the items on that list in a hierarchical layout. The posts are written in bite-sized, easy-to-digest chunks. They're enticing, and readers eat them up, especially if you pick compelling items for your lists but stick to your premise. And, if you place a picture with each of your list items, they serve a pictorial purpose, entertaining those readers who don't feel like diving into intense text.

Infographic

Gather a pile of facts, figures, and statistics about a topic, and if you're a pretty good Photoshop artist, you can put together a large, visually pleasing graphic that'll be packed with information that's easy to scan. This kind of visual presentation has gained considerable popularity lately. If you come up with a good idea for an infographic but your design skills won't quite let you execute it yourself, find someone who can, and the resulting boost in traffic might be well worth your time, effort, and expenditure. We noticed at *Mashable* that the most successful infographics are more than just a page full of graphs. Sprinkle fun facts within, along with amusing illustrations, and you'll have yourself a winning formula.

Commentary

Go ahead, rant! This is your chance to sound off, telling them what you really think. Of course, nearly all of your posts and articles will contain your opinions, but this category lets you dive into the controversy, raise new talking points, and get your readers worked up. Don't be afraid to take a stand on an issue, but keep in mind that if most of your readers disagree with you, you could be wrong. When you're writing your commentary, it helps to cite facts to back up each of your points, along with links to your sources so readers can see the information for themselves. Don't just pull a bunch of statements out of your ass whose sole factual support is "because I said so"—well, unless you're a proven expert in the field. Don't be "Captain Obvious," stating opinions that are so well-trodden that everyone knows about them and has heard them over and over. The goal here is to introduce viewpoints to your readers that they might not have ever considered. At the same time, if readers have considered your opinions themselves and wondered if anyone else ever thought that way, they'll get a lift, enjoying the commiseration and validation. You get extra juju if you think up a topic that's bugging everyone but few have written about it yet. Just be sure you clearly mark your missive as "opinion."

Poll/Quiz

When you're first starting out, your number of readers will be so small, it will be embarrassing to create a poll, but a quiz will work with any number of readers. Polls and quizzes have the underlying advantage of adding to your pageview count, because most require more than one page to register votes and display results. Quizzes are a ripe opportunity for humor, slipping in some absurd answers along with the right ones. Be sure to congratulate those who did well on the quiz, while gently ribbing those who didn't.

Polls will entice those readers who don't normally take the trouble to comment to participate. They can be versatile, occupying a small space on your front page, or turning into an entire demographic study within your site. Polls are easy to insert on any site, and at *Mashable* we've had good experiences with *Polldaddy* (http://polldaddy.com), which allows us to customize the look of the poll. You create the poll on the *Polldaddy* site, and when you're done, like *YouTube*, you're provided with code to embed on your own site to display the poll. It's an easy way (and free for those just starting out with less than 100 responses per month) to create quick polls, and we recommend it highly.

> ### Pro Tip
>
> If you want to get more in-depth with your readers and find out demographic information, their story preferences, or anything else about them, you'll need to create a survey. A popular online survey service is Survey Monkey, whose basic free plan lets you create a ten-question survey with up to 100 responses per survey, probably enough for a site that's just starting out. But to get a large enough sample for validity of your data, you'll need to spring for at least the "Select" plan, giving you unlimited questions and responses for $17 per month.

Caption

If you find a video, picture, or sight gag that tells a story by itself, a caption underneath that content consisting of a half-dozen words or less might be all you need. Other times, photos or videos need more setup and explanation, but keep it simple and let the pictures do most of the talking. You might even dive into the latest click-whoring gallery scheme where you present a group of twenty photographs or videos in a slideshow or gallery format, with each pic earning you a click. Go ahead, write your story within the captions for each of the gallery items, but know this: Many readers are increasingly annoyed at this obvious ploy for more pageviews. You might consider placing all the photos or embedded videos on one easily scrollable page with captions attached, just to keep your readers happy (at *Mashable*, we offer a single-page option for all of our galleries). On the other hand, if you're looking for a bonanza of pageviews, see what happens when you write a blockbuster post with thirty photos, each earning its own pageview. So here it is: Should you make your site easy to navigate and please your readers, or go for the gold? The decision is yours, Captain, but we'd say keep your decisions user-friendly most of the time.

Interview

If you get lucky enough (or if you're aggressive or well-connected enough) to have a chance to talk with a newsmaker, important person, or generally interesting industry maven, you might want to transcribe that VIP's words into a text interview, just like the ones that appear in *Playboy* magazine. And yes, we do read the articles in that girlie mag. Get yourself a voice recorder or use an app on your smartphone, and record that celebrity's every word, later transcribing it faithfully for your readers. Try making it punchier by publishing only the most pithy phrases and sentences, but don't edit it so much that the content is distorted. If it doesn't play well as a full verbatim interview, write a story with numerous quotes. If you're up for it, shoot video of your interview for the full face-to-face effect, or you can go for a combination of transcript and audio file, giving your readers a choice of hearing or reading the interview.

How-To

How-tos are some of the most popular posts you can write. People love them. The goal of a how-to (some people call them tutorials) is to explain a process in step-by-step fashion, describing each step in as much detail as you can muster. What kind of how-tos can you post? Beer bloggers can write about how to pour the perfect pint. Knitters can describe special stitches. Bike bloggers can describe brake upgrades. Anything you do and want others to learn is fair game.

Battles

Will your blog be a pugnacious, fighting publication? Will you be constantly on the offensive, aggressively attacking anything and everything? Picking fights with everyone and anyone is not necessarily a strategy—it's just aggression. On top of that, if you always go negative, your writing becomes predictable. Pick your battles. Attack a product or a person only if something outrageous has happened. Keep in mind that it's always easier to tear things down than to build them up, and you might discover that you're going negative just because it's easier. Finally, protect yourself from libel lawsuits by refraining from attacking someone with false accusations. Truth is the best defense, so if you're going to get into the negative game, be sure you have the truth on your side.

Graphics and How to Use Them

Find a graphic for every post. If you're writing about a product, this is easy, because companies are usually more than happy to provide you with high-resolution shots of their products from all conceivable angles. In that context, feel free to use any company-supplied pictures you want.

With conceptual stories, commentaries, and features, graphics can get a little trickier. In our experience, if we use a picture found on another website, simply linking to that site at the end of the article is not enough—you must ask the owner of that graphic for permission to use it. If it's a unique, clever graphic, you're better off creating one of your own.

> **War Story**
>
> At *Mashable,* Charlie never once had anyone refuse to allow him to use a photo, even if it was an exclusive. But that was on a major site where a link back to the picture's originator was valuable. It might not be so easy if you're just starting out.

In other cases, combining or modifying graphics using Photoshop (or any other image editor) usually turns those graphical elements into a new-enough image, especially if you're making fun of those depicted within—copyright law calls it "parody." The Fair Use provisions of U.S. copyright law will usually protect you when you want to use pieces of images, particularly if they're small, otherwise known as "thumbnails."

If you're in doubt and feeling paranoid, ask the organization that owns those images for permission before publishing. That's not good enough for some corporations and those who want to follow the letter of the law. Each site has its own philosophy; for example, at *Mashable* and at one NBC site, each graphic we used required written permission from its owner. Within the same company, at another NBC site, we were allowed to grab graphics from wherever we wanted, regardless of whether we linked to its owner. At *Mashable*, we used only graphics we bought from iStockPhoto or Getty Images, and graphics or photos we'd created ourselves, were provided by companies, or were licensed for Creative Commons. Many of those images can be found on the photo-sharing site Flickr.com, and are easily found by using search engines such as CC Search (http://search.creativecommons.org/) or Compfight.com.

Snark and the Single Blogger

Comedy and snark are defining characteristics of blogs, but they're not necessary to write interesting posts. Because both of your humble narrators spent many of our formative years at the snark capital of the world, otherwise known as Gawker Media, we sometimes find ourselves spewing out geyser-loads of snarkcasm. Here's how we've controlled that urge: if you do choose to go snarky, remember to use a light touch. As we described earlier, the Cynicism Trap will capture you in its clutches when you least expect it, resulting in less humor and more bile.

The easiest way to decide on insult humor is to remember the old rule of thumb for comedy: saying "I suck" is funny, saying "You suck" is not funny. While there are many insult comics who make a decent living, there are far more comics who focus more on introspective humor.

Use humor and snark the way you'd use any writing technique. Repetition can get boring. However, it's always fun to end a post with a quip or include a funny graphic that closely relates to your topic. Serious blogs are often too straight-laced for many readers, and the wellspring of most early blogs was snark, wit, and anger. Poking fun at your subjects or yourself is the soul of blogging.

However, remember that sarcasm doesn't translate well in the blogging arena. Users read your posts quickly and often with minimal comprehension. Parodies can work well as long as you're over the top. Imagine that blogging is like mime—to express emotion, the emotion has to be exaggerated to the point of being grotesque. For example, users who may not know your position on a topic may see your sarcasm as support or condemnation of a competing viewpoint. This, in turn, leads to angry comments hurled in your direction.

Post Length

Mashable, *TechCrunch*, and *Gizmodo* were all built on the concept of variety, where long posts have always been juxtaposed with medium-length and shorter posts. This works because you're giving busy readers a way to quickly entertain themselves with the short posts, while offering in-depth coverage to those with longer attention spans and higher interest levels. This also gives you the ability to write longer pieces for more complicated topics, and fire away short, punchy posts that make just a single point.

Some say longer posts gather more readers—we disagree. Longer posts require real dedication from a busy reader and unless your writing is top-notch, you can expect a reader to stop at the third graf. If you haven't held a reader's attention for that long with your prose, you're sunk.

Many bloggers focus primarily on longer posts, writing one or two items per day. This is one way to go, but these bloggers often include large, enticing photos and lots of commentary. The best examples of these include the aforementioned *BikeSnobNYC* and *ABlogToRead*.com, a blog about watches.

Being a Better Blogger

As you blog, constantly strive to improve. Reread old posts for typos. Plan new posts. Assess, through analytics, what gets the most attention. See which posts attract the most visitors—those are your readers telling you what they want. Give them what they want! Write posts that *you'd* like to read. Create goals and match them. These are steps you need to take to become a better blogger. If you do this every day or do this as a source of livelihood, all of these improvements will come naturally. However, if you don't treat blogging as a daily exercise you will not succeed.

Here are some tips for better blogging:

- Write punchy: Not every sentence has to be fifty words long. Write text that is short, concise, and rhythmic.
- Remember the pyramid structure of news writing and use it as often as possible.
- Use quotes: Quotes from your original source are an excellent way to propel a story along without much work.
- Use short paragraphs: Your lede and nut should be as short and concise as possible.
- Write as if no one wants to finish your stories: Remember that your readers don't have a lot of time. You are vying for their attention. Unless you give them a good reason to keep coming back, they won't.
- Write for the F: Studies have found that the average reader looks at two words in a headline and reads in an F pattern—sliding their eyes along the first line, then barely

grazing the remaining lines, until they hit the end of the page. The remainder of the F, the downstroke, is them skimming the rest of the story. Put your most important news in the top bar of that F.

- Modern readers love brevity over longer stories: This is a fact of journalism. Your beautifully wrought tick-tock about the rise of a political figure will be overshadowed by pictures of that figure *in flagrante*. This does not mean we want you to pander—we just want you to understand what makes news. Building a great story out of great news is excellent, but, to quote the bard, "Be brief, I pray you."

- Look at the rest of the story: What are other sites missing when it comes to your story? What can you add?

- Leave your office: Go and meet people—even PR people. Go and explore your beat by going to a conference or meeting. Hands-on posts are much more valuable and widely read.

- Do no harm: Don't be a battle blogger, always itching for a fight. Do your own thing and work with other bloggers. Competition in the blogging space is real and it's tight, but you don't have to stoop to "beating" the other guy on news items that everyone shares. Shine with your exclusives and scoops, and work together on the news that may or may not bring readers. You should always keep the competition in mind, but in many cases it's far better to link to another blogger and create a relationship of mutual trust. Many people try to fake links in hopes of better rankings on search engines. Why not ask a friendly blogger to link to you because she owes you a favor for linking to her? It happens every day, and it's a helpful way for a blogger to gain traction.

Writing So Someone Will Read You

Imagine your ideal reader. That reader is who you need to be writing for every day you blog. The ideal reader could be your dad. She could be your wife. She could be a blogger you particularly admire. Aim to write things that readers will understand.

The moment you write solely for Google or keywords or other SEO claptrap is the moment you've stopped writing for humans. There are far too many examples of news sources that focus primarily on getting pageviews, clicks, and advertising impressions. Those are secondary to your goal and come organically with good work. Let no one tell you different.

Write for people. Learn about your audience and ask them what they need or want. Create a mailing list for your blog and send surveys every half a year. Use systems like Mailchimp and Survey Monkey to create these feedback loops.

Your goal is to be indispensable to your readership. Understanding them completely does this. Writing specifically for them ensures they will read you again and again.

As bloggers we're given permission to write in any way we see fit. We can be crazy, we can be wacky, or we can be deadly serious. It's this freedom that is so frightening to the average journalist who grew up in an era of editors, deadlines, and free coffee in the newsroom. Those days, it's sad to note, are long gone.

Most important, however, is write things you'd love to read. If we can offer any advice to you, the fledgling blogger, it's that you must believe that what you have to say is important. You're doing yourself a disservice by not sharing it.

Email and Its Discontents

Not exactly sure you want to create a public blog? You can follow all of these same rules while creating an email newsletter, essentially building a digest of stories that you blast out to your followers. While this technique isn't as popular as building a blog, it does have its advantages, especially for more business-oriented sites.

What does an email newsletter get you? Well, you have a dedicated swarm of readers who are, on the average, going to read your posts. It also lends an air of exclusivity to your content. One blogger, Jason Calacanis, even capped his email list at a certain number of people to exude a sort of exclusivity associated with fancy handbags and secret night-clubs. If you have to earn a place at the table, you tend to eat whatever's given you.

So how do you create an email newsletter? I'd recommend using something like Mailchimp, a mailing list service that lets you send a massive number of emails for about $40 a month. Mailchimp allows you to embed "Subscribe" code in your web page so people can sign up to your newsletter and then offers multiple templates and other goodies to contact your list regularly. Email is a great contact medium. While many love social media, it's not quite there in terms of reach and return on investment. Building an email list is a great way to maintain contact with your audience.

Should you just use an email newsletter and not a blog? That's up to you. Some of the best blogs have an email component, and it's become more and more important to have a great list of avid readers. In short, it's a good idea, but offering email-only content depends on your goal. Are you aiming to be an expert that sells your expertise to a certain audience? Do you write about a very specific niche? Are you willing to forgo advertising revenue for reach?

Create

First, familiarize yourself with your mailing application. Many systems allow for rich emails that include images and nice-looking text. We'd recommend creating two newsletters and allow users to opt-in for a text-only version. You will also need to build a list. Don't steal or buy email addresses. Your email newsletter needs to grow organically or you risk being banned from your email provider and angering a whole mess of people.

Email once a week, but fill the newsletter with a week's worth of content. Daily emails are horrible, and monthly emails are easy to forget. Your goal is to create an experience for your readers, something they expect to see and enjoy regularly.

Write your emails like you would write a blog post. In fact, we'd recommend leading people back to your blog. Reading long-form writing in a mail window is a tough sell.

Solicit

Now you have to find those readers. As with any online endeavor, you will find yourself preaching to an empty room until you grow your audience. This is natural and shouldn't frustrate you. We'd recommend creating a website for your newsletter and placing your text up there a few days after you email it out. You can also truncate articles and encourage readers to get the whole thing by requesting they sign up for your newsletter. You can also create an interstitial ad requesting that people join your mailing list. In this case you can treat your blog as a secondary location for your hard-won content.

Distribute

Now press send. And repeat. An email newsletter must appear regularly and at approximately the same time on the same day of the week. Imagine it as a television sitcom. *Modern Family* doesn't just appear whenever the station feels like it. Instead, it appears at a set time and location. This familiarity is key and will keep people coming back.

What's the most important thing? You now have a huge list of emails you can use to contact your readers about special content and offers. In fact, this also allows you to monetize by offering products right inside your emails—but be careful. Today's email newsletter is tomorrow's spam.

Note

1. www.time.com/time/covers/0,16641,1101660408,00.html

Mob Rule, Inciting a Riot, and Freedom of Speech

It's a common perception that in the old days, journalists resided in their ivory towers, typing out their sacred texts and knowing their readers would absorb their scribbling without question. Some readers wanting to raise a stink about what was written would sit down at their typewriters and peck out a letter to the editor. Those journalists who received such screeds would often toss them in the trash, but every once in a while a few of them would find their way into print. Those were published alongside the sacred texts, completing the circle of communication. The cranks had one page in the paper while the journalists had the other hundred.

This mode of communication in which writer is disconnected from reader created an aura of permissiveness, and more important, an infallibility that gave rise to images of "papers of record" recording every important thing happening in the world. But papers of record are fallible, and without oversight these journalists became egoists and felt beholden to no one except, perhaps, the grouchy editor at the top.

There were reasons this system existed. It protected journalists from outside attacks and allowed for some truly groundbreaking stories—stories that redefined the paths of nations and history—to appear in print. However, it created an exclusive club of journalists who looked down on so-called citizen journalism and the voice of the rabble. They controlled the conversation.

This is clearly no longer the case.

Fast-forward to the present, where letters to the editor, now called "commenting" in the text of blogs and websites, have been completely transformed into instant reaction. Depending on how you set up your blog, usually readers can immediately and anonymously pound out their opinions, appearing directly below what you just wrote. It's a conversation, where you receive instant feedback. Welcome to the roller-coaster world of blog comments. As a blogger, one day you'll love them, and sometimes, even a few seconds later, you'll loathe them.

One reason to love them: They let you dip your toe into the tremendous power of what's called "crowdsourcing." The collective IQ of a large group of readers who've been inspired to comment about your post is mind-boggling. It's a level of intelligence significantly higher than any individual could ever muster, and can serve as an amplifier for your posts, a wellspring of new information you might never have considered. Unfortunately, sometimes this crowd can be a cruel and instant editor, notifying you of just how wrong you really are.

In blogging, the crowd acts as your copy editor, your fact checker, and the crabby boss upstairs. By creating an open forum for people to express their views, opinions, and education on a particular topic, you, the blogger, are able to get much more done in a shorter time and with a smaller budget. This is not to say you can write junk and expect the crowd to fix it for you. Instead, think of the crowd as both cheering section and inquisitor. Heck, it's almost like a jury of your peers. They are not interested in what you *meant*; they're interested in what you *wrote*.

What does this mean? It means that everything you write must have context. You cannot assume your reader knows anything about your topic or that your reader assumes *you* know anything about the topic. Your reader assumes you are an idiot on the Internet unless proven otherwise and vice versa. The age of civil discourse has, sadly, passed, and your every foible will be fodder for wild rants.

But don't let it get to you. Our rule of thumb is this: for every rude comment there are ten innocuous comments and two positive comments. Take these other twelve to heart and learn from the rant or, barring that, ignore it.

But sometimes you'll hate the comments you get. Sure, many of them are instructive and constructive, and will effectively show you the error of your ways. Others are simple *ad hominem* attacks, making you feel so bad that you'll be ruminating over some of these insults all night long and well into the next day. Yes, we've been there, receiving criticisms so harsh that we've never forgotten the pain they cause. But as a blogger, know this: you will be criticized, and you will be praised. Develop a thick skin now, because no matter how perfect and great a blogger and writer you are, sometimes you will be wrong, you will be criticized, and you will be hurt, badly. Get used to the idea now, and steel yourself for the torture that rains down upon you when you're being attacked by an angry mob.

Before we begin exploring the madness of crowds, we want to offer two ironclad rules of conversational blogging.

It is a bad idea to delete comments. There are good reasons to delete comments for content and tone and we'll explore them, but unless we're talking about spam or crazy talk, you are doing yourself and your readers a disservice if you delete more than one comment per week.

Also, do not delete a post that appears to have drawn criticism or anger. Deleting a post for fear of retribution is a dangerous precedent to set on your site. If necessary, strike out the offending text using the <s> </s> tag in HTML and update the post, stating clearly why you updated it either in comments or in the post itself. Do this even if the story ends up being an entire post full of crossed-out text. You can correct or transparently modify a story, but to delete it raises problems of control and potential chilling effects.

Gizmodo's Commenting Evolution: A Case Study

In our early days at *Gizmodo*, the privilege to comment, appearing in the form of a coveted invitation, was rare. Before the "invite" system was implemented, Gawker blogs did not have comments at all. The pages were barren. It was a single voice braying to the multitudes, and sadly, that held the company's sites back for almost two years. Then the invite system was formed. We would require readers to *apply* to become a commenter, asking them to write a sample comment or two. We'd want them to tell us why they'd like to express their opinions at the bottom of our posts. We needed them to assure us they wouldn't be stinking up the place. If they passed through our gauntlet, we'd grant them access—a valuable privilege indeed, one they would guard carefully. Oddly enough, we were also encouraged to send comment invites to old-guard journalists. The men and women who wanted their readers to have no voice were suddenly faced with the alien concept of having one online.

The early *Gizmodo* commenters were part of an exclusive club, and took that honor seriously. They remained faithful to us, even though some of us Gizmodians (especially the site's second editor, Joel Johnson) would ridicule them, pretending they were mindless drones who blurted out whatever first came to their feeble minds. Of course, the gentle ribbing we sent their way was all in good fun, because we appreciated what they wrote. They often took more time writing their comments than we had spent writing the posts to which they referred.

It was easy for us to love them. What's not to love about a pack of sycophantic lapdogs that rarely criticized anything we wrote? Why risk their exclusive club membership by pissing on those who have bestowed it upon them? Every once in a while, they would object to (or correct) what we'd written (which was not a bad thing), but generally their criticism was constructive, albeit skewed toward the delicate, as far as criticism of us bloggers was concerned.

What was the result of this love fest? How did that work out for us? Well, the comments we received were generally astute, often surpassing what we had written by orders of magnitude. Because we chose our commenters carefully, most of them were knowledgeable, and some were even luminaries in their fields.

But there was one problem with that. We had set up such a tall barrier to entry that we weren't getting *enough* comments. Hungry to build traffic, we wanted more people involved in this instant criticism/praise/amplification, because more comments attract more traffic. Why? Once a reader had written a comment, that reader would usually return to the site repeatedly to see if there were any responses, reactions, praise, or criticism of the comment.

And so we opened the floodgates to commenters. Gone was the requirement that they pass some sort of test we had constructed. Our next technique was to let just about any commenter blurt out whatever they wanted, but then we would revoke their commenting privileges if they did something that displeased us. They would be banned. The banhammer was born.

An interim experiment involved a technique called "disemvowelling."[1] Just as it sounds, it involves removing the vowels from an offending comment, turning it into barely readable gibberish that can still be vaguely understood if someone wants to go to the trouble. It's an intermediate step before deleting a post, which lets you deny suppression of unpleasant posts, but stops short of permitting it full run of your site. We've tried using this technique once or twice, but it seems to have an odd effect, where it only makes the offenders angrier, and confuses a lot of readers. If this sounds like something you'd be interested in trying, you can get plug-ins for content management systems such as Movable Type and WordPress that make the technique easy to implement.

Sometimes disemvowelling seemed too mild a remedy, so it was time to get out the banhammer. What would constitute grounds for banishment? At first, we had vague and general guidelines—for example, if somebody was "being a douche," we would ban that person. Other capital offenses included attacking a writer personally, repeatedly writing incorrect information, attacking other commenters, spamming us with links to their own sites, writing a bunch of clichés such as "I for one, welcome our ___ overlords," annoying comments such as "How is this news?" or bragging how they were the first ones to comment—boom! Down came the dreaded banhammer.

Interestingly, these are problems faced by most well-developed websites but rarely encountered by smaller sites. If a reader cries out "FIRST!" on your growing website, you're probably going to welcome the excitement. By the ten-thousandth time, however, you're going to get tired of it.

So, as you can see here, we were dealing with two ends of the spectrum with a few stopgaps in between. The first approach was the most restrictive. Going beyond moderating comments, we were moderating the commenters themselves. We created a club of quasi-journalists who added significantly to our content, but unfortunately didn't add much to our traffic. Our reaction to that was the second approach, to swing open the doors to all who desired to comment, and then we'd weed out the trolls. But that wasn't perfect, either—there would still be lots of inane comments sitting on our site until someone removed them.

What was *Gizmodo*'s solution to this problem? In those days, the site developed one of the best and most highly effective commenting systems on the web. Just like the technique that's commonplace in kindergartens across the country, a gold star was awarded to commenters who proved themselves worthy. Once a commenter had earned that gold star, he or she then had the right to moderate other comments. How could commenters get one of these coveted baubles? According to *Gizmodo*, "You just need to blow away the moderators with some great contributions in the comments and they'll reward you with a star." That gold star appears next to the commenter's name with each entry.

Effectively, *Gizmodo* returned to the comment auditioning system, where user comments didn't show up on the site unless they'd been approved by either a *Gizmodo* editor or one of the commenters who possessed a gold star. This caste system turned out to be extremely effective, making all lower-ranked commenters strive for the gold standard. This rising tide lifts all boats. The site also implemented profile pages for each commenter, where all that person's comments, replies, private messages, profile picture, and friends appear.

Since then, *Gizmodo* has further refined its commenting system, turning it into what Gawker Media calls Kinja. It allows readers to turn their profiles into blogs, and lets them use the company's commenting system. This lets them curate and moderate comments as if they were an editor on one of the main Gawker sites. This is a comment system taken to the extreme, almost like a comedian inviting hecklers onstage to see if they can do any better.

Short of building an elaborate and wonderful system such as this, there are other ways of using peer pressure to accomplish roughly the same thing. One effective technique is used on the explosively popular site Reddit, and the once-popular social journalism site Digg. It uses crowdsourcing to elevate or demote comments. Readers can choose to click on either an up-arrow or down-arrow (or on one of the many custom icons created in many of Reddit's "Subreddits"), and as a commenter gets more votes, a number designating the vote count is prominently displayed. Comments with too many down votes become invisible (but can still be accessed with a click), and the threshold of negative votes resulting in invisibility can be set by each user. It works well.

Now, the system of other readers voting their approval or disdain of another comment with a single click is more commonplace. Even a simple system can have a positive effect, such as an option to recommend a comment by a single click on a "recommend" or "like" button, a technique used by *The New York Times*.

We've had success at *Mashable* and *TechCruch* with Disqus (but *Mashable* and *TechCrunch* have since moved beyond that to a Livefyre WordPress plug-in), a commenting system by Big Head Labs that's gaining popularity on a variety of sites such as *CNN*, *Wired*, and *The Daily Telegraph*. Disqus is an online service that embeds a commenting system into your blog. It's integrated with Facebook, Twitter, and Yahoo, and users can log in using those accounts; then their Disqus account can be used across any of the 500,000+ communities that have already installed the service. Our favorite part of Disqus? Its easy moderation tools, and its "like" button, letting others vote in support of a particular comment. The only thing missing is the downvoting capability that's been so popular on Reddit.

There are many companies offering to "manage" your conversations for you, including Disqus and Facebook. Although there are often major concerns about abusive commenters, what usually ends up happening is that most beginning bloggers just depend on the standard mode of anonymous or account-based comment systems available on most content management systems. Having to depend on third-party systems to prevent abuse and general douchebaggery is a good problem to have—it means you have lots of amazing discussion on your site that's being slightly ruined by a few bad apples.

You're in Control

These are all methods to moderate anonymous commenters. Beyond these crowdsourced methods, you can also moderate comments the old-fashioned way: Read them yourself, and delete those that displease you, or are contrary to your terms of service (which we'll discuss later in this chapter). Or, you could engage in an activity that we wish were the standard throughout the Internet, and that is requiring your commenters to reveal their real names.

This is a controversial topic on the Internet at this writing, with those who are against using real names saying that many comments would never be made if people would be held accountable for them. Politically persecuted commenters won't want to express negative feelings against their governments (think Arab Spring or the later conflicts in Syria or Egypt) unless they can comment anonymously. Keep that in mind if you're running a political or world-news blog. Barring that, however, we think people's behavior when assured anonymity is skewing toward the antisocial, and often veers into the obnoxious, abusive, racist, homophobic, and even illegal. On top of that, the cowardice of the anonymous commenter is something we'd rather not support. However, banning anonymity will cost you comments, and the fewer comments you have, the less traffic.

One way to banish anonymity is to require people to use a Facebook profile if they want to comment (Disqus doesn't *require* the user to log in using a traceable account such as Facebook). That way, their real reputation is at stake every time they type anything on your site. Or you could simply require people to use their real names, and confirm their identities via email. This is not perfect, but many times it's better than nothing.

Some form of comment moderation is necessary, even if it does feel like censorship. Let us remind you that the First Amendment forbids only *government* censorship of writings and speech. It doesn't apply to your blog, where you're allowed to censor whatever you want. This works just like it does in the workplace, where you're not allowed to say anything you want there, either. Call the boss an asshole to her face, and see what happens. Yes, she can fire you, First Amendment be damned. If you must, you can do the same thing with those visitors to your blog.

It's hard to get around the obnoxious commenter problem. Each way to deal with the problem is imperfect. Whatever method of moderation you pick, make a serious attempt at encouraging your readers to enhance your site, rather than detract from it. After all, that's your ultimate goal.

Some comments might be okay for some sites, but not for others. For example, there are the borderline commenters who might add insights from time to time, but generally seem to have a mission of self-aggrandizement. These are the ones who gainsay over other commenters (or you), and constantly attempt to pump themselves up into some sort of superhuman wonder boy. "I've done that, I've seen that, I have better than that, I'm better than you." Bah. Depending on how closely you want to moderate your comments, these douchebag braggarts might also be part of the useless detritus you'd like to eliminate with extreme prejudice. We wouldn't blame you.

Again, we encourage restraint when removing comments or commenters, especially at first. The potential value of every new comment far outweighs the annoyance wrought by these selfsame comments. It may bother you to see someone so overtly annoying using your site as a sounding board for such insane ideas, but what is the Internet but a repository that consists of 99 percent ridiculous ideas and 1 percent gold? Your goal is to tease that 1 percent out of your readers. Let the rest of the world maintain the rest.

Encourage comments, but let everyone know what you expect from them. The best idea is to be transparent to those who would like to comment on your site. Set up explicit ground rules, in the form of Terms of Service, a special post with a permanent link to it prominently displayed on your front page. Let this guidepost be a manifesto for commenting on your site, laying down exactly what's permitted and what isn't.

What kinds of guidelines will you use in your comments manifesto? That's entirely up to you, but we'd suggest choosing from the following:

1. Tell them how much you want and appreciate their comments, and how valuable they are.
2. Remind them that this is *your* blog, your home on the web, and you will treat those who comment on it as visitors in your home. If a visitor to your home does something rude that you find unacceptable, that person will be asked to leave.
3. Remind them your site is not a democracy, but more akin to a benevolent dictatorship. In your little fiefdom, you reserve the right to delete any comment for any reason.
4. Reassure them that you won't delete comments just because their writers disagree with your posts. In fact, you should *encourage* disagreement, especially that which is constructive and furthers the discussion.
5. Spell out specifically what kinds of comments will be deleted; for example, what sort of profanity or vulgarity will or won't be tolerated, whether you'll allow personal attacks and smear tactics (let's hope you won't!), and so on.

6. Encourage them to keep the conversations relevant, on-topic, and civil, with a promise that violating comments will be removed.

7. Remind them you will delete commenter accounts if necessary, and in extreme cases you'll even ban the IP addresses whence those offending comments came.

8. Encourage them to report abusive comments and commenters when they find them. Eventually your site will be big enough that you won't be able to police all these comments yourself.

Dealing with the Angry Mob

There are many ways for the conversation to go sour. Perhaps you posted an unpopular opinion about a popular topic, either based on your own feelings or in an effort to raise ire and incite conversation. Both of these are valid methods to create an online presence, and these methods have been used by many of the best bloggers. You are not out to make friends, nor are you out to specifically please your audience at every turn.

While this is a Machiavellian idea, it also further expresses your role as journalist and pundit. You do not have the resources available to the big guys, but that does not mean you have to be beholden to their ideals. To quote Fleetwood Mac, you can go your own way.

So What Did You Do to Unnerve Your Readers?

You hold an opposing viewpoint. Your readers, for the most part, are used to a unified wall of opinion that comes at them from multiple media. These opinions, as we will explore shortly, have the habit of creating internecine wars between two camps. This can be Democrat vs. Republican, Mac vs. PC, or this season's hot starlet vs. last season's. It literally does not matter: you will face strong opinions *no matter what you say*.

You offer a review that is not enthusiastic about a subject that engenders enthusiasm. Saying a band sucks is considered fighting words in many parts of the world. Saying you liked a movie when everyone "knows" it was bad can endanger your life. Saying a product is bad when hype says it is good is grounds for homicide. Your shield in this case is truth.

You are trolling. Trolling is the process by which you express an opinion or perform an action just to get a rise out of people. Done well, it can be an art form. Many of the best bloggers troll at least a few times a month, just to keep the conversation flowing. However, we wouldn't recommend espousing an opinion you don't support just for the sake of luring in higher traffic numbers.

By trolling on everything that is not Apple, for example, Jon Gruber of Daringfireball.com encourages interaction between blogs. How? Many people look at his acerbic posts as calls to action, and as such, they post about what he has written. For example, he often cites statistics about Android that support his view that the iPhone is better. This angers many Android supporters to no end and encourages them to respond to him in their own post, thereby encouraging cross-pollination of his ideas. He may be called an idiot on other blogs, but at least someone is paying attention.

The bedrock of a blog is its conversational nature. That means once you've finished writing your post, you're not really finished. As your blog gains popularity, comments will soon proliferate. They'll start rolling in soon after you've published your post, and some will be addressed to you. Go ahead! Respond. In fact, some posts will collect comments long after they've been read. So-called "evergreen posts" include reviews, bits of conjecture or rumor, and longer think pieces. Check your reviews for occasional updates.

If you've written a particularly controversial post, sometimes the first few comments set the tone for all the rest. Just like mob behavior in the physical world, one person's online anger becomes contagious, spreading to everyone until it festers and accumulates into a huge gang of aggressive slanderers, all attacking you for your "thoughtless post," where you failed to "do your research." Often, in an irate commenter's mind, "your research" means you haven't read exactly the same things that commenter has read, and don't agree 100 percent with that reader's opinions. Sometimes, they gather on a message board, and all plan to attack you in concert with each other.

You talk back to the backtalkers. The best way to defuse such a riot is to get involved in the discussion. When you, the author, show up in the comments area, we've noticed things instantly cool down. Now, the commenters see a real person behind those opinions, and it usually softens them. This works especially well if you're completely transparent. Be honest. If you've made a mistake, apologize. If you've changed your text after publishing it, after some people had already criticized you for your errors, own up to it. Even the most sadistic readers tend to forgive you if you're honest with them, and if you apologize for any transgressions you've actually committed. Admitting a mistake shows readers what kind of person you are, and can bolster their respect for you. After you've made your apologies, it's time to move on, and either close the comments on that post, or just ignore subsequent abuse.

But you're not always required to respond to each comment. No response is also a response. Many unhinged comments deserve nothing but icy silence from you. Those that are direct questions are probably the most obvious candidates for a return volley. Other times, you might see fit to react to an insult, defending yourself and clarifying what you've written. However, sometimes your response will only beget more comments, often devolving into a flame war that's more akin to simple fist fighting than an illuminating discussion.

If you find yourself the victim of a particularly caustic comment, assess its merits and demerits, and put it on the back burner. If you can get back to it later and still feel the same way about the comment, feel free to add your opinion. But realize you are pulling on a rope with many people attached.

You are a fanboy. The culprit behind many flame wars is the fanboy. You've heard of him (and it's almost always a male), the fanatic who's so attached to a particular brand that showing affection for any others constitutes blasphemy. The most rabid fanboys cling to Apple as their deity, and now there's a rising army of smartphone operating system Android acolytes. There are others following celebrities. Some of these people have serious psychiatric problems, while others are just in the throes of an obsession. The best way for you to think of this is to consider these obsessions a religion. Handle this delicately, because these people can't see any other opinions as being valid except their own. They've been so intensely brainwashed that anything you say or write that doesn't completely agree with their worldview is met with astonishment and vitriol.

People become fanboys for many reasons. First, fanboyism is fun and safe. If you are online, you want to be part of a networked community. By choosing a side, you are guaranteed a seat at the table regardless of your opinion. But the key thought here is to understand that fanboys have chosen sides to protect a few things. First, they must protect their investment in a technology. While many of us wouldn't think twice about which operating system we use, many have invested time, money, and effort into one of their choices. Perhaps they are simply fans—maybe they really like a particular politician or point of order. Or perhaps it is a matter of faith (and some nonreligious choices can take on aspects of faith). Or perhaps they have already bought thousands of dollars' worth of gear, or maybe they don't have much money at all and they made a choice to support one side or another. It is not our place to judge or fear these folks. It is our place to avoid fanboyism at all costs and offer opinions tempered with intelligence and wit. You can hold an opinion, but fall into fanboyism at your peril.

You've been targeted for abuse. In fact, there are way too many blog readers who get their jollies by marauding around the Internet, trying to incite such controversy with lots of insulting, rude remarks, and crazy stuff. They troll the bottom, often making comments just for the sake of eliciting a reaction. That's why they're called trolls. Either that, or they resemble the villains of fairytales, ogres who live under bridges and lick their chops in anticipation of eviscerating some innocent passerby.

Remember, you can immediately handle trolls with a fell swoop of your mouse. Being the god of your blog has its benefits, and if some readers seem like they're just making comments solely for the purpose of starting useless fights, you can delete their comments forthwith. Unfortunately, this often draws you into a game of whack-a-mole, where your little troll friend will make more comments, accusing you of censorship, and then you delete those comments, eliciting even more. With a determined sicko, this game could go on for hours, days, or even weeks. If you're using a commenting system such as Disqus, you can bring out the nuclear weapon and ban that person's IP address. But keep in mind that particular IP address might be in use for an entire company, and your fell swoop might accidentally forbid a large group of innocent readers from commenting. And your nemesis might just continue commenting on a smartphone, or simply turn off his cable modem for a few minutes, long enough for his service provider to assign a completely different IP address.

Sometimes these conflicts even devolve into stalking, with a hateful reader virtually following you wherever you write, sabotaging your every post. Occasionally, these issues can be dealt with one-on-one, where you ask the offender to contact you offline, via email. The vast majority of times a quick email ("Hey, what's going on with your comments?") is enough to send a troll packing. We've used this technique and received consistent results. Sometimes you get a heartfelt, if inappropriate, excuse ("The wife has been sick and I was just angry at work and I don't know why I told you I wanted you to

War Story

Once I had a commenter who was so angry at me about a post I had written that he stalked me for days, continuing his hate-filled comments on our site. He wouldn't respond to anything I wrote to him. Perhaps coincidentally, during those days there was a veiled death threat sent to me anonymously via Facebook. I had to take action. After a bit of searching online, I found the offending person's phone number and called him. He was defiant at first, but then calmed down. He still refused to stop harassing me, though, until I threatened legal action. He remained defiant, but it was all bluster. I never heard from him again after that conversation.

die of cancer when you wrote Archie was better than Jughead"). Other times they curse you out a bit more and then stop commenting entirely. It's a win-win.

Sometimes contacting an angry commenter helps to humanize you; other times, a phone call will do the trick. At its worst, it might be a good idea to call the police. Other times, the heat dies down as the commenter moves on to another target. Don't ever agree to meet a disgruntled commenter face-to-face, though. Better to cut off communication and let the lunatic wear himself out first. The best advice is to refrain from escalating conflict, instead diffusing it whenever possible and answering verbal violence with silence most of the time. *Blessed are the peacemakers, for they shall inherit the blogosphere.*

Should You Turn Off Comments?

The short answer is "No." The long answer is "Why would you?" Turning off comments is convenient for your own ego, but it reduces online interaction and makes you look, at best, scared of your readership. Some sites refuse to allow comments for historical reasons—DaringFireball just never had them—but most sites need them. Even the smallest town newspaper can benefit from commenters (even though comment forms tend to bring out the cranks). If you are doing a good job and you are an expert in your niche, you shouldn't have a problem with commenters online.

Understanding Spam

At the very least, we'd recommend you use a CAPTCHA ("Completely Automated Public Turing test to tell Computers and Humans Apart"), a challenge-response system that requires prospective commenters to decipher twisted graphics that are hard for machines to read, and then enter those nonsensical words or phrases before any comments are accepted. This will prevent boatloads of spam comments infecting your site. Some spammers are so determined that they'll hire low-paid workers to decipher and enter CAPTCHA text, and then try to slip links to their employers' sites into your comments. To deal with comment spam, most bloggers use nofollow[2] tags to prevent spam links from gaining spammers any traction in their wild-eyed quest for web domination. This is usually a setting in your content management system.

For your site, you'll probably choose something between these two extremes—perhaps starting out with admitting almost all comments, and then as your site grows and comments proliferate, you can begin pruning those who aren't adding much to the conversation. This work is worthwhile, because you want comments, and you need them. Comments are content, and at their best, add knowledge to your posts. They have entertainment value, often add clarity, boost your credibility with praise, and sometimes even scold you when you deserve it.

Comment spam can also be reduced by using a filter such as Akismet for WordPress and other content management systems. Akismet compares comments to a known body of spam and spam-like comments. It is one of the most effective ways to maintain comments without much work. It is free for small sites, but if you have a larger site it may begin to cost you. Check the current terms on Akismet's site.

How does spam work? When a commenter posts a spam message, it usually includes a link to his own website. This link from your well-respected site allows spammers to gain some of your hard-earned respect. This rarely if ever works, but that doesn't mean that you won't get hundreds or thousands of spam messages daily. If something is in your spam queue, delete it. You can occasionally go through your queue to confirm that a real comment hasn't slipped through, but in general, delete spam from your site immediately.

Rewarding Loyal Fans

We like to thank our readers by holding contests and giving away freebies. In almost every industry there will be someone willing to offer your readers something small. Don't force your readers to jump through hoops to get something good. Just create a comment contest—ask them to comment on a post and pick one reader at random. Or, encourage better commenting by choosing the best one of the bunch.

We often single out commenters and contact them via email to ask for a mailing address. We then send them something from the odds-and-ends pile that quickly builds up in our offices. Many folks may be delighted to receive a USB key or a hat from a popular brand you cover. Imagine the value you're creating with this singular act of kindness. You're not only thanking a friendly face in the "crowd," you're creating a vociferous and enthusiastic defender of you, your site, and your practices. Politicians of old probably called this glad-handing. We call it a love letter to your readers.

Finally, **listen to your readers**. If they send you tips, thank them in the post. The best feeling in the (Internet) world is to see your name under a post. We remember the days before we got to run large blogs. It was a real treat to see a "[*Thanks, John!*]" or "*Hat tip to Charlie W.*" When thanking someone in a post, it is customary to put the person's name at the bottom of the page and italicize the note, simultaneously calling it out while ensuring it's not confused with the actual content of your site.

Notes

1. http://en.wikipedia.org/wiki/Disemvowelling
2. http://en.wikipedia.org/wiki/Nofollow

Building Traffic, Making Money, and Measuring Success

There are plenty of people who will sell you snake oil they claim can gain more traffic. You don't have to go far on Google to find plenty of balderdash about keywords, secret algorithms, and traffic-boosting tricks. In our own history as bloggers we have rarely had much truck with those sorts. **In fact, there have been times when we've ignored search engine optimization (SEO) completely, writing stuff that we know will appeal to humans and not robots.** That's our trick.

Here's our piece of advice: **write good stuff, tell people about it, keep writing good stuff.** As one of our favorite authors Farhad Manjoo once wrote, "Optimizing for Google results is a little like going out and buying the best VCR on the market."[1] Are you going to invest in something that will soon be obsolete? Google's algorithms change regularly—it's something the SEO-heads call the "Google Dance"—and anything you do today will be obsolete a few months from now.

SEO for Bloggers

However, we didn't want you to feel short-changed, so we approached well-known search expert Eli Feldblum, CTO of RankAbove, to explain a bit about SEO for bloggers.

One of the most popular ways to get traffic to your blog is through search engines. People are always searching for stuff online, and if you're writing about that same stuff, they probably should come to your blog. That theory is correct; in fact, it's the theory that the major search engines such as Google, Yahoo!, and Bing were founded on: connecting searchers to results.

But if you want to be in those results, and especially if you want to be at the *top* of those results, you need to make sure the search engines know what your blog is about—and you need to ensure that once they do, they think your blog is the most relevant site to show a searcher. That process is called search engine optimization, or SEO. Simply put, SEO is the process of explaining to search engines that your site is relevant (there's that word again) to specific queries, which are primarily defined by the keywords people use when they search for stuff online.

The Key Phrase

The first step to SEO is making sure your content is truly relevant to what people search for, and that takes knowing what people search for. Let's say you just bought a new iPhone. You start getting into it, and you start buying accessories and apps, and pretty soon you're the guy your friends with iPhones ask for advice. You think you can turn the knowledge into cash by starting a blog about iPhone accessories. The most popular question you get is about hooking up an iPhone to a car stereo, so your first post is about iPhone car cables.

If your content is good, your page is optimized (we'll get to that in a minute), and you get some links (we'll get to that, too), you should bring in visitors by the thousands. So you're pretty surprised when no one shows up. What gives? Your post was the perfectly optimized answer to any queries to any searches about iPhone car cables. Does Google just not like you?

The problem is this: no one searches for iPhone car cables. Lots of people want to hook up their iPhones to their cars; they just don't use the word "cable." Searchers prefer, in descending order, "iPhone car chargers," "iPhone car mounts," and "iPhone car kits." According to data from Google, "iPhone car chargers" gets more than 27,000 searches every month in the U.S.—while "iPhone car cables" gets a mere 700 searchers monthly.

The bots look at how often the key phrase and its variations are used. That will occur naturally when you discuss a topic, and there is no need to force it. Your content needs to appeal to users first, and then search engines.

Keep in mind that the perfect key phrase describes your story accurately, and also predicts which terms your readers will use to search for your story. When you're choosing your key phrase, think of what you would search for if you were looking for the story you just wrote.

However, if the story you just wrote is a story that thousands of other bloggers are also writing at the same time, try to think of a slightly different angle that will attract readers searching for a key phrase that's not so heavily populated.

For instance, if you're writing about the new iPhone 7, your first instinct will of course be to use "iPhone 7" as your key phrase. But you will be competing against literally millions of other posts if you decide to use that key phrase. Think of a different angle, such as "iPhone 7 compared," and then you can tailor your post around those keywords, comparing and contrasting that product with its competitors.

Isn't determining keywords before you've written your post getting into "gray hat" SEO? Not exactly, because what you're doing is trying to figure out a way to best reach your readers, and you're not misrepresenting the content of your post with your key phrase. Of course, you'll have to want to write a post comparing your product to others if you're going to use our foregoing example, but you won't be dishonest to your readers and those who have searched for your article by using that key phrase.

When optimizing SEO, keep honesty and integrity in mind. There are shady characters on the Internet who are abusing SEO. There are certain topics that you can't search on the Internet and get a reliable result, because SEO has been gamed so much. For instance, try searching "SEO," and you'll see how SEO experts have made it impossible to find reliable information about that topic, just because of their unparalleled expertise.

On-Page

So now that you've picked the correct keywords, the ones that meet audience demand, it's time to let Google and the other search engines know that your post is about those keywords. That's called on-page optimization.

At the same time, think about the supply of readers. If there are a million people searching for a certain keyword and a billion blogs playing to that keyword, you're going to get lost in the crowd. Look for niche keywords that are less competitive, giving you a fighting chance of grabbing a share of the audience.

No one from Google will come and read your site to determine how relevant you are—it's all done via automated "bots" that crawl the web, jumping from link to link and reading the content (to the best of their ability) on each page, called "spiders." (Get it? Spiders crawl the web? Funny people, those Google guys.) Because they are not people, the spiders are not perfect readers. They can't read everything that appears on the page. And they rely on you highlighting specific sections of the page, called "signals," to alert them to the most relevant content on the page.

These spiders operate by a few basic rules:

- They read only text, not images or Flash video or audio (at least, not fully, and not yet).
- They read from top to bottom.
- They look for signals to tell them what's important.

Our friend Farhad was so right when he said Google's search algorithm is a moving target. However, there are some basic parts of the search algorithm that can't really change. For instance, the title of your post will always be the best place to find out what your post is actually about.

So that's the first basic rule of our SEO philosophy: state the topic of your post as early as possible in the title. For instance, if you're writing about the new Krazy Kikz shoes everybody's talking about, you'll want to have the words Krazy Kikz as close to the beginning of your title as possible. For optimum SEO, you'll want the term Krazy Kikz in the first paragraph of your post, and in the first sentence if you can swing it.

You'll want to add the term "Krazy Kikz" as an "alt" to all of the images on your page, and then in your content management system (CMS) such as WordPress or Blogger, you'll want to be sure to include the term Krazy Kikz in your meta description of the story. Finally, be sure the term Krazy Kikz is part of your permalink for the story—that is, be sure the URL of your story includes it.

If you follow the routine of creating a thoroughly descriptive key phrase (often called "focus keyword") and then use it in those specific places in your post, you'll be well on your way toward SEO perfection. Let's go over each of the specific places where your key phrase should reside in your post, and explain why each is significant.

Article heading: This is the title you use to populate the Title field of your page. It's the SEO title as well—unless you would like to use a separate SEO title. There's a place for you to change it to something different in most content management systems.
Page title: If you leave this blank, your article heading will also function as your SEO title. Why would you want to change it? One good reason is that the display in most search engines is limited to seventy characters, so if your display title is longer than

that, it will get cut off when people are searching for your story. In addition, for best SEO results, your title should be at least forty characters long. The page title is important, so if you can't part with your display title, write a separate one for SEO and be sure to place that key phrase at the title's beginning.

Page URL: Otherwise known as a permalink, this is where your post will reside on your site. You can set defaults for what all of your permalink's look like, but you'll always want to contain your key phrase in that permalink for maximum optimization. For example, when I'm writing about the iBarge, here's how that post's permalink will look: http://charliewhite.net/2013/08/iBarge/.

Inside the content: You'll want to include that magic word or phrase in the first paragraph, and even in the first sentence if possible. You'll want to mention it a few times within your post as well, but don't go overboard. There is such a thing as mentioning your keyword too many times, for which your post will be downgraded. In our experience, using the key phrase before it feels forced or awkward is usually a good rule of thumb.

Meta description: If you've written a tight first sentence to your post, that will usually serve you well as a meta description. It's usually limited to 156 characters, so stay within those parameters, mentioning your key phrase at least once.

Other SEO enhancements:

Outbound links: Include at least a backlink—that is, one link outside of your own site, and the SEO gods will smile upon you. We'll tell you more about backlinks a bit later in this chapter.

Image Alt: Whenever you place an image in a page, there's always a spot for alternate text, so place your key phrase in there, too. Try to add it to all of your images in the post. Before you've added it, you'll see this in the code: alt="". Between those two quotes is where you'll add your key phrase. Here's an example:

<img src="http://charliewhite.net/wp-content/uploads/2013/08/Apple-iWatch-02.png" **alt="iWatch"** width="1280" height="720" class="aligncenter size-full wp-image-630" />

Subheadings: If you find it aesthetically pleasing or editorially necessary to place subheads within your text, the more times you include your key phrase in those subheads, the more SEO power you'll have.

Post length: Three hundred words seems to be the magic number for some SEO mavens, but there's little if any research that supports that number. However, as an esteemed colleague pointed out, a 300-word minimum is a good way to urge you to expound upon your post topic. Write more, add context, and make it yours on the way to getting the length up to 300 words. However, this rule is made to be broken, because many photos and factoids do fine with just one sentence or a short paragraph.

Writing style: You can adopt some styles of writing that will help, like the "Inverted Pyramid," which is what some journalists use for news articles. In the Inverted Pyramid, all the crucial information is imparted in the first paragraph and then examined and explained in depth throughout the article. Because the spider reads a page from top to bottom, this style quickly alerts them to the content of the page, and it ensures the bots don't give up on a long page before getting to the point.

After all that, we come back to this: **the most important thing is good content.** In the world of SEO, content is king. The foregoing rules will help Google understand your content, but if it's not good content to begin with, it's worthless. The search engines look for content relevant to what people search for, but that also abides by the rules of good—or at least pretty good—writing. And good content will also naturally get other people to link to your blog, which, as we'll soon see, could be the most important part of all.

Overall, Google is looking for three things from your content: relevance, uniqueness, and freshness. Write good content frequently, using these rules, and you'll soon see visitors from SEO.

Off-Page

Okay, so your blog is now relevant for the keywords people use when they're interested in your topic. Here's a dirty little secret. You're not the only person reading about SEO. Lots of other bloggers and webmasters have also been working to optimize their sites. They may all be equally relevant to the keywords you are going after.

Once the spiders figure out all the pages that are relevant to a certain query, they need to rank the pages in a way that benefits the user. They want to show the user the best page first, and "best" is usually synonymous with most popular. The more people who like your site—and express that sentiment by linking to your blog—the higher you will rank for your relevant content. Google's big innovation when it came on the scene was looking at the web the same way kids look at high school. The coolest kids are not just the ones with the most friends, but also those with the coolest friends (defined the same way; Google loves recursion). The kid with lots of friends on the football team and cheerleading squad is usually more popular than the one with friends on the chess club and the debate team. Google applied this to the web. Sites with more links—especially links from sites that also had lots of links to them, called backlinks—were more popular. Google gave each site a popularity quotient, called PageRank (named after co-founder Larry Page, no kidding).

Given two identically relevant and equally optimized pages, the one with better backlinks wins.

The SEO Bottom Line

So you've got three steps to make sure your blog ranks and gets traffic from SEO:

1. Make sure your content matches up with the keywords people are using for their search queries.
2. Make sure your content is optimized so that the search engines can read it and know what the important parts are.
3. Make sure other sites know about—and link to—your content.

That's basically it, with an emphasis on "basic." There are a host of other factors and signals the engines use to rank pages, but everything is based on keywords, relevance, and links.

Social Media

When you've written all your wonderful guff, you need to get the word out and let everyone know it exists. This is where you can leverage social media to spread the word about your shiny new site, alerting all those information-hungry visitors to click into your world. The beauty of social networks to market your site is that you get other people to do your marketing for you. In fact, for blogs that are just starting out, social media can refer more traffic to blogs than search engines. For example, many news startups get as much as 40 percent of their traffic from Facebook and Twitter. Even for sites that have been around for a while, social media experts are starting to see Twitter and Facebook as the fastest-growing way to refer traffic to your blog.

All the social networking in the world is not going to do any good if you can't get people to click on your links. This points back to creating a compelling headline. You're going to need to lure those people with Twitter links, especially if you're generating them automatically with the headline and link. A catchy, punchy headline will go a long way toward facilitating all of your social networking.

But using social media to promote your site is not the sort of thing that just happens overnight. You first must build a following on Twitter and gather your friends on Facebook. Before you're going to direct the crowd to scurry over to your website to read that fascinating story you just teased them about, you're going to need to gather that crowd first. How's that done?

Social Media Tips
Promoting with Twitter

If you want to promote your posts on Twitter, you need followers, and the more you can get, the more promotion you can do. Every Twitter user started with zero followers. How do you build up that list? You need to organically expand your list of Twitter followers by giving them a reason to follow you, read your stuff, and click on the links you provide. There are automated tools that purport to boost your followers on Twitter, but they result in low-quality followers who all require you to follow them at the same time. This results in a high follower count, but not a whole lot of clicks will be coming from those followers you bought. That's not really going to help you much in the long run. What you really need are engaged followers who look forward to your next link or comment.

The best way to gain followers is to offer compelling content. Twitter is known as a microblogging service, so treat it as such. Give your followers real content in the short space allowed, constantly tweeting a sampling of content from your site, 140 characters at a time. That doesn't mean just pushing links onto your growing list of followers. Offer analysis, and include fun facts and maybe a few words of pithy commentary. Whatever you do, after they read that actual information, make them want to read more. Lure them to your site; get them into the tent. The more you engage, the more followers you'll get, and the more people will pay attention to whatever you share, resulting in more visitors driven to your blog.

The number of followers is important, but the quality of your followers is even more important. Says Stephanie Haberman, social media producer at NBC news, "I'm passionate about quality over quantity. I would much rather have five people who will retweet your tweets, share and talk about them and create chatter and interest in the brand, rather than having twenty people who are ignoring you." Find those valuable followers, and they will help you build your brand.

One way to gather followers quickly is to follow others. There are varying schools of thought here, where some Twitter experts think it's a good practice to follow everyone who follows you. However, if you follow Twitter power users who have thousands of followers, they're not likely to follow you. Start out by following those power users anyway (because of all the great info you'll gather from them), but don't forget to also follow people you know, and they'll probably be willing to reciprocate.

Treat your Twitter stream like an alternative blog, albeit in miniature. You can engage with your readers using Twitter, and the interactions you have using the service are often surprisingly rich.

When you want to promote a post using Twitter, in most Twitter apps and tools, your link will be automatically shortened, giving you more room within your 140-character allotment to offer some actual content along with that link. And keep your total character count below 120, so your followers will have room to retweet (RT) your tweet and add some of their own opinions alongside it.

Should you tweet every headline you post? Yes. This is the bare minimum of expected Twitter interaction, and even if you think Twitter is just a fad, your posts should appear there and on your Facebook page. Says Haberman, "I will tweet out the headlines of a post at least once. The first time I will tweet out the headline, because if you write your headline as well you should, that does encapsulate everything you want to say."

Beyond that, Haberman says that it's okay to tweet about a post more than once. However, she says, "When you're repromoting it and when you're resharing it, you can add an interesting quote from it, or something that's a lot more grabby." Chances are, if you Tweet about that post again, and delay it by a few hours, most of your followers won't see it twice. Even if they've already seen it, Haberman adds, "that quote might make them think they should revisit the topic."

Establish your presence on Twitter throughout the day with your pithy prose, and over time, people will begin to know you and respect you. Interact with other Twitter users by responding to their tweets. Interject your opinions into conversations that are happening within your chosen topic area. Find the most interesting links about your topic, even if they aren't from your own site, and place them on your Twitter feed along with an opinion or two of your own. Some experts even recommend sending private Twitter messages to those who might find a particular piece useful, adding a personal touch that goes a long way. But beware: being a pest on Twitter is worse than undertweeting.

Automate It!

An even easier way to promote your Twitter and Facebook feeds is using an automated site such as twitterfeed.com. You create an account, point it to your site's RSS feed, and then you designate when and where you'd like your tweets and Facebook entries to be posted.

That's the easiest way to automate your Twitter posting, but not the best. Twitter posting tools are becoming increasingly more sophisticated, and now there are services such as Buffer and SocialFlow that give you even more control over what you'll be tweeting and when.

Buffer is a service that lets you tweet at designated intervals during the day, or allows you to schedule when each of those tweets will occur. A free account lets you choose how many post-times during the day you need, spreading them out so followers won't get

Config Buffer Schedule

Days

☑ Mon ☑ Tue ☑ Wed ☑ Thu ☑ Fri ☑ Sat ☑ Sun

Tweets Per Day: 5

Minimum Interval: 02:40

Optimum tweet schedule:

06:30 (21% Online followers)
09:30 (34% Online followers)
12:10 (32% Online followers)
14:50 (31% Online followers)
18:30 (27% Online followers)

Close   Save Settings

tired of hearing from you over and over again. Buffer even has a way to interface with a service called Social Bro, which shows you statistics about your followers and community, and creates a "best time to tweet" file you can use in Buffer.

However, for the ability to configure different time intervals for different days of the week and post unlimited numbers of tweets with twelve social profiles, you'll need Buffer's "Awesome Plan" for $10 per month.

When your traffic increases and your operation becomes more sophisticated, you might want to try a tool we used at *Mashable* called SocialFlow. Working with either a browser-based version or a browser plugin, you designate a story you'd like to tweet about, and then tell SocialFlow you'd like for it to optimize your tweet over the next hour, number of hours, or days. Then, SocialFlow figures out the optimal time to tweet that story, not only gauging the engagement of your usual readers but also determining the time when that story is most likely to attract the most traffic to your site. It's not cheap, with prices starting at $99 per month for one Twitter account and one Facebook account, but it's the most sophisticated Twitter software we've used so far. While we didn't get the 40 to 60 percent increase in click rate the company touted at SocialFlow's launch in early 2012, we found the tool easy to use, especially when dealing with multiple tweets.

Facebook Promotion

Promoting your blog posts on Facebook and getting people to engage with them is a great way to build traffic to your blog. This is the most valuable of all social media for promotion, potentially giving you more visitors than you can get from search engines. Build up your list of friends on Facebook, and you'll have a ready-made group of people who will be likely to spread your links far and wide. Beyond those people you know, there are more than 500 million active users on Facebook. Obviously, this is where the people are, so this is where you need to promote your site.

On Facebook, you have a bit more room to write a tease than you'll get on Twitter, and there are certain ways you can encourage discussions on Facebook, as well as entice those readers to click on your link and come to your website. Try asking those Facebook readers a provocative question, luring them into the discussion. Or consider placing an exclusive fact on your Facebook tease that points toward your article, giving people more information as you convince them to click on your link. You'll find that a pithy quote from your post will often do the trick. Don't give away the whole story with your teaser sentence or question. Most importantly, try to think of something that can compel someone to click through to your blog or "like" your update, in as few words as possible.

After posting on Facebook for *Mashable* over a period of more than two and a half years, Charlie's in a position to tell us about a few idiosyncrasies of the mainstream Facebook audience that you might want to know about. One area of special concern is when someone has died. If your blog is in the business of writing about stories like that, be extremely careful how you present any Facebook posts about the death. It's been my experience that people don't go to Facebook to find news of death, and are often angered when they see stories like that posted (see the following War Story). Our advice: avoid posting about death and mayhem unless that's part of your site's stock in trade. You might get lots of engagement with a post about death, but it's likely not the kind of traffic you actually want.

War Story

Charlie was promoting a post on Facebook he wrote for *Mashable* about a tragic incident where a football player shot his wife and then himself. In an attempt to maximize sensitivity, Charlie wrote in his Facebook tease, "Our deepest sympathy goes to [player's name] and his family in this tragic incident." Seems innocent enough, doesn't it? Immediately, a firestorm of anger erupted in the comments underneath the Facebook tease. "Where's the sympathy for the wife who was shot, Mashable?" said a few readers. "Completely insensitive not to mention the wife, Mashable!" said another. "Why did you even post this at all?" said even more. After a few comments like that, a chain reaction erupted with even more readers piling on, and the anger began to approach the level of a raging mob. Realizing his mistake, Charlie deleted the Facebook update. It was not an ideal way to handle a Facebook problem, but this was such an explosion of anger that it was the only solution. Sometimes you just have to punt. Never mind that Charlie had thought the words "his family" would include the guy's wife–apparently that wasn't sensitive enough for readers who were going through the stages of grief over this incident, and unfortunately were stuck on that stage that has to do with anger.

Stories about rival social services don't do well on Facebook, either. Many in the mainstream Facebook audience are mostly concentrating on Facebook for their social media needs, and tend to be only mildly interested in stories about Twitter, for instance. So if you're writing about Twitter, Facebook, or other social media services, you're better off posting Twitter stories to Twitter, where they invariably do well, and Facebook stories to Facebook, where the same is true.

Pro Tip Hits and Misses of Facebook Promotion

Positive stories do best: The neighbor's cat that just had a litter of the cutest kittens ever will make people smile. The litter of kittens being run over by the garbage truck will make people cry, and they won't want to see your face on Facebook for a while.

Showcase a photo: Research shows that Facebook users are more likely to "Like" or click a link associated with an image than an update where you merely link to your blog post. So if you have a dramatic picture, post it along with a description of its accompanying story, and be sure to place a shortened link in the description to direct readers to your post.

Ask questions, but not too many: If people catch onto a pattern where you're always asking questions and trying to get them to engage, some of them will grow angry, and be more interested in criticizing your question than answering it.

Sometimes you just have to delete: Facebook is touchy, and sometimes your entertaining clip might be completely misunderstood, or roundly hated by your audience. Better to delete the post before it gets out of hand and have it shared far and wide, at the expense of your reputation.

Police this area: Just like comments on your blog, sometimes Facebook comments can get out of hand, too. Treat your Facebook readers as if they're visitors in your own home, and eject them if necessary. A feature on Facebook allows you to "almost delete" an offensive post, making it visible only to whoever wrote it and that person's friends. Its usefulness is extraordinary—deploy it liberally.

Don't overdo it: Whenever you write a post, share it on Facebook and all your other social platforms, but don't overdo it. At *Mashable*, we've noticed that people start complaining if we place updates on Facebook more often than every hour or so. Don't wear out your welcome, posting multiple times each hour, because you'll reach a point of diminishing returns, annoying more potential readers than you entice.

Contribute to other posts, discussions, and interactions on Facebook, so it won't look like you're just there as a promoter and a spammer. Participate. The more you put into it, the more you'll get out of it.

A new addition to Facebook is the ability to add hashtags to keywords. An example would be when you write a sentence such as this: "Check out the new #iPhone6—we have pics." The strength of this is, whenever someone clicks on #iPhone6 in another Facebook update, it will result in a list that includes your update, too, theoretically giving it wider exposure. However, hashtags on Facebook are relatively new, and according to authoritative source Edge Rank (http://edgerankchecker.com/blog/2013/09/hashtags-on-face book-do-nothing-to-help-additional-exposure/), they haven't helped anyone gain much additional exposure yet. But it's still early in the game, and hashtags might become more important on Facebook as more users become aware of them.

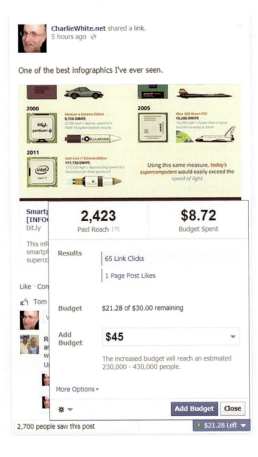

Facebook Advertising

If your posts aren't getting promoted fast enough on Facebook, now Facebook allows you to buy favorable placement of your updates on the gigantic social network. But can't you get this anyway? Not exactly. If you update your status, it won't be seen by all your friends, but will be displayed according to a proprietary Facebook algorithm. Whether it will be displayed to your friends has to do with how they interacted with you, whether your friends have chosen to avoid your posts, what sorts of things they're interested in, and how quickly your post experienced engagement after it was first shared.

You'll see at the bottom of each of your Facebook updates an invitation to "Promote." Click on that, and you'll see an offer to promote an important update, making it move higher on your friends' news feeds for $6.99. You're able to pay with PayPal or credit card.

Once you've established your site, it's a good idea to start a Facebook page for your site. This gives you additional promotional capabilities, letting you plunk down higher amounts of cash to spread your reach across people you don't know yet, such as friends of friends. We've tried some of this promotion, and you'd be surprised how many visitors you can get for, say, $45.

How's the best way to spend this advertising money? One winning strategy is to wait until you have a post that resonates much more than most of your posts do. That would be the one to promote, spreading the word to between 10,000 and 20,000 Facebook users who might be tempted to click on that link. It can start getting expensive, but this is a good way to get a new site off the ground quickly, and get additional people to "like" your site's Facebook page.

Buying advertising for a post can become seriously addicting. You put money in here, and the pageviews come out there. However, spending $30 for every single one of your posts might not be sustainable for you. We've noticed that even with posts that are wildly popular, at first we weren't able to profit from the pageviews as much as we spent on the advertising to get them.

Some bloggers promote many posts. For example, Crystal Ponti of MommiFried.com selectively promotes posts with a few bucks. "I religiously promote posts on Facebook— mostly between $5 and $15," she told us. But she is more likely to buy ads for particular topics. "Facebook advertising responds well to topics that have a family/personal nature. So I frequently promote my posts related to cooking/recipes and parenting," she says. Other topics don't do as well for her mommy blog. "I've tried promoting posts related to social media and blogging, but even with targeting they didn't do nearly as well as the others."

If you have a little extra cash, it's a good idea to experiment with Facebook advertising, but we think it's better to use it as a seasoning, just for special occasions. If you have a post that feels like it's on fire, give it a rocket engine to propel it into orbit with advertising. However, we've also noticed that a post that isn't particularly resonating with the readers doesn't do much better no matter how much advertising money you throw at it.

The more people who are attracted by your ads, the more you can earn with the ads you've placed on your site. But the advantages of advertising can go beyond short-term monetary gains, too. Says Crystal Ponti, "I've recovered the costs in terms of referral traffic; not monetary. But there is a long-tail to blog monetization. The more readers and unique visitors, the greater the chances of attracting the interest of an advertising or brand. So a clickthrough from Facebook doesn't necessarily monetize, but the traffic is one part of the larger puzzle."

Whether you promote every post, just a few, or none, the object of this game is to get your Facebook updates in front of the largest crowd you could possibly gather. Unless you have a huge following on Facebook already, you'll need that advertising to get people to come to your site. Get as many people liking your Facebook page as possible, and then you'll have a ready-made group with whom you can share each of your posts. Once you have a few hundred fans who are eager to read your next missive, you'll see a delightful difference in the traffic you can lure with your posts on your site's Facebook page.

The ultimate goal is thousands more "likes" than that. Once you get up to 1.3 million likes, every time you place something on your Facebook page, hundreds—and sometimes thousands—of people will come flocking to your posts. At that level, Facebook becomes a spectacular promotion machine.

The downside? You're depending on the vagaries of one social network (which some people believe is just a fad) for most of your site promotion. Spread out your promotional efforts, also sharing each of your posts to LinkedIn, Google+, Twitter, and if the post's content has an eye-catching picture or two on board, Instagram.

Your two mainstays will be Facebook and Twitter. Become familiar with their intricacies, and if you need help, there are thousands of articles on the web and books in the library that will fill you in on all the details. However, the big picture is this: It doesn't matter if you're feeding Facebook, Twitter, Google+, LinkedIn, or some other social network, if you don't have that hot title or that compelling hook, then it doesn't matter where or what you're promoting—nobody will care.

Contests

Want thousands of readers? The closest thing to buying them is to put on a contest. One advantage of this technique is that it attracts readers who normally wouldn't visit your site. Hopefully, after they've visited for the contest, they'll stay for the content.

You've probably developed contacts with companies that supply products for your chosen topic, so you can approach them for prizes, assuring them lots of promotion during the process. As your site gets bigger, those companies will come to you with contest ideas. If you're looking for a high-impact prize that might be too expensive for a company to provide, you might need to buy that yourself. However, offering something like an iPad might be such a huge enticement and audience builder, it could be worth the investment.

There are a variety of contests you can conduct. The most basic contest is simply offering prizes to randomly chosen winners. That works to attract readers, but even better for a blog is a contest that gets readers involved. For instance, a sewing site could have an annual Halloween costume contest, with promises to showcase the top ten entries, and a complete how-to article showing how the winning costume was created. If you promote it right, the prize for this contest is the exposure, giving the winner bragging rights and prestige. Best of all, entrants will certainly ask all their friends to come to your site and vote for them. This results in the ideal situation: Your readers are promoting your site for you. In this case, they're even supplying content for you. In this sort of contest, both you and your site visitors win.

Promote!

Once you become microfamous, you might have radio stations or other broadcast outlets contacting you for interviews. If you get a call to do such an interview, you've struck gold. You might not see an immediate benefit to your blog's traffic, but to have your name mentioned on radio or television, or in a newspaper, is a tremendous boon to your brand.

Another way to promote your brand is when you're reviewing products. Once you've finished your review, if you liked the product and gave it a positive review, mention to the people who sent you the review unit that they would be welcome to quote a few words of your review in their advertising materials. There's nothing quite like shopping around in Best Buy and seeing one of your comments next to your name on a product box.

Spreading the word about your blog can take an infinite number of forms, where you're limited only by the amount of creativity you can bring to bear on the subject. We're not saying you have to transmogrify a bus into a cigar-shaped vehicle to promote your cigar blog, but any sort of wildly creative publicity stunt—as long as it's legal—leaves a lasting impression.

Measuring Success

How do you know if your blog is doing well? Analytics. Analytics measure your visitors, your reach, and the time individual users stay on your site. When you're a new blogger, the difference between 1,000 pageviews and 10,000 is huge. However, before we discuss the various services, remember that focusing too much on pageviews can become frustrating at best. By writing to "get Google juice," as the analytics-fanatics call it, you may fall into the trap of writing to please machines and not humans.

Also note that we are not here to offer a foolproof method for monetizing your blog. We're trying to teach you how to write for blogs and make your blog a success, and making money is part of it. However, there are plenty of online resources for monetizing and analyzing your blog. Here are a few notable ones.

Google Analytics

Google Analytics is the premier free analytics service. We recommend that everyone use it to keep track of traffic to their blogs. To add it to your website, simply create a Google Analytics account (use your Gmail account to do this) and paste the tracking code into your site (where on a page you place this code varies, so be sure to read the instructions). The site you're seeing to the right is WristWatchReview.com, a property that sees a fairly regular stream of traffic on a daily basis (about 1,000 visitors a day) who view an average of 1.5 pages per visit. Most users spend a minute on the site, and most of the traffic comes from searches.

That little box there, the Top Content read-out, is probably the most interesting and addicting. It shows you what content performs the best and can become a problematic source of obsession for many bloggers.

It gets even more interesting when you watch visitors interacting with your site in real time. On the left column of Google Analytics, click on Real-Time, and you can get a live look at your active audience. Here's a real-time tracking tool that shows you traffic numbers as they happen, organized in a useful and constantly updating list. If there's such a thing as exciting website analytics, this is it. It's a thrill to post a story and then see the immediate reaction of your readers, watching that story climb to the top of your Google Analytics chart after you've published it.

Our favorite mode is "Overview," which gives you a look at the locations where your traffic is originating, pageviews per minute and per second, and the number of active visitors on the site right now. To show you what's driving the traffic to your site, there's a live list of where your traffic is coming from, as well as your top social traffic. You can get closer looks at visitor locations, traffic sources, content, and more using this live tool, a service so powerful it hard to believe it's free.

Want to know more? We'd recommend taking a few hours on a weekend to study Google Analytics, learning how to customize it to your liking, and how to use it to track traffic. Don't worry—it's nowhere near as complicated as it looks at first. Google provides excellent free training for new users at "Conversion University" (look it up on Google), a site featuring a comprehensive suite of video tutorials that show you everything you need to know to take advantage of this powerful and free tool.

Woopra

Woopra beat Google Analytics to the live traffic monitoring game, and it has a variety of tools that Google Analytics Real-Time can't match. Like most analytics tools, Woopra requires you to slip a snippet of JavaScript code onto each of your site's pages (or install a simple plug-in in a CMS such as WordPress), and then you're good to go,

with each page communicating with Woopra's mothership and delivering the numerical goods to you, lickety-split. Even with all that number crunching, it doesn't seem to slow your site down at all. And, if your site is still in its beginning stages with less than 30,000 pageviews per month, Woopra is free. Once you've graduated into the big leagues of pageviews, the price goes up, from the "Startup" plan—$79.95/month for 1,000,000 actions, up to the "Small Business" plan that handles 4,000,000 actions per month for $199.95.

Let's take a close look at how it works.

Here's the browser-based version of Woopra's main screen, where the Active Pages area on the top right shows you exactly how many visitors are reading your posts, listed in hierarchical order. You can see which search terms people are using to get to your site on the bottom-left Recent Search Queries window, and the handy Today vs. Trend window in the upper left shows you how you're doing compared to your site's historical averages. Imagine all of this data moving and updating in real time. It's a kick.

War Story

Here's an example of how this real-time data proved itself to be extremely valuable to *Mashable*. It was Oscars Sunday, and in Woopra's Recent Search Queries window we noticed a tremendous number of users searching Google for the term "Oscar predictions." Looking over to the right Active Pages window, it turned out that it was last year's Oscars story that was attracting increasing numbers of users. Uh-oh. Users were searching for these terms, finding them on *Mashable*, but quickly leaving our site because they were getting information that was a year old. Still, they were coming to the site in constantly increasing numbers. We acted quickly on this, writing a post with as many Oscar details as we could muster in a half-hour. After posting that story, we modified last year's Oscars story with a prominent link at the top of the page to this year's new Oscars post. Instantly, Woopra showed the crowd's reaction, showing us in real time how visitors were landing on last year's Oscars page, and then immediately clicking the link that took them to this year's Oscars page. Suddenly, we were getting twice the pageviews for this timely topic. By knowing exactly what was happening in real time, Woopra allowed us to enlarge our audience.

Woopra does a lot more than just track traffic, though. It offers in-depth analytics, letting you see how stories performed, and letting you filter them by any combination of dates or geographical area. And it offers an odd feature that some users might find creepy: it allows you to chat with your visitors, live. Take a look at Woopra's map view, depicting each visitor with a red pin:

Click on one of these pins, and you'll see live information about that user.

Click "start chat" and as administrator of your site, you can try to initiate a live conversation with one of your visitors.

The visitor sees an invitation to chat, and if accepted, the interrupted and surprised reader will probably be asking you what the heck is going on. This feature could be useful—Woopra reports that some people are using it for contests, notifying winners via live chat. Others are using it for answering questions about a visitor's orders or other customer service functions. Be careful how you use this, or your readers will soon feel like they're under surveillance.

Compete.com

Compete.com is another interesting source for information about competing blogs, but the data found at Compete can't be taken completely seriously.

Take the foregoing comparison, for example. We've just confirmed that WristWatchReview saw 39,000 visitors over the past month or so. Therefore, the estimate there is far from correct. However, Compete describes its service (signup required) as similar to the Nielsen Ratings. The company explains:

Compete's data comes from a statistically representative cross-section of 2 million consumers across the United States who have given permission to have their internet clickstream behaviors and opt-in survey responses analyzed anonymously as a new source of marketing research.

Clearly Compete's base of 2 million consumers is not representative of the entire Internet, but for general assessments of site performance, it's a great intelligence tool. Even though its data seems to skew low, showing fewer visitors than you really have, true to its name, its data is useful for showing competition, displaying the ongoing traffic differences between sites.

Chartbeat

Chartbeat.com is one of the more interesting "web dashboards" available for standard websites. As you can see on the next page, it gives you a speedometer of active visits as well as views on individual stories. It also maintains a history of your average performance over time and allows you to replay days the way you'd roll back the tape in a sports game so you can understand when—and why—posts do well.

Chartbeat costs $9.95 per month after an initial trial period, but if you're serious about analytics and truly paying attention to what's going on at your site minute-by-minute, it's a stat aficionado's dream come true. John has used it for more than a year, and it's a useful way to see what exactly is happening on your site at any time. For folks used to "old" analytics, it's amazing.

Give Them What They Want

One last thing about your web stats: Use these tools to find out what people are looking for when they come to your website. Are they looking for reviews? Are they looking for specific terms in articles that you've written? Keep those terms in mind, and even write more articles about them if they're appropriate for your topic. Give your visitors what they want, but first, be sure to find out exactly what that is.

How to Make Money

So how do you make money blogging? First, as we said at the outset, there is no magic bullet. Living off the proceeds of your blog requires you to be one part hustler, one part entrepreneur, and two parts lucky. And it can take a long time to reach the point where you're making money blogging.

Crystal Ponti with MommiFried.com has a multipronged approach. "I do sponsored reviews and posts that come in directly from brands and indirectly through organizations like BlogHer and Mom Central," she said. But she gives mixed reviews to affiliate programs that give her cash when people click on (and then buy) products mentioned on her site. "I've tried several affiliate programs, with little success," she said.

When we asked her what was the most effective thing she's done to enhance traffic, she answered, "Syndicating on some of these larger sites has helped considerably. They are great sources of traffic and referrals." That reveals an important fact about blogging and competition: teaming up with the biggest and most formidable competitors in your topic space can pay off.

You can also attract some attention to your blog by commenting on other blogs. Says Ponti, "Blog commenting is also another huge source of traffic and referrals." She says the combination of blog comments and syndicating her posts on other blogs "bring in a large percentage of unique visits to MommiFried."

Notice, too, that besides being a writer and a mom, Crystal is a businessperson—that's a crucial component of blogger success.

War Story

Once, when John was on a media trip with another writer, he asked what the hardest thing about running your own "writing business" was. The wizened reporter replied, "the hustle." Freelance reporters have to always hustle and always sell their wares. Bloggers are no different, although they already have a place to publish their work. The real key for both the freelance writer and the blogger is to get paid for writing.

The Brick Wall

There's more than a mere line between editorial and advertising—it's more commonly characterized as a brick wall. In larger operations, it's customary for those who are selling advertising to separate themselves from those who are writing, reviewing, and posting. If you're part of a one-person staff, make a special effort to separate your ad sales activities from editorial.

You might be tempted to review your main advertisers' products in the best possible light, but you're probably better off not writing about that product at all if you've been brainwashed by an advertiser, manufacturer, or source. If you find yourself falling into a situation where there are too many conflicts between advertising and editorial, perhaps it's time for you to accept only brokered advertising on your site through services like Federated Media or Google AdSense. Sadly, these brokered situations are often less lucrative, but they do ensure journalistic integrity. Bloggers cannot live on integrity alone, but be careful when crossing the line from writer to sales manager.

Any sense that you need to maintain a brick wall between advertising and editorial, especially if you choose to sell your own ads, could go out the window once you start thinking about your blog as a money-making venture. However, do not allow yourself to be pulled to the dark side of marketing.

Another thing to consider is the lure of monetization to the detriment of your content. Is your desire to monetize strangling your need to produce strong posts, at least in the first few months of your blog? If this is the case, step back, take a breath, and work through some entry-level advertising systems like Google AdSense, explained ahead. There is no reason to go chasing big money when there is none to be had.

We recommend hitting at least 5,000 pageviews a day before considering approaching outside advertisers—unless your niche is razor-focused and you personally know the major players in it. You may be able to sell an inexpensive ad to a knitting store, but don't try the same thing with Sony if you run a headphone review site. We leave weighing the pros and cons of these methods as an exercise for the reader, and there are many excellent monetization websites out there, including the well-known ProBlogger.com. Running a website and monetizing it are, in the end, jobs for two different people, and if your site becomes popular at all you will eventually need to take the steps necessary to hire an outside ad sales manager.

You Don't Have to Sell Your Opinion Tonight

As an Internet journalist extraordinaire, your opinion is not for sale. What you are selling is your credibility, and your readers will stop believing what you say if they find out someone paid you to express an opinion that's not necessarily yours. Some bloggers accept a certain kind of advertising that looks like a blog post, but here's where transparency comes in. As long as you're clearly designating which stories you post are paid for by advertisers and which are your own work, you're probably in the clear. However, it's up to you to decide just how desperate for advertising you are, to the point of posting paid reviews from various manufacturers on your site. You're on thin ice here, so just be sure to completely divulge any pay-for-play relationships. Advertisers often try to convince online journalists to blur the line between advertising and editorial, but don't let them do it.

One writer I know refuses advertorial but will sell his time as a consultant to companies who want to break into his portion of the market. This sort of advising relationship should also be disclosed but is not as wildly inappropriate as accepting money for a good review.

In general, don't sell advertorial. It helps no one in the end and makes you look like a shill.

AdSense

If you're looking to start advertising on your site right away, you can always begin by serving ads from Google AdSense. It's relatively simple to apply the ad codes to your site, and you can start earning a few bucks right away.

After a quick application process, you can quickly get approved to place a maximum of three ads per page on your site. With a CMS system such as WordPress, it's simple to place the AdSense code onto a post page, and suddenly you're in the ad business. Best of all, Google helps you along every step of the way. However, Google doesn't have any phone support, so if you need additional help for a complicated matter, that must be done over email.

One reason AdSense works so well is because of Google's system that scans your blog post's text for keywords and inserts a text or display ad on your website that's related to the content. For example, if you write about fishing, AdSense will offer your readers ads for fishing lures, rods, and spinners. It won't offer them deals on mopeds (unless you suddenly write about mopeds).

You'll find yourself going to the AdSense dashboard often, checking to see how many clicks your ads have gotten. On that same "estimated earnings" page is a helpful scorecard from Google, letting you know if you're using the most effective ads, if your site is fast enough to rank high on Google, and congratulating you if you link its ads to its own service, Google+.

There are a variety of plug-ins you can use on your content management system for placing ads on various parts of your site. Or, as we like to do, you can copy the specific code Google gives you for each ad type and paste that directly into your site.

As your traffic grows, you can begin to make good money with Google AdSense. You're paid according to the number of clicks or views each ad gets—whichever is greater. In our experience, the clickthroughs make the most money. The return you get on each of the clicks and traffic varies widely each day, with some days more lucrative than others. To give you an idea of how much you can earn, we've received around $30 for each 5,000 pageviews we get. John's been able to make about $100 to $200 per month on a site with 1,000 pageviews a day with very little updating.

That doesn't sound like much, but as your traffic builds and you persevere day after day, it adds up. It's not exactly free money, but it's the easiest way to start. Build and sustain your blog, and before you know it you'll have enough income to replace that full-time job you just left.

Remember that some blogs are immune to AdSense, especially if you're working on an esoteric topic. AdSense may not work if your topic is not easily monetizable or particularly offensive or lurid. Covering murders in Georgia or the porn industry may not endear you to certain advertisers.

A competing service with Google AdSense is the Lijit (pronounced "legit") Network, a division of Federated Media, a company that serves as a clearinghouse for selling ads on larger sites. Until you make it to that uber-site level, for smaller sites, Lijit performs the same function as Google AdSense. It delivers eyeballs to advertisers, with Lijit furnishing the advertisers as you furnish the eyeballs. Like AdSense, you place the code on your site, and get paid for a combination of clicks and pageviews. You can choose to ban certain advertisers and ads from your site, and you can get paid automatically with direct deposit, replenishing your bank account every thirty days. There are many more such services, all operating in basically the same way.

Advertising Partnerships. Do you write about cigars? Partner with a cigar company. Sell your ad space to them and review the products they have available. But wait, you say, isn't that shilling for the cigar company? No, because you will make it clear from the very beginning that you are not part of the partner organization. It is instead a pooling of resources to build traffic for yourself and your partner.

Take care, though, because partnerships can quickly become overpowered by an over-zealous partner. If you're not able to maintain your editorial integrity—or if your readers notice you tend to prefer your partner's products versus the competitors—then you're sunk. You can obviously take a salary from your partner and focus primarily on their business in your blogging, but that is hardly a partnership.

Sponsorship. Related to partnerships are paid sponsorships. Some of the best bloggers offer sponsorships for multiple news sources on their blog. For example, you can sell a sponsorship to your RSS feed, your podcast, and even offer sponsorships for certain tags, categories, or posts. Make it clear at the beginning that this sponsorship does not allow editorial control, and you can safely accept a bit of cash for your hard work.

Donations. Oddly enough, few people try to accept donations for their hard work. Pay-Pal offers ready-made buttons for webmasters who want to accept donations. You could also bank on your popularity to run a Kickstarter or Indiegogo campaign to raise money when starting your site or sell merchandise branded with your site's logo. This assumes, of course, that you have an excellent and hardcore fan base, which shouldn't be hard if you've been following our advice. If you need help, ask for it. The Internet is great at helping the little guy.

Affiliate Sales

Affiliate sales come from people purchasing something based on either your post or your direct recommendation. The most popular source for affiliate sales is Amazon, whose affiliate program is simple and easy to understand. You can either place a standard ad on your site or you can select items from the Amazon catalog tagged with your own affiliate ID. When you mention those items in your post, you link to the item on Amazon with your Affiliate ID. Get readers to click, and it could be lucrative. In fact, a percentage of any sale that happens on the reader's computer within twenty-four hours of clicking on the link goes into your coffers. Hey, this could amount to some cash!

Google has a similar affiliate network, and another popular site is Commission Junction (cj.com). If performed correctly, this can be an excellent source for many bloggers to make a little cash. For example, you can create a little store containing items you use every day—gardening items, knitting items, fishing items—and send people to Amazon to buy them. If you are careful and don't make affiliate marketing the absolute reason for your blog, you can steer your readers to some good products and earn a few bucks.

Ad Networks

There are many so-called ad networks, and choosing among them can be difficult. Ad networks aggregate ad sales for many sites and try to get their editors better deals by selling many pageviews over many sites rather than focusing on one site. The most popular purveyor is probably Federated Media, although a network like Chitika.com could also offer beginner bloggers a break. It is often hard to "join" ad networks—a more apt term would be "accepted by"—because the managers require a certain level of involvement and a large number of pageviews to get through the door.

However, the number of pageviews required to become involved with an online ad network is not so astronomical that you couldn't reach it—once your site has grown to about 10,000 page views per month, for example, it's possible to successfully apply to the online advertising network Federated Media. *Mashable* got its start this way, earning enough money to grow to a staff of about fifty employees. *Mashable* severed its relationship with Federated Media and hired its own sales staff in February 2011 (http://adage.com/article/digital/mashable-breaks-federated-media-hires-ad-sales-force/149123/). The site got to be a tremendous success, even while using a syndicated advertiser for its first six years.

Personal Ad Sales

The highest echelon of monetization is direct ad sales. By connecting with the manufacturers of the items you write about the most, you can create a relationship that would potentially allow you to write about their products objectively while still accepting ad money for banners on your site. How is this done?

First, you need to create a Media Kit and Rate Card. The Media Kit will describe your site and mention some pertinent facts about your readers (age, salary range, geographical location), and some information about your traffic.

This, for example, is *Mashable's* media kit.

ABlogToRead's media kit is shown on the next page.

You'll notice that both are fairly compact. Think of this as a "top-level presentation" to ad buyers. The real work and detail will come when you present your case to them in a

Media & Advertising Kit

Why Mashable?

Founded in 2005, Mashable is the top source for news in social and digital media, technology and web culture. With more than **40 million monthly pageviews and 11.5 million unique monthly visitors**, Mashable is the most prolific news site reporting breaking web news, providing analysis of trends, reviewing new Web sites and services, and offering social media resources and guides. Mashable's audience includes early adopters, social media enthusiasts, entrepreneurs, influencers, brands and corporations, marketing, PR and advertising agencies, Web 2.0 aficionados and technology journalists. Mashable is also popular with bloggers, Twitter and Facebook users — an increasingly influential demographic.

- Top 25 Blog of 2009 by Time.com
- Top 5 Blog on Twitter and Technorati
- Winner of 3 Webby Awards
- A Unique and Important Social Media Savvy Audience
- Mashable is a Top Influencer on Twitter *(Web Ecology Project)*

aBlogtoRead.com offers readers:

- Highest traffic watch blog, covered by countless other websites
- Earned credibility from watch buyers and the watch industry
- Real editorial, and trusted opinions from leading voices on the watch industry with a real passion for watches
- Industry's finest detailed, hands-on watch reviews complete with original images and video
- Attention from serious watch collectors and new buyers alike with complete industry coverage

Advertisers can expect:

- An extremely focused audience of watch lovers and regular watch buyers
- Ideal demographic for all watches, no matter if they are very high-end or targeted toward mainstream buyers
- Advertising receptive audience interested in learning about new products or promotions
- Placement on the highest traffic dedicated watch blog on the Internet
- Regular covered "republication" of aBlogtoRead.com articles on many other popular websites
- Support from a reputable watch expect
- 100% editorial integrity and independence - aBlogtoRead.com will always be a resource to readers by keeping advertising and editorial separate.
- A much higher value to impressions ratio than traditional print media.

more personal fashion. Also prepare a rate card for a number of placement opportunities. We recommend sticking with banner and skyscraper advertisements on most blogs—banners being the long, thin advertisements that appear between stories or at the top of a page, and skyscrapers being the long, tall, and skinny ones that feature text or graphics.

Other sites sell "roadblocks," essentially rebranding the entire site to an advertiser's wishes during a set period. In many cases, this is an excellent way to sell a large ad for a period of time—a day or a week—that will prevent all other ad inventory from being visible, and it gives your intended advertiser the run of the site. For example, all of the banners and skyscrapers would belong to one advertiser, all AdSense ads would be turned off for that period, and the site background will change to suit the theme of the roadblock ads.

All of this is theoretical, however, if you can't get advertisers. Start small. Approach PR people you know asking to be put in touch with their ad-buying and marketing teams. Introduce yourself, offer your media kit, and a rate card noting your "cost per thousand" or CPM, and follow up every few months. Your job is to produce quality content, not go chasing every dollar. As your site grows you may find advertisers beginning to approach you. It will take work and dedication, but monetizing through personal ad sales is possible.

Advertorial

We didn't want to have to discuss this, but advertorial—essentially "paid content"—is **not okay**. Anything you write for an advertiser to showcase its brand or product is advertorial, and it should never be done for any money. It jeopardizes your respectability and objectiveness in the space and turns you into a shill. **Don't do it**. Don't accept a product for a "good review." Don't accept "corrections" because an advertiser requested them (unless your error was wildly egregious).

Another problem to consider is the misuse of affiliate links. If you write a post just to plop in a potentially lucrative affiliate link, scrap it. There is no reason to risk the reader's ire at your crass commercialism over a few dollars made from selling a box of diapers or a steak knife.

A more acceptable way of getting companies involved in your advertising—but not selling out—is with "sponsored posts." You can create a series of posts that would be supported by one advertiser with its logo and graphics all over each post. However, none of the articles within that series would be about that particular advertiser. This is a favorite technique of *Mashable*'s. For instance, you could write a series of ten articles about "Back to School," and all of those could be sponsored by a company that makes lunchboxes.

However, don't cross the line into writing about those lunchboxes, because that would be the same as taking part in an advertorial.

This can backfire. For example, *The Atlantic* once posted a "sponsored post" about Scientology that expressed some charming hagiography about the religion. Regardless of which side of the religious debate you fall on, *The Atlantic* couldn't afford to be seen as supporting Scientology, no matter how rich the payoff. The outcry forced *The Atlantic* to rescind the article.

There are varying schools of thought in regards to advertorial. If you can avoid it, avoid it. It might be hard and it might lose you money, but it's often better to post advertising in more traditional ways.

Merchandising

Depending on your chosen topic, merchandising might be a huge way for you to make money. One blogging guru we know makes a killing selling T-shirts on his comic book site. He had the T-shirts specially designed with unique graphics that have widespread appeal, and he sells dozens of them every week at a hugely profitable markup. Perhaps you can think of a particular piece of merchandise that could sell well on your site. Include your site logo on those items, and you can get your readers to advertise for you when they wear that shirt or carry around that tote bag. If you do decide to have custom merchandise made, we'd suggest having it created locally, saving yourself some shipping costs. Then take care of handling and shipping the items yourself. Even though you might spend your weekends boxing up products and mailing them out, if you create the right products and make them appealing enough, this might be a good profit center for you.

"Donate" Button

You've probably seen those PayPal buttons on websites, asking for donations, but did you know that they actually work? Yes, readers donate cash to websites using this simple method. One of our blogging friends says he gets about a 10 percent donation rate from his visitors using this "Donate" button, compared with a 1 percent clickthrough rate for his ads. Not all his visitors donate huge sums of money—many of the donations are $1— but as his number of visitors grows, it's paralleled by the number of contributions.

Handle this tactfully. We advise you to add just a small amount of text near your "please donate" button, eschewing the guilt trip or high-pressure public-television-style tactics, and keeping your begging short and simple. Try to make your pitch for donations more like the highly skilled guitar player at the train station, busking with his case open and passively inviting contributions, rather than the pushy wino, tapping you on the shoulder while hustling you for spare change.

Indirect Monetization

Remember when we told you, early on, that bloggers were experts in their fields? This is your chance to shine. By giving away the content on your blog, you become more likely to pick up freelance writing contracts, book deals, speaking engagements, and consulting opportunities. In fact, many individuals and companies use a blog as a way to advertise themselves, thereby informing their readers and the world at large about their skills and expertise.

Say you're a garden planner. By creating a gardening blog (and noting in the sidebar that you're available for consultations) you can talk about your favorite subject and build your business. This sort of work—simple, basic, and eminently scalable—is the kind of monetization we like best. Take what you love to do, add blogging, and you create a synergy unavailable to nonbloggers in the same field.

Note

1. www.slate.com/id/2284353"

Ethics Problems and How to Solve Them

We wish ethics questions in blogging could exist in a vacuum. "Is it okay to keep a source secret?" "Is it okay to publish business secrets? State secrets? Personal secrets?" "Is it ethical to take money for a blog post?" All of these questions would be easier to answer if we didn't have to answer the primary question in modern blogging: "Is this going to get me sued?"

Libel and Slander

Blogs are journalistic endeavors—but they aren't. You are free to write what you want, but you must always understand that you have neither the might of an organization nor the law behind you. However, you have the laws of the country where you're blogging on your side (or against you, as the case may be). In one recent example, a blogger named John "Johnny Northside" Hoff wrote a blog post about mortgage fraud involving Jerry Moore,[1] a former community leader in Minneapolis whom Hoff wrote about three times on his local blog. Moore sued for libel and was unable to make the charge stick. Instead he sued for $60,000 for "meddling" with Moore's employment after he was fired, and he won that original case.[2]

Hoff appealed the case in 2012, and the court reversed the award, because that old saying about how "truth is the best defense" turns out to be, uh, true. The appeals court found that Hoff's statements about Moore were true, and under the First Amendment of the U.S. Constitution, you can't be found liable for true statements (www.startribune.com/local/minneapolis/166762386.html).

So what have we learned from this? What is libel and slander, and who are public vs. private individuals? Let's go over a few definitions.

You'll notice all the scare quotes here. That's because we're basically dealing with uncharted territory. Anything you write can get you sued, and you may or may not have legal recourse.

Libel, according to the *Random House Dictionary*, is "defamation by written or printed words, pictures, or in any form other than by spoken words or gestures." This means printed or written matter that scandalizes a person. This could include images. The key point here is falsity: What you are trying to prove in a libel case is that the libelous party is writing something false about you. The same goes for libel's talky cousin, *slander* ("The action or crime of making a false *spoken statement* damaging to a person's reputation"): both of these require *falsity*.

Here, then, is the rub: If you are publishing rumor or hearsay, you will inevitably publish false information. This is fine if you mess up rumors of an upcoming electric car, but not so good if you're talking about a public or private person.

The vast majority of libel and slander threats are never taken to court. Persons finding their good names besmirched on the Internet often send "cease and desist" (C&D) letters, ostensibly from a lawyer, that politely (or impolitely) require that a blogger take down this or that post or comment. **As a rule of thumb do not remove anything you have written, unless you know it is false, or it has been proven false and potentially damaging by an impartial third party, usually a court**. Thus, any C&Ds—unless followed by real legal wrangling on the offended party's part, should be quietly ignored. Don't get in a shouting match with someone who has a big legal budget, but don't concede defeat, either. The chilling effect created by these C&Ds damages the business of blogging (and all journalism, for that matter) by causing real newsgathering to wither due to fear of retribution. You will write unpopular things, and the best thing you can do is be accurate, truthful, and have well-documented sources.

Bloggers often receive C&D letters for one reason and one reason only—the rumors they reported are true. In most of the cases when we've received C&D letters, they were sent by companies who found that we had acquired internal information through an informal leak, the most memorable case being a letter from Apple about images of the iPod Nano we had received from a tipster. The C&D confirmed the rumors as true and we published the C&D alongside the news.

Libel and slander cases are notoriously hard to win, and those who feel themselves wronged usually decide against continuing the cases once they realize the expenditures involved. But to bring people to the point of consulting a lawyer is not in an independent blogger's best interest.

Getting Called Out

So you've written something that disagrees with something someone else wrote later on, and they call you out. What do you do?

Well, are they right? Did they add context to your piece that you missed? Did you mess up? If any of these are true, a correction is in order but not a retraction. There are plenty of people out there who will take pot shots from the sidelines, but if you did your job right you have nothing to fear.

This happened to us recently: A post we did a few months prior was called out as an example of how "bad" our work was. The post was written on good faith with details supplied by people in the know. The takedown, on the other hand, was written from the perspective of disgruntled former employees of the operation we wrote about. Therefore, our post looked nice and saccharine, and the other reporter looked like a hard-working muckracker. In the world of media, both posts should exist, but we were not wrong for posting our slightly more supportive piece. In context, we were both right.

If you value your integrity, don't cave to online pressure. That's the long and the short of it.

Shield Law

There's one other legal right you might have as a blogger called a shield law,[3] applying to you just as it does to news reporters. Those laws, different in every state, give you the right to refuse to reveal your sources during the newsgathering process. There is no national shield law, but forty states and the District of Columbia offer those protections, otherwise known as "reporters' privilege." So unless you live in Idaho, Iowa, Massachusetts, Mississippi, Missouri, New Hampshire, South Dakota, Vermont, Virginia, or Wyoming, you won't need to worry about being subpoenaed or forced to reveal your sources in a court of law. For those other states, all except Wyoming have court-recognized privilege, which varies from state to state. We hope a national shield law will soon be enacted, something that's been under consideration for several years now.

Mr(s). Cellophane

Transparency is just a newfangled word for being candid and telling the truth. Transparency means not doing anything sneaky, tricky, or sleazy. You're going to be writing some quick stories on your online site, and being human, it's inevitable you'll get something wrong. If you're entirely transparent, rather than sneaking in and changing something that you got wrong, you'll let the readers know you've changed it.

When you've written a post and you discover you've made a mistake, the urge to edit those errant words or phrases without saying anything will grip you like a vice. "Maybe nobody will notice if I go in and change 1,000 to the correct number, 2,000," you say to yourself as you go back into your publishing program and start editing stuff. Maybe they won't notice, but then you won't exactly be telling the truth to your readers, now will you?

In a fast-moving news environment, new facts tend to emerge, and you can call attention to those either inside the body of text or at the end of the story. When you publish an update to your story, it gives readers a good feeling, assuring them they are getting the latest information. Sometimes an update is so crucial to the story, you'll want to put the word "updated" in the story's headline to call attention to the new stuff. Sometimes that headline modification can draw in more readers, looking for new information. You can tweet that new headline, announcing the new information, and visitors will come to your site to read it.

Other times, you mistype something—for example, writing "teh" instead of "the," and we think it's okay to fix typos without correction notices or undue fanfare unless the whole meaning of the story is changed by that one typo.

Whether you go to great lengths to apologize and correct your mistakes is up to you. There are different variations on such corrections, such as striking out the errant word and replacing it with the correct one. If you want to do that, just place an <s> before the word you'd like to strike out, and a </s> after it, and then it will be plain for all to see exactly what you've changed. It's a little humiliating and looks messy on the page, but this is the most straightforward way to call attention to changes and updates you've made since the piece was published.

An emerging standard on serious news sites is to keep a list of all the changes you made on a special page on your site. Each item in that list includes a link to the corrected article. It's also helpful to formulate a corrections policy, and post that on the site as well. Make your corrections policy and corrections page accessible with one click from any

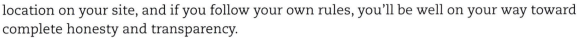

location on your site, and if you follow your own rules, you'll be well on your way toward complete honesty and transparency.

Going back into your text and correcting yourself—admitting you're wrong—is a tough thing to do, especially for someone just starting out. You might ask, "Won't that take the site's credibility down a few notches every time I make a correction?" Not necessarily. If you have to correct almost everything you write, your readers will stop believing you. But if you make an occasional correction, in our experience we've noticed that *readers love that*. You're reminding them that you made a mistake, but at the same time you're confirming that you're honest and transparent.

Are there exceptions to this corrections rule? Like most things, there is a gray area where you've published a story mere minutes before, and you suddenly realize you've left out information, or that you needed to edit some grammatical errors, or that you would like to polish up that last paragraph. Our rule is akin to the "five-second rule" when you drop food on the floor—any correction you make within five minutes of the publishing time is okay. Depending on how fast your server is, sometimes the story might not have even become available to the public by then.

An exception to that rule is when someone has commented on your story within those first five minutes. For example, what if a *Mashable* blogger misspelled former Egyptian president Hosni Mubarak's first name (oops, spelled it "Mosni"), and then made the correction within five *seconds* of clicking "publish?" Complicating matters: a reader spotted the error, commenting about it even within that short five-second exposure. Would it be okay to delete that comment? Technically, no, but it's a gray area, one where you as king of your blog will have to make an executive decision. Here's our take: If a commenter points out that error you made, and then you change it underneath him, you'll leave him hanging, and subsequent readers of the comments will wonder what the heck happened. Don't do that to your readers. They will always know that *you* were the one who made them look silly. It's not worth it. Simply add a comment thanking your eagle-eyed reader and move on.

As the ultimate grand poo-bah of your site, you'll be the one who decides whether that five-minute rule holds sway, if there is zero tolerance for any sneaky corrections, or if you'll just go ahead and correct whatever you want and never tell anybody. Maybe we're wusses, but we've always thought the best way to do business is with honesty and transparency. Do what you want, but in our experience with numerous successful blogs, we've noticed that the more transparent you are, the better.

Whichever route you take, it's usually the best idea to fess up, letting the readers know you made a mistake and that you're fixing it. It's simply the right thing to do, just like they used to teach you in kindergarten—when you make a mistake, take responsibility for it, apologize, and then do your best to make it right.

When Hosting Providers Attack

If your hosting provider ever pulls your plug because of something you wrote—and we're assuming that the thing you wrote isn't 100 scanned pages of a Harry Potter novel (i.e., pirated material)—then find a new host. In some cases hosts like Wordpress.com receive Digital Millennium Copyright Act (DMCA) takedown notices from malicious organizations that want to, say, silence debate. This is not okay.

If your provider tries to censor you, it's time to get a new provider. Pulling your post is never "within their rights," and shutting down your site is even worse. The unwritten contract between us and the Internet states that information must be free. Providers ignore that at their peril.

If you find yourself in a position where you have to fight a hosting provider to let you post something, quit that host immediately. There is no reason to fight them on points they will eventually lose.

Junket Junkies

The same level of transparency is required in dealings with trips provided by companies that want to share news with you in some exotic locale. Sometimes corporations are so awash in cash that they elect to take a group of lucky journalists on a trip, showing off the company's products and generally bathing those ink-stained wretches in the glow of corporate largesse. Some might even call it brainwashing.

This is a tricky area for you, Mr. or Ms. Watchdog. You want the info that's doled out on these fancy trips, many of which will include brand-new facts, figures, and products. But you don't want to get too close to the company. As a rule of thumb, you must make your reader understand what free stuff you were given while writing a story. Disclose.

What's wrong with taking a trip with a company to cover a bit of news? Well, first, let's talk about what's *not* wrong. On the positive side, accepting an invitation to a junket usually gives you a close-up look at products or services before they're introduced to anyone else. You'll get firsthand experience with the latest stuff, and usually the engineers, developers, and executives who brought the product from idea to reality will be right there, ready and willing to answer all your questions. This can be a valuable source of information, giving you the ability to relate your firsthand experience to your readers before they hear it from anyone else.

There's a social value to traveling on these junkets, too. Besides the original content you'll be able to glean from such trips, it's also advantageous to you as a journalist to hobnob with others of your ilk. And, once you establish a congenial face-to-face relationship with a corporation and its agents, product managers, executives, and engineers, they'll be more likely to place a name with a face when it's time for even more new products and information to roll out. As long as you realize that the companies are trying to bribe you into writing positive articles about their products, you're probably okay.

As a practical matter, most bloggers don't have the financial backing of a large organization, and can't afford a lot of travel. A freelance travel writer would go out of business after her first trip to a five-star resort in Burma. It's not financially feasible for much "lifestyle" journalism to exist without this relationship. It is not completely savory, but it happens all the time anyway.

So what does that mean? It means a company comes to expect coverage of a certain tenor from the authors they fête at their ranches and on their yachts. Clearly, the balance of power is out of the journalist's favor in this case, and the resulting disparity creates the worst kind of writing: bespoke or access journalism. If company A offers you a trip with the promise of more to come, what are you going to say about company A? That its product is subpar? That it misses the mark? That it sucks? If you do end up publishing a negative article about that company, would that be your last junket with that company?

The primary mission of any journalist is to comfort the afflicted and afflict the comfortable. It's hard to afflict the comfortable when you're rubbing shoulders with oligarchs and drinking fine wine from the CEO's private cellar.

So what to do? Keeping your credibility intact is not that hard. All you have to do is maintain a level head, remembering that you can't be bought and that you're on a search for truth. Keep things ethical when you write about what you've learned on the trip by revealing that the company paid your way.

You don't think you can maintain credibility and judgment on such a trip? Then don't go, or if you do, don't write about what you saw. If you're working for a larger organization, you might be completely forbidden from attending any paid trips by manufacturers. Some organizations (such as *The New York Times*) will not let you write for their publications unless it's been a set amount of time (sometimes two years) since you've been on any paid junkets. Others such as *Mashable* insist on paying their journalists' way to these events. But as an online journalist or blogger, if you're in charge and you do decide that junkets are okay, it's in your best interest to divulge this free travel, entertainment, wining, and dining to your readers when you write the articles describing the products and experiences you've had, seen, and touched on those trips. Beyond the transparency of divulging a company's attempt to bribe you, the most important thing of all is not to let your own opinion be swayed by such luxuries.

The bottom line is this: PR people, during business hours, aren't your friends. Their goal is to maximize the reach of a piece of news, and if they can get you to practice bespoke journalism, gaining their client a bit of free advertising, so be it. With advertising rates high and the value of online presence increasing, there is a recently popular trend to send product out to almost everyone and his dog. Five hundred good reviews are better than 499, at least when it comes to Google and other ranking sites, and so PR people depend on some laxity of morals to ensure that less experienced journalists will support their position in hopes of receiving future free products. Don't be one of those corporate stooges.

Your goal is to tell the truth. If the truth as you perceive it matches their pitch, then everything is fine. But don't be pressured to change your mind by a fancy steak and whiskey chaser.

A few more tips:

Should you ever befriend PR people? Yes, but don't let them pitch you.
Should you ever date PR people? The heart wants what the heart wants, but don't let them pitch you.
Should you ever take gifts from PR people? No.
Should you ever take calls from PR people? No. Make them email you.
Are PR people valuable? Yes, when they help you achieve a coverage goal. They are at their worst when they get in the way of your work.

Free Stuff

Review units: Do you send them back or not?

It's tempting to simply keep review units, giving yourself free perks for your trouble. The problem with that is the appearance of impropriety when you accept free products from companies, which could be construed as bribes. In most cases, you're obligated to send a product you reviewed back to its maker, and it's customary for the company to pay for shipping costs on any review units, both ways. For more valuable products, companies will often ask you to sign a product loan agreement. At the end of the designated loan period, they'll usually nudge you to send the review unit back, which you should do promptly.

War Story

There are exceptions to this quandary of hanging on to review units. Many times, there are updates, bug fixes, and modifications applied to products. For example, Logitech sent us its Revue Google TV set-top box, which we promptly reviewed. As product development continued, the company continually updated its operating system, added applications to it, and generally improved upon its usability. We wanted to write about these incremental improvements to this important device, so we held onto the review unit, and Logitech wasn't asking for it back anytime soon. This is still ethical, because a reviewer must continue to possess the hardware to do further reviews of the product. Other times, you need to use those products longer than just a few days, so you'll be conversant about its particular characteristics. These sorts of arrangements can be worked out with companies, but it's your obligation to immediately return any review unit upon request.

If you're writing favorable comments about a product that was given to you for free, that could be seen as advertising, but it's deceptive only if you're praising the product simply because you got it free. That's why some journalists go to great extremes to avoid even the appearance of bribery.

War Story

At the end of a dinner we enjoyed with former *Wall Street Journal* tech guru Walt Mossberg, we saw the sage columnist paying cash to our corporate host for the price of the dinner we just ate, and for the Las Vegas show we were about to attend. To be fair, the *Wall Street Journal* probably has an impressive entertainment budget, but the spirit of his action should guide your dealings with PR folks.

Your ultimate desire should be to serve your readers, and tell them the truth about the products you review. Your credibility hinges on the fact that you are incorruptible; that no matter how hard companies try to sway your opinion with gifts, travel, expensive dinners, and plenty of drinks, you're an ironclad journalist who can't be bought. According to your own set of ethics and morals, you'll need to decide for yourself how you'll handle the issue of journalistic integrity.

What if you've reviewed a product, and like it so much you'd like to keep it, but the company is asking for it back? Again in murky ethical territory, you could ask the company for what's known as an "editorial accommodation price," allowing you to settle accounts with the price that is usually around what it costs for the company to manufacture it. Companies are often eager to do this, because shipping costs and the fact that you'll be returning a used product make it unprofitable to return review units, especially if they're bulky yet inexpensive.

This opens up a larger discussion of bribes and payola. Should you accept *anything* free from companies you're writing about? It's complicated. For example, some publications such as *Consumer Reports* don't accept free samples, instead hiring secret shoppers to buy all their own review units from the same stores where consumers will buy those products.

That's not practical for a blogger just starting out. You'll need to convince companies to send you free review units if you want to write reviews, but that doesn't give those companies the right to expect you to suddenly be under their control. Ultimately, you need to maintain your own distance from the companies that supply you with products to review.

The U.S. Federal Trade Commission (FTC) has addressed this issue, and it's put together its Revised Endorsement Guides[4] for bloggers using review units and free services from companies. The Guides say that affiliation must be disclosed if the writer strays from typical "just the facts" reporting. So "this widget is blue" requires no disclosure, while "This beautiful widget is a rich, cerulean blue and will remind you of your first love [Disclosure: The company gave me 500 of these widgets for my friends and family]" does.

While the Guides are detailed and contain lots of useful suggestions, the gist is that the FTC recommends transparency. That means if you review a car, for instance, and you got to use that car free for a month, mention that in your post. The FTC even goes so far as to say if you borrowed a review unit and then returned it, you should mention that, too.

Contrary to rumors, the FTC will not be levying fines of $11,000 per post against those who don't choose to follow its Endorsement Guides, and the agency will not be monitoring bloggers for compliance, nor does it have any plans to. Go ahead, read the government gobbledygook recommended by the Federal Trade Commission—it's enlightening. Or skip it, and remember the most important lesson: **keeping your journalistic activities transparent will serve you well in every aspect of your blog.**

Whatever you decide about review units and how you'll handle them, it's difficult not to be influenced by someone who bestows lavish gifts upon you. Resist that influence. Ideally, every reviewer would buy all review samples like *Consumer Reports* does, and not accept any advertising. But this is the real world, so we'll leave this topic here: Remember, your obligation is to your readers, not to those companies whose products you're reviewing. Tell the truth, no matter how much companies try to bribe you. Readers will trust you to do the right thing, if you'll just be straight with them. The government's not going to bust you for being dishonest, but your readers will.

Caught in a Trap

"Oh, what a tangled web we weave, when first we practice to deceive." You've lied, and now you're caught. First of all, just don't lie. Stop it. Now. You're a blogger, on a search for truth, and lies are anathema. Now that we've gotten that out of the way, how do you control damage from a lie you told on your blog? The easy way seems to be to just stonewall it, and keep insisting that you didn't lie, and that whoever says you're lying is himself a liar. But that doesn't work. Forget that. The first thing you need to do is much like what you do when you make a mistake and correct it: Take responsibility for your falsehood, apologize for it, assure your readers that you won't do it again, and then don't. And make it a sincere apology, none of this half-baked, "mistakes were made" crap. Use phrases like "I was wrong," "For that I sincerely apologize," "I take complete responsibility." These earnest apologies will let the readers know you are truly contrite. Just don't lie.

Leaks and Trust

As you get to know more PR reps and company officials, they'll start letting you in on secret products, ideas, policies, or plans. No, they usually won't trust you with that information, requiring you to sign a nondisclosure agreement, known in the industry as an NDA. Inside the NDA are provisions that will allow them to sue you if you reveal this information before the agreed-upon embargo date. Signing an NDA can be a great help to you as a writer, giving you time to write a well-considered and carefully crafted review or story that you can publish the instant the product is announced. However, in our fast-paced world, an embargo can make or break a scoop. Perhaps someone isn't as scrupulous as you, or maybe the news appeared on a rumor site. It's couched as rumor, but you know it's true. What to do?

The easy, glib thing to say in this situation is "Stick by your agreements and don't reveal any secrets until the embargo date." But sometimes it gets tricky. What if you and twenty other sites have signed this NDA, and then one of the sites publishes a story a couple of days before the embargo lifts? Under those circumstances, is it all right to go ahead with the story, since the cat's already out of the bag? Technically, no, but realistically, if one major website has already told this secret story, it's no longer a secret. Careful, though—you could get sued (although it's highly unlikely). You signed that NDA that promised you wouldn't reveal any of this information, not that you would keep it a secret as long as everyone else did.

The solution to this, obviously, is to refuse to sign NDAs on principle, and for the same reasons that disclosure is important: an NDA is a restraint, as is an embargo. Embargoes started out for a good reason: it was to allow journalists far from the major news hubs to receive and digest information before a nationwide release. However, now embargoes often allow bigger names "exclusive" rights to news while the rest of the rabble waits out the embargo time. While not particularly fair, this is a bad habit that crops up quite often on many beats. For example, many electronics companies release products on Wednesday nights so the big papers—*The Wall Street Journal* and *The New York Times*—can have first crack at publication on Thursday. This sort of tacit collusion, while unseemly, is fairly commonplace.

Again, because of this gray area, many bloggers and website editors refuse to sign NDAs. Their argument is that NDAs give companies too much control over the dissemination of information. At the same time, numerous companies abuse the concept of an NDA, making you sign such an agreement months before a product release, and then controlling what you can and can't write about that product in the ensuing months. The tail wags the dog. Now, many companies are asking writers to sign NDAs even for the slightest trifle of a product release. Honestly, it's getting out of hand. You can refuse to sign NDAs, or do what we do, and play the NDA game on a case-by-case basis.

Stand Up Straight, Private

You'll notice we spent quite a while on the maintenance of propriety in blogging. There is a good reason: blogs, for the longest time, have not been taken seriously. Long seen as side projects and hobbies, it took us and the other blogging stalwarts years to gain status in the journalistic world. Some, like *Mashable*, don't even want to be called "blogs" anymore, opting to be called "digital news sites."

We remember the early 2000s when the Consumer Electronics Show would barely recognize bloggers, let alone offer them journalist credentials to cover the show. This started to change in about 2004, but it was only in the past four years or so that blogs far out-reported mainstream sources in terms of word count and access. Local papers are folding left and right, while companies are finding the web to be a much more comfortable outlet for many of their messages. As a result, bloggers are seen as, if not valuable, then necessary. For every major newspaper review of a new product or vacation spot there are three or four—or forty—blog posts. Marketers have begrudgingly begun to accept that maybe, just maybe, we know what we're doing.

Not to sound rude, but we don't want you ruining a good thing. Once you get into our shoes, you will want to maintain blogging's integrity and value as a medium. If you came into this so you could get free stuff and trips to Hawaii, then you're in the wrong business (we hear sweepstakes entry is an up-and-coming industry). Sure, you'll get your share of fun doing this job, but the satisfaction that your work is read and appreciated and actually makes a difference is worth far more than a new iPod, no matter what anyone else says.

We are telling you how to act because we want you, as a new blogger, to make us proud. As we mentioned before, blogging is a big deal. Scandals only reinforce negative stereotypes and reduce our value in the ecosystem of information.

Be Nice or Be Right

Remember when your mom told you that if you didn't have anything nice to say don't say anything at all? She was partially right. If you have solid evidence of wrongdoing, malfeasance, messiness, or mendacity and you can prove it beyond a shadow of a doubt, you should. If you hear rumors that someone did something to someone else, then maybe you should hold off until you hear more. In short, be nice or be right.

Blogging's Golden Rule

You can't work in a vacuum. Blogging is now mainstream, and what you write can potentially damage blogging's reputation. The new golden rule is this: **respect the blog and the blogger.** The days of trolls, cranks, and lonely guys in their basements posting cat videos are over. Blogging is mainstream. You are entering a strange new world where media is not owned by massive corporations and where bloggers are becoming massive corporations in their own right.

Blogging is the front line of a new journalistic model. You are its vanguard. Make us proud.

Notes

1. www.citypages.com/2010-08-18/news/jerry-moore-has-a-controversial-past/
2. www.startribune.com/local/117805398.html
3. http://en.wikipedia.org/wiki/Shield_laws_in_the_United_States
4. www.ftc.gov/bcp/edu/pubs/business/adv/bus71.shtm

10
Expanding Your Blogging Horizons
Blogging Perks

Blogging is not all grueling drudgery and gnashing of teeth. Once you get the heavy lifting done in the beginning, it's time to set your mind free, relax, be yourself, and find fascinating topics where you can show everyone your stuff.

While blogging yourself into a notable presence (or a notorious one) takes a long time, you'll be able to get a taste of the sweet perks of blogging early on. Watching Google real-time analytics gives you a cheap thrill right at the beginning, showing you how many active visitors you have on your site, what they're reading and where they're reading from. Here's where you are reminded that the web is truly worldwide, with dots appearing on the global map from nearly everywhere on earth. It's a humbling feeling.

One of the lasting perks of being a blogger is the education you get from covering your chosen topic. Because you're a driven and determined engine of expertise, you'll be digging into your topic deeper than anyone else, perhaps uncovering brand-new knowledge with your own experimentation. At the very least, you'll be talking to the luminaries of your subject, finding out what the current deep thinking is, and spinning along this information to your readers. Before too long, unless your topic is so vast that no one will ever get a firm grip on it, you will know practically everything there is to know about your topic area.

This might not seem like a perk, but as soon as you press Publish, you're suddenly plugged into the most gigantic fact-checking machine the world has ever known. If you've been diligent about writing that post, you'll have all of your facts correct. However, no one's perfect, and when your audience gets bigger, there will always be one reader who knows more than you do about the narrow subject you're writing about. That reader might decide to admonish you in the comments, but take it as a perk and not an affront, learning from the experience and adding it to the most valuable asset you possess: your memory bank.

Perhaps the best part of being a blogger is the visibility you get. Most jobs that require deep thinking also require sharp writing skills, and your blog will be the perfect showcase for those wondering if you can concisely express yourself with words on a page. If you have picked the right topic and written compelling blog posts, your blog can serve as the ultimate writing sample. Not only will it show those who might want to hire you that you are knowledgeable, but also they will get a good look at your personality just by reading through your blog.

The Job Hunt

You're reading this book, so you're probably considering blogging as a way to make a living. If you persevere and have talent and a little luck, you could make sensational money from a successful blog. However, instead of starting your own blog, you might want to get a job at one of the established websites on the Internet. Or you might want to work for a big corporation, helping it communicate with its customers on a corporate blog. In this chapter we'll offer tips about how to get hired at a big blog, and show you how to build your brand so you'll get noticed. We'll explain how networking can make all the difference for your blog and for your future employment, and how to make a career change to blogging in the smoothest possible way.

So what's the best way to get a job at one of those top-flight blogs? There are many routes to the same destination. For instance, at *Mashable*, the best way to get hired is to get a job there first as an intern. The company hires more interns every semester, and the latest "internapalooza" saw thirty-five interns hired. That's remarkable, considering that *Mashable* has only about ninety staffers total.

As you work through your $10-per-hour gig, lots of friendly people are more than happy to be your mentor. *Mashable*'s interns get to work on the front lines, writing posts from almost their first day working at the site. They're given tremendous responsibility, writing for 15 million unique visitors every day. This is the kind of internship you want. While the morality of using $10-per-hour interns to do the same work its paid staffers are doing is questionable—and if you can afford to live in New York City with that kind of income—you could work at a major blog for a semester or two, and that could be your ticket to the big time.

Another way to get noticed at the top blogs is to become an astute commenter. Find a story you know something about, add your own special brand of insight, and if you're consistent in the quality and frequency of your comments, you will be noticed. Be sure not to simply write a post and paste it into the comments section. That's bad form. Instead, add a pithy two-paragraph response to the post under which you're commenting, showing that your mindset is similar to those who are writing the blog.

In fact, as we worked for three of the top five blogs in the world, we were always on the lookout for promising writers. Most of those strong writers we noticed were writing posts on their own blogs, showing us every day that they had the chops to make it in the big time. Starting up your own blog is your chance to show your stuff. If your destination is one of the major blogs, the best thing for you to do first is to start your own blog, write 1,000 words on it every day, and see if blogging is actually a career path you want to take. If you turn out to be spectacularly successful, not only will you be noticed by industry luminaries and big-time blogs, but also you might consider keeping your blog going for yourself, and perhaps even turn it into an empire.

War Story

When we were working at *Gizmodo*, there was one small blog that kept grabbing all the scoops. Who was this secretive and anonymous "Boy Genius" (whom we now know is Jonathan Geller) who seemed to find out about every cellphone and hot gadget before anyone else? Certainly he would like to step up to a major-league tech blog like *Gizmodo*, abandoning all he had done for his site, *Boy Genius Report* (now known as *BGR*). It turned out the Boy Genius had already been through *Gizmodo's* rival blog, *Engadget*, and was so successful as an anonymous columnist there that he started his own website. He was not interested in leaving his blog, and it continued to grow, rivaling *Gizmodo* and all the other tech sites. It was so successful that in April 2010–less than four years after he started the blog–Geller sold *BGR* to Los Angeles-based media company PMC for an undisclosed sum. Now, he's probably worth millions while *BGR* is "the biggest mobile news destination in the world."

Networking

Looking for jobs on LinkedIn, other job sites such as Glassdoor.com (www.glassdoor.com/), and Monster.com can sometimes work, but there is no site that can match the magic of a recommendation from someone you know well when you're looking for the perfect job. Most of the best jobs are never advertised, and are filled solely by word-of-mouth.

We've been on both the hiring side and the job-seeking side of the employment equation, and the hiring side is a lot more stressful than you might think. Whenever you bring someone into your organization, you're taking a risk. Will you be spending money on someone who will not work hard enough? Will you be introducing more trouble than benefit by hiring someone? As a job hunter, it's up to you to show hiring managers that you will be a significant benefit to their organization. However, the company might not be willing to take on the risk of taking your word for it when you say you're going to be an ideal employee. Hiring managers are looking for a sure thing, and a recommendation from a trusted colleague has extraordinary value.

Your best bet in finding an appropriate blogging job is to seek out those you know who are blogging, and ask them if they've heard of any opportunities that might be suitable for you. You never know—a friend of yours who is working at a blog might be able to get a finder's fee for recommending you. That happens at *Mashable*, where anyone finding a person who ends up being employed at *Mashable* gets a few hundred bucks as a finder's fee.

An important way to tap into this word-of-mouth power is to be sure your friends know you're looking for a job. You might even consider placing on your LinkedIn profile something along the lines of "looking for online reporting opportunities." If you follow our advice and build up your LinkedIn network, a simple change in your profile could suddenly be viewed by thousands of your connections and result in job leads.

There's no shortage of editorial jobs in today's employment market; however, there is enormous competition for the best ones. That's why you need to make yourself stand out by knowing someone at the company. That's another area where LinkedIn can help; if you look up a particular company on LinkedIn, you'll see how many of your connections either work there or know someone who does.

Usually when you apply for a job as an online journalist, you'll be asked for references. Of course, you'll want to include those trusted colleagues you've worked with in the past who are sure to put in a good word for you. But it would be even more helpful to get a recommendation from someone who works for the company to which you are applying. Either way, always check with someone before you list that person as one of your references, and if you're applying to a company where someone you know will be your reference, be sure that person is liked and admired by those who are hiring you.

Beyond online networking, trade shows and industry events are where you'll find your richest job-hunting targets. Your humble authors rarely go to a trade show where they're not offered jobs, and the same can happen to you if you know enough people and have established a viable network.

If you can be seen at important events, that serves as its own endorsement—it means that you care enough about your topic to either spend money to get there, or you're important enough to have a company paying your way. However you can get there, be seen at these events, and you'll notice more opportunities coming your way.

Follow Your Own Dreams

Before you decide to try to get a job with an established blog, don't give up on the idea of building your own blog to the point where it makes money. While the benefits such as health insurance, vacation days, and holidays you get when working for a major-league website are enticing, you'll be working for someone else. You won't have control over what you do, and you won't be able to implement your vision for the site. Sure, it means you'll be able to contribute your ideas, but never forget that when you're working for someone else, your mission is to fulfill that person's entrepreneurial dreams, not yours. Unless you're lucky enough to have the exact same dreams as your employer, you're not going to have control over what happens in that job. And even if your dreams are similar, it often works out that your employer gets the gold mine, and you get the shaft.

On the other hand, if you start your own blog, everything on that site is yours. There is a risk—and often there's an opportunity cost—to starting your own blog, but unless something is risked, there's no opportunity for reward. Would you rather be earning $300,000 per year for your employer and then paid $50,000 in salary, or earning $300,000 a year for your blog, and then get to keep all of it for yourself? You'll be working for something you built, something that belongs to you and that you can show to the world as completely yours.

The feeling of total ownership and responsibility is profound. The spirit of entrepreneurism is what you'll need to start your own blog and see it through to success. The reward of entrepreneurism is the ability to visualize what will happen, put lots of sustained and focused work into it, and then see the result. If you don't like what's happened, it's your responsibility. At the same time, you will be the one receiving the kudos when it's a success.

Get Rich Quick?

Blogging is a long-tail career. As in most "writerly" pursuits, you're going to face the facts: most bloggers aren't making much money. Even given all of their clout, many blogs can support a single editor and little else. Although there are plenty of amazing bloggers making lots of money, most of them treat blogging as a labor of love.

That's why you need to expect to be paid very little (if at all) if you sign on with a prominent blog. John's niche blog, WristWatchReview.com, gets about 30,000 pageviews a month, barely makes enough to pay one writer—and John doesn't see a penny of income from the site. It is important for John to keep it going because he likes watches but the writer who helps him out, Patrick Kansa, is basically doing it for the love of wristwatches. Could he be making more? Probably, but given both John and Patrick have day jobs, it's hard to dedicate the hours to ad sales necessary to truly become profitable.

There's the rub: ridiculous claims can be made about the lucrative nature of blogging, and there are plenty of people who will sell you snake oil. But trust us: it's hard. It's not impossible, but it's hard.

War Story

John joined *Gizmodo* because he got laid off and the editor at the time, Joel Johnson, liked pierogis. Before his work at *Gizmodo*, John was technical editor for *Laptop* magazine (yes, a paper magazine). Because that magazine apparently no longer needed technical expertise, he got the boot. After a few weeks of frenzied job hunting, he saw a post on *Gizmodo* looking for writers. John drove to Brooklyn, where he and Joel ate Polish food and talked tech. In an hour John was sold. Joel's life was exciting, fascinating, and looked exhausting. But even though Joel–who is a hale and hearty writer with a heart of gold–looked like he was about to have a heart attack because he was so far from his computer for that hour, it was clear that this was a life that offered quite a bit of freedom and a lot of future. Fast-forward nearly a decade, and Joel is still blogging and now John is that exhausted but exhilarated writer.

Changing Careers

What if you want to move into blogging as a full-time profession? We've met a few people who have done it with success, so we can address a few major concerns and give a bit of advice.

Blogging, like any profession, requires conviction. We have seen too many sites fall by the wayside simply because the creators didn't follow through. Your blogging goal, defined in Chapter 1, can be to become an expert in your field. Maybe you don't need the cash. If that's the case, skip ahead.

Still with us? Good. So here's the truth: making money blogging is easy if you have the right niche. There are multiple monetization strategies that we've discussed in previous chapters but here are our favorites.

Consulting. The easiest way to make money blogging is the most indirect. Because you are considered an expert in your field you can parlay your recognition into speaking gigs (mostly unpaid) and consulting gigs (always paid). While creating a consulting career is outside the scope of this book, rest assured that we've met popular bloggers who blog to further their "second" careers. Think of your blog as a public portfolio; if you write regularly and using the tips we've described in previous chapters, you will get noticed. Some businesses buy billboards. You've chosen to make Google your billboard.

War Story

John owns a 3D printer. It's a printer that makes objects out of plastic. In his years blogging he's followed the 3D printing industry with avid interest, and recently his posts have driven a great deal of traffic to an odd place—John's own 3D printing service website. While he doesn't make much on the services, he is number three in Google for "3D printing in Brooklyn" and he gets a steady stream of small clients who need small things printed on the fly. While 3D printing is little more than a hobby for John, imagine the damage he could do if he put his mind to growing the business.

Building a Brand

You might think corporations and products are the only ones who have brands, but you have a specific brand to promote: you. Your name and the name of your blog are both parts of your brand, and your reputation is what makes it shiny and appealing, or repugnant and off-putting.

Keep your personal brand in mind with every action you take. Minding your brand is crucial at every turn, even if it's the smallest interaction such as a reply to a comment on your blog, a comment anywhere on Facebook, the way you carry yourself at industry events, press conferences, and trade shows, and all of your interpersonal interactions with readers, other bloggers, and anyone else.

You might not be famous yet. You might not even be micro-famous, or even nano-famous, but starting from the beginning, you need to think this way: that you're not famous *yet*. You never want to do anything to besmirch your good name, a valuable brand that will serve you well if you treat it with tender loving care.

Successfully building your brand hinges on how giving you are to everyone else. For instance, do more than just promote yourself and your blog posts on social media. Point your followers toward other sites' posts, or point out happenings that you found interesting. Give people content they can use, and that they'll want, beyond simply promoting your posts. In fact, some stories you're thinking about posting might work just as well or even better as a tweet or a Facebook update. Give people these morsels of content and information—things you know that they don't—and that will build your brand.

Pay attention to detail if you want your brand to shine. If your blog is full of misspellings, poor grammar, factual errors, and posts that no one cares about, your personal brand will emerge as something people would rather avoid.

Be consistent with your brand. Create a logo or look that people recognize as yours alone. Then spread that logo around as much as you can without being a graffiti artist. Place it on your business cards, make sure it's always spelled and capitalized the same way, and treat it like gold.

Speaking of business cards, you never know when a branding opportunity might emerge, so any time you meet someone, make it a point to hand that person your business card. He or she might not be someone who can directly help you, but it's hard to predict when someone will know someone else who could approach you with a great gig, assignment, advertiser, or story tip.

You don't need to be an annoying and pushy salesperson with your brand, but reminding everyone that you're a blogger, you write great stuff, and your site is worth a visit is crucial to your success.

11

Building an Empire

The hardest thing you'll face while blogging is realizing that it's just too much work to do alone. While your 1,000-word regimen will allow you to post four or five items—or one big one, if you're in the mood—you'll soon realize that the amount of news you're missing is becoming a detriment to the growth and evolution of the site. It's a good problem to have.

We bloggers are often loath to admit we need help. We do. Blogging is difficult and constant work, and even the best bloggers eventually bring on teams of people to help them cover the day's news. Add personnel when you've picked up enough traffic to pay yourself. Once you're making a few hundred dollars a month on your site and you have good (or bad or any) relationships with your sources, you may be ready to take on an assistant, paid or unpaid.

Sadly, the current blogging model rarely supports paid interns or assistants, or even co-editors. If you're making enough money to pass a little cash on to another person, however, no matter the amount, try to pay that person. If blogging is to be taken seriously it cannot depend on the kindness of strangers. As the boss, you might even consider paying other bloggers to work for you before you even pay yourself. Consider this unpaid work an investment in growth, part of the cost of boosting your blog from obscurity into a powerful force of the blogosphere.

Knowing When to Call in Reserves

If your beat is big—technology, fashion, or film, for example—you'll probably need help off the bat but can't afford it, or can't find the right people. Do your best alone until you hit about 1,000 pageviews a month. The difference between 10 pageviews and 1,000 is fairly small—it just means more people have made you a daily read—but the difference between 1,000 and 10,000 pageviews is immense. Getting to that number is hard work.

Why do you need help? Because you can't do everything. You need to be writing, photographing, interviewing, and reviewing. As a solo blogger, your three or four posts a day amount to your own personal statement, but if you want to build an empire, you're going to need more than just a personal statement. To catch that shark, you're going to need a bigger boat. You're going to need to cover your topic comprehensively, and that can be done only with a highly motivated team of enthusiastic journalists. If you don't know any such people offhand, find some at job boards such as problogger.com, freelanceswitch.com, or elance.com. Or ask around on Facebook or LinkedIn, especially helpful if you've built up a big list of friends or contacts there.

Is it time to start hiring? To quote the White Stripes:

> *Well you're in your little room*
> *And you're working on something good*
> *But if it's really good*
> *You're gonna need a bigger room*

The bigger room, in this case populated with a scintillating writer or two in addition to yourself, is a better support system for your site and your work. By the time you reach the point where your blog is starting to generate some income, it's probably proven itself to be an entity poised for even more growth. That's especially true when your blog is nurtured by extra ninjas at your side, adding additional content, putting forth more effort, and making their numerous points with a variety of voices.

Posts equal traffic. To spur additional growth, increase the number of posts your blog presents to its readers every day. Generally, the more posts you have, the more popular your site will be. A blog that publishes twenty high-quality posts a day is going to be a lot more attractive to potential readers than one that cranks out a mere five equally high-quality posts a day. But there are limits to the number of posts a blog can handle in one day, organically restricted by the amount of content that's worth covering and the amount of money available to pay those writers who are stoking this furnace.

Where is that sweet spot, where there are enough posts per day on a blog to adequately cover the news, yet not so many that your team of bloggers has to scrape the bottom to find suitable content about which to write? There's no hard and set rule for the sweet spot of post-count-to-audience-growth, because it varies with each topic niche. Some subjects are so vast and general that even 100 posts per day won't cover the topic thoroughly, while others can be completely covered every day with just 10 posts. Some are completely covered with one or two per day.

You'll know when you're approaching that sweet spot. You know that feeling when you're solo blogging, and when you first start your day, it seems like there are dozens of topics you could write about? That changes drastically when you build a team of bloggers. If you've built up your post count, it gets to the point where by mid-afternoon, when you're looking for something to write about, every conceivable news story of the day has already been covered. That means you're getting close to that sweet spot, if you haven't already passed it.

Another indicator that you've reached that sweet spot: When you add posts, your traffic numbers stay the same. Unless that new writer you added isn't cutting it, or you've done something else to offend your readers and slow down traffic, you might have gotten to the post-count saturation point for your blog.

In the early days of our work with *Gizmodo*, we were cranking out about thirty posts a day with five bloggers. As the site grew, we added more writers, until about a year later we were publishing fifty posts per day with about ten bloggers. We noticed a sizable jump in our traffic when we raised the post count from thirty to about forty posts per day. It's difficult to pinpoint if that traffic growth was due to the increased number of posts, improvement in the quality of the writing, or maybe the growing buzz surrounding

Gizmodo. We suspect it was a combination of all three, but it felt like a big part of that boost was directly attributable to those additional posts. When writing about technology and gadgets, it felt like we were thoroughly covering our topic at forty posts per day. But when we raised that to fifty posts a day with an even bigger team, it felt like we were getting in each other's way, and it often seemed like we were desperate to find worthy topics to cover, especially on a slow news day. Worse, it felt like our posts were competing against each other for the limited attention of our visitors. It felt the same way at *Mashable*, which in 2013 was blasting forth around seventy posts per day.

Here's the dirty secret to blogging: posting more makes you look bigger online. When people return again and again and see an entirely new front page with brand new stories they see your site as a source for up-to-date information and therefore more valuable. *Huffington Post* didn't get big because it posted a few big stories a day. It got big because it flooded the webwaves with information. *Drudge Report* is popular because new content appears on it seemingly every minute. That's how web content works—by engulfing the user in stuff.

How to Be a Blogger Boss

The key to being a blogger boss is letting go of some things while holding tight to the core principles of your blog. It's a loose/tight leadership that lets your writers flex their own style while you take care of the big picture. Trying to control everything your writers do, editing their work to the point that it's not their work anymore, and micromanaging everything that happens with your site is not a good way to motivate your chosen bloggers. That's why you have to choose the right people, and then let them work their magic while you keep an eye on the direction your ship is headed.

The concept of teamwork is popular these days, but when it gets down to it, blogging is about 95 percent parallel work and 5 percent cooperative work. Your blogging team will need to coordinate its topic choices to avoid duplication of effort. And ideally, you, as editor-in-chief, will want to edit their work and offer constructive suggestions. But the actual writing of complicated, tight, and entertaining blog posts is a solitary activity requiring intense concentration, and doesn't lend itself well to teamwork, which tends to devolve into distraction. There's no shortage of starry-eyed managers who envision a tight-knit group working together like a well-oiled machine, cranking out a cohesive website with impressive teamwork. For sure, that 5 percent of the time spent on teamwork is crucial, like the 5 percent of the time pilots spend taking off and landing airplanes. But the rest of the time, a group blog is not like a band playing together, blending in with each other in perfect harmony. It's more like a continuous concert with a series of highly skilled and expressive soloists taking the stage, one at a time. Yes, they're all playing a similar kind of music, but each person is expressing him- or herself individually. Each soloist even gets to choose which music he'll play, with your approval. Your job is to decide what *style* of music everyone will play, help clean up any sour notes that may find their way to the audience's ears, fill the concert hall with eager listeners, and supply the concert hall building at the same time.

That means you're going to have to hire a team of self-starting individuals—people who are knowledgeable about your chosen topic, can write coherently enough not to require rewriting of everything they do, and have a likable and agreeable demeanor. Of all the eccentric personalities we've seen floating through the blogging world, these knowledgeable, borderline-obsessed creative types are the kind of people who are the most successful in a group blogging environment.

The most important quality we looked for when hiring bloggers was the ability to write quality content with a minimum of supervision. All other considerations were secondary. We didn't need some hotshot reporter with a long resume writing in-depth stories about tax policy. We needed a person with energy who was able, in a few minutes, to pump out a post or two during a lull in the news. We needed someone who was like a speed chess player, who could write quickly, with smart style and wit.

How do you supervise these people? At the core, a blogger boss must be able to send out a quick message—do this, shoot that, take a look at this—and expect that your employees will be able to accurately carry out your wishes. Managing writers is a dicey proposition. Criticize them too much, and you'll break their spirit, making them paranoid every time they sit down to write. Praise them too much, and they'll either stop believing you, or will get so pumped up they will have less room to improve their work and might stop trying as hard. But if you must overdo something, err on the side of too much praise rather than too little. It's best to couch criticism inside a sandwich of praise, and let a writer find his or her own style. If you don't like that style, you might have hired the wrong person. However, don't hire a seasoned writer hoping to mold that person into the blogger you want. Save your molding for interns or beginners you might take under your wing. Even then, these are human beings, not trained seals. Give people ownership of their work, trust them, and let them develop their own voices, and your team will be inspired to operate at its peak efficiency.

How to Find Bloggers

The best bloggers come from the ranks of your readers—those who already know and love your work will be most willing to supply their time and effort to your cause. Publish a post on your site asking for help, and more often than not, you'll receive a few emails from qualified people willing to help.

Pay close attention to those who comment on your site. Sometimes there's a standout who might already be writing comments good enough to be blog posts. Pursue that person. It won't be that much of a leap to turn your best commenter into your best blogger.

Trade shows and industry events are fertile ground for finding suitable blogging partners as well. If you're attending a trade show about your chosen topic, you'll be meeting a ready-made crowd of other writers working the same beat who might be interested in blogging with you. Keep an eye on sites that compete with you—you never know when one of your favorite bloggers might be looking for work.

The blogger interview process is simple: Send your candidates a few links or story ideas, and ask them to write sample posts. There's no reason to ask for anything much longer than 300 words, and if the turnaround and intent are clear and the writing is good, give them a bit of a trial period blogging for the site. It's literally that simple. The best bloggers aren't professional journalists. They are students (like one of John's writers, Nicholas Deleon), stay-at-home dads, retirees, Best Buy employees (another one of John's writers), or frustrated video producers (like Charlie).

In our blogs there is usually a "hazing" period—albeit electronic—when a blogger's work is picked apart with an intensity that is usually exaggerated. This process ensures that the new blogger understands the importance of his or her work, and understands that the writing will be judged by even more vehement readers—namely, an audience accustomed to seeing words spelled correctly and the rules of grammar followed. That's not to mention the readers' craving for posts that have their facts straight.

Blogging bosses must be on the lookout for cynicism as well. Blog posts that skew inordinately toward the negative crop up often in new bloggers, because it's more fun to be snarky and write negatively. That's a dangerous place for a new blogger to descend into. Catch cynicism early and prevent it by offering easier stories to write.

We usually ask new bloggers to start out writing "straight"—that is, without humor or opinion. This ensures they are able to at least find the basic facts of a story, and express them succinctly. Only after a few weeks of that do we consider allowing those fledgling bloggers to begin their inevitable flights of lyrical fantasy.

Keeping Connected

Now we're getting to the teamwork part. For your blog to function at its maximum efficiency, you must all become experts at communicating. For everyone to communicate with each other as a group, we use the web-based chat room we mentioned earlier, called Campfire by 37 Signals (free thirty-day trial, $12 per month after that) to keep up with what our writers and colleagues are doing. That's not the only one—others include IRC, Hipchat, and Yammer, a group communication app that is like Twitter for closed groups. Most of these web-based chat rooms function in a similar way, and all have one key ingredient: privacy—you don't want outsiders stumbling into your private virtual clubhouse.

Campfire works well if everyone using it is aware of some basic etiquette. When you get more than four or five people using Campfire, it can be distracting—each time someone enters an instant message on the service, it makes a dinging sound on everyone else's computers. Imagine three conversations going on at once with all that constant dinging. That's why everyone using Campfire should also be using an instant messaging client at the same time (*Mashable* uses Google Talk; *Gizmodo* uses AIM; *TechCrunch* uses Skype), so only conversations that are necessary for everyone on the team to hear take place on the group chat application.

Campfire is generally used to pitch or claim stories. When one blogger on the team finds a story that he or she deems postworthy, a link to that story is pasted into Campfire, where the editor and other bloggers can click that link and take a look at the story. Depending on how you set up your blog, this can be an active notification or a request for permission. In most blogs where we've worked, the act of pasting a link into Campfire is akin to staking a claim on that story, but it's no fair pasting more than one story into Campfire at a time. As editor-in-chief, you have the right to veto any story proposal. Here's where some lively discussions begin on Campfire, but it's best to move that discussion to individual instant messages, sparing the rest of the group the distraction of a heated discussion where every volley is accompanied by Campfire's dinging sound effect that gets more annoying with each iteration.

As your group of bloggers begins to coalesce, some individuals will gravitate toward certain topics. Encourage this individual interest, and even delineate beats for each of your bloggers to cover. That'll make it easier for them to stay out of each other's way when selecting and pitching stories, and you can begin to develop an expert system where your writers specialize in certain topics, products, and people. If someone on your team is an expert in a certain area or topic, pass ideas or leads onto that person, rather than muddling through it yourself. Maybe even pass along an idea for an angle on that story, too. But don't offer too much detail—it'll seem like an order. People don't work as passionately when they're following orders. Give them ownership of their stories.

As a leader, you'll be there to mediate disputes between your bloggers. When you're dealing with talented, high-strung individuals, it's inevitable that conflicts will arise. These disputes usually have to do with two writers wanting to write the same story. This is where you'll be the one to make the decision about who does the writing, but choose carefully. You'll need to know your writers' strengths and weaknesses to make a valid decision about which writer will cover which topic. It's up to you as boss and facilitator to celebrate the strengths of your writers while downplaying their weaknesses. Whatever you do, avoid pitting one writer against another, or showing favoritism. There will already be enough natural competition between writers on your team without you stirring up more conflict.

Networking for Bloggers

Trying to meet bloggers? Trying to enter the blogging "upper echelon?" Trying to get noticed? Fine, but don't be a pest.

Bloggers, like so many other cliques, have a certain way of approaching the world. Most bloggers respect quiet humor, wit, and friendliness over crass chest-beating. In short, be nice.

Want to meet a blogger? Tweet. Don't email. Emailing a blogger will get you nowhere. In fact, if you have any questions we'd recommend you tweet us before you email (I know, we gave you our email addresses, but trust me on this). Twitter is far more direct than any other social network. Facebook posts tend to get buried, and LinkedIn is a black hole.

When you reach out, be nice. Don't tweet or email, "HEY I SAW YOUR POST, YOU SUCK. THIS IS WHAT I WROTE." Try emailing something like "Saw your video on XYZ. Can we chat? I'm familiar with XYZ and maybe we can collaborate on something."

One of John's closest blogger friends, Ariel Adams, approached him via email and explained that he might have some information that could help him with a research project. John, being John, ignored repeated emails until finally relenting. Now Ariel is a boon friend and trusted confidant.

Charlie approached John for a job at *Gizmodo* by offering to copy edit for free. John, knowing a good deal when he saw one, called him on his offer and Charlie joined up. Almost a decade later, the pair of us are some of the best bloggers in the business.

In short, be nice, be friendly, and be persistent.

Firing

Every blogger needs to be a self-contained universe. Each must produce content that is self-contained, context-aware, and 99.9 percent free of typos—if not 100 percent.

Sometimes, no matter how hard you try to nurture and mentor one of your newfound bloggers, things just don't work out. Firing a blogger is hard. Assistants who usually come from your readership will count you as a friend rather than a boss, and even if you pay them, it will be difficult to pull the plug.

Every situation is different, but most bloggers who aren't cutting it will know almost immediately. If a blogger doesn't have time to help you, that person usually drops out of the group voluntarily rather than sustain the agony of disappointment.

However, sometimes you just know it's not working out, but the blogger refuses to go. It's time to pull out the big guns. First, offer the blogger a month to shape up. Offer clear instruction and discuss what's disappointing you. Do this on a private channel—in person—if possible. Do not make this a public scolding. Make it clear to your errant blogger that he or she is being watched.

A month later, either pull the trigger or give the newly improved blogger a reprieve.

Paying Bloggers

There is no way for us to tell you how to pay your bloggers, but we don't recommend paying per post. Paying per post is great in theory, but in practice it encourages a certain amount of "spamming" by new or less scrupulous writers. The only way to truly do it is the way one blogger boss did it: He expected a certain number of posts from his minions, read them all, but accepted and paid only for the ones he liked. While this makes some sort of ruthless and Darwinian sense, it's not the best way to run a blog. But it does ensure quality, and also ensures your bloggers won't go firing posts at you at an unsustainable clip.

We recommend a flat fee monthly. If that's not possible, you can use the foregoing survival-of-the-fittest method. We usually request 1,000 words per day and one or two posts on weekends. There are no baseline salaries we can recommend, but $4000–$6000 per month if you're really cooking is on par with what most bloggers are making in 2014. Some big-name bloggers earn $10,000 per month at top sites.

If you do have unpaid interns, treat them well and with kindness.

Who gets on your masthead or About page? Our rule of thumb is to add new colleagues to the About page after they've worked with us for a month. It's nice for people to get recognized for their dedication, and it doesn't cost you much—just a few seconds of typing.

Also remember: This industry is small. We know most of the professional bloggers on our beat, and we count them as friends. Don't cause disorder and strife just because someone didn't work out. Offer good, solid recommendations and always look out for fellow bloggers. When the time comes and you need some help, they'll be there for you.

Group Blogging Workflow

There are a variety of ways to set up workflow for your blog. It seems so simple when you're blogging by yourself, picking out topics, writing posts, publishing them, doing your own copy editing—you're in charge of everything. Now that you have colleagues, you can keep everything individualistic, or with a larger group, divide the labor and specialize.

If your bloggers are less experienced than you, or if you are one who must control every aspect of your blog, you might want to set up a more traditional workflow. In this scenario, writers pitch story ideas to you as editor-in-chief, and then you approve or disapprove. You sometimes assign stories to your bloggers, and other times they pitch stories to you by placing a link in Campfire along with a proposed headline. At this point, especially if your bloggers are new, you might want to suggest story angles, recommend sources, and generally shepherd the process. When they finish writing their posts, they're saved in "unpublished" mode and the writers send the link of their work to you, where you edit for content, grammar, and spelling. In this system, you will be the only one who pushes the Publish button.

If you're working with more advanced bloggers, or you're striving for a more egalitarian workplace, each blogger functions as both writer and publisher. Writers place links in Campfire as notifications, letting everyone else know which stories they'll be covering. Once they've written their stories, your bloggers do their own copy editing and line editing, and publish their stories when they're ready. This is the most satisfying setup for writers, giving them full rein over what they post. However, this system works only if you completely trust each of your bloggers to consistently pick compelling story topics and creative angles, something that's more appropriate when you've put together an all-star team of blogosphere veterans.

There's a middle ground. Once your team grows larger, you might have the budget for specialization. This is the way *Mashable* works today, where each of the site's main areas (business, social media, tech, lifestyle, etc.) has a channel editor. Each one of these people presides over his or her subject area, editing the posts and mentoring all those working for that channel. In addition, the channel editors assign stories received from the email news tips box and sources, and gleaned from RSS and Twitter feeds. After a story's written, the writer sends the post to the channel editor for editing, who line edits for content and style, cleans up typos, and checks for other errors. Next, it's passed along to the associate editor, who hits the Publish button at the appropriate time, and immediately after that, the community manager and his or her colleagues share the story by placing witty prompts, lures, and links on *Mashable*'s extensive Twitter and Facebook feeds.

Story Tips via Email

At first, it will be easy to handle your email tips, because there won't be many. But as your blog grows, those valuable tips will blossom, giving you story scoops with inside information that you might be able to use in a blog post. Decide whether everyone will be allowed to receive these tips, or if they will be handled by one person. At *Mashable*, whoever is the associate editor at the time is also responsible for the tips mailbox, news@mashable.com. Having one person handle all those emails, which are often rife with junk, is an efficient way to handle large volumes of email, because only one person must take the time to sift through it. As long as that person is diligent about forwarding tips to those who might be able to act upon them, the system works well.

CrunchGear did this differently. John created two email addresses, everyone@[domain]. com and tips@[domain].com, that both go to every writer on the site. When an outsider emails the tips email box, everyone in the group can read it. Even though it requires more time from each individual, the strength of this workflow is that everyone gets to decide whether each email tip contains a story that's appropriate for publication, rather than one person deciding for all, and perhaps not thinking of an angle that others on the team might have considered.

In this *CrunchGear* workflow, the "everyone" box is for internal communication, but you'd be best served by changing the word "everyone" to, for example, "everyoneWWR" if your website is WristWatchReview. John has also created editors@ and writers@ email addresses, so team members can send email blasts to specific groups in the organization.

Communicate!

To be a great communicator, you need to use more than one medium. Instant messaging is quick and easy, but sometimes nuance is lost amid all the typing—emoticons can go only so far to convey subtle meaning and emotion. If you find yourself typing long missives in IM or Campfire, maybe it's time to pick up the phone. This is especially true when there's a conflict, or if a complicated situation arises that's hard to explain in just a few words. We know that it might sound old-fashioned, but just pick up the phone. Have all of your cobloggers' phone numbers on your favorites list, and talk every once in a while.

But don't talk too much—especially in that culprit of timewasters that's the bane of many a corporate existence: meetings. We suggest avoiding regular meetings, and getting together on a conference call, videoconference, or at a meeting table only when there's a specific and important reason for doing so. Hopefully you'll build your organization in such a way that it's not overpopulated with middle managers whose only job is to attend meetings. Within some of the corporate giants where we've blogged, meetings take on lives of their own, wasting a multitude of hours while accomplishing little. While there are differences of opinion about the necessity of meetings, and their importance changes with the size of an organization and the topics covered, we'll leave this hot topic with three suggestions:

1. When you get together for a meeting, set a timer for thirty minutes. Point to the timer when someone gets too long-winded.
2. Have a stand-up meeting, where everyone remains standing until the meeting is over.
3. Everyone must report to a meeting with a full bladder—no stopping off at the bathroom beforehand. This tends to speed things up.

Joining a Blogging Team

How did we get our blogging jobs? We found out about them either through personal contacts or through a quick email to an editor. Many blogs post want ads right on their front page. When you see one, jump. If you find a job posting looking for a blogger and you want the job, reply immediately with two posts written in the style of the blog. One post should be on an item the blog has covered in the past, and the other should be on an entirely new topic. Also include a short blurb about yourself. That's all. You can include a resume, but we wouldn't. If you have a particularly impressive resume, though, put it online and add a link to it, or point to your LinkedIn profile.

Blogging bosses don't want to hear about your ability to juggle on a unicycle or train wolves. Regardless of what your mom told you, you are not a special, unique flower. You are a random voice howling out from the Internet. Make it worth the editor's while to open and read your email.

Be Careful What You Wish For

If you've managed to sidestep the whole business of starting up a blog yourself, and have somehow landed in a bustling, ongoing blog that has firmly established itself already, consider yourself lucky. It happens. For instance, Charlie got his start at *Gizmodo* by contacting John and bitching about all the typos on the site, offering his services as a copy editor. To his surprise, John asked him to start the next day. This could happen to you—a prominent blogger is suddenly looking for writers, you happen to live in the right city or have the right qualifications, and boom! You suddenly find yourself in the middle of a screaming team of swaggering A-list bloggers. What to do?

What got you there? It was probably a combination of your blogging prowess and networking capability. Maybe you have a lot of connections. You're probably a kind, outgoing person, so it won't be hard for you to blend in. Our advice is this: Work together. Help one another. Share. Do unto others as you would have them do unto you. The rules you learned in kindergarten (or in Sunday school, if that applies to you) are helpful here. If you see a mistake someone has made, fix it. Tactfully let that person know you've corrected the error if it's something you've noticed before. Or another approach: just fix it and don't say anything if it's a one-time mistake. Find out who normally covers certain stories, and tread lightly when pitching an idea on that topic. Familiarize yourself with the local blog politics—are there other blogs to which you're never supposed to link? When we were at *Gizmodo*, it was considered taboo to ever link to our blogging nemesis and fierce competitor, *Engadget*. And our number one tip for getting along in a new blog: It's simple—don't be a jerk.

Appendix
Tips and Tricks of the Trade

Multitasking: When to Use It and When to Avoid It

It's hard to avoid multitasking if, say, you're waiting for an email reply, you're instant messaging with a source, and you're in the middle of a blog post. But if you're writing a complicated piece, turn off the email notifier for a while, close that Facebook tab, and put your cell in the other room. Everyone's different, but solid, constant concentration is often the way important things get done, well.

Seven Ways to Enhance Your Blogging Efficiency

More screen real estate: Numerous studies say that if you have a bigger screen, and preferably two (or maybe even three), you'll be more productive. That's because you don't need to keep switching between documents, clicking around just to peek at something. For instance, one smaller monitor could be dedicated to email, half of another could be the home of your instant messaging and Campfire communications, and front-and-center could be your word processing area, with a browser open next to it. Even if you're using a laptop, determine what is the biggest screen its graphics card can accommodate, and plug that in. You'll see an immediate result of enhanced efficiency.

Comfortable chair: It's been called the most important component in your computer/office setup, and in our experience it rings true. Buy yourself a good chair—you'll be sitting in it for so many hours that it's a huge quality-of-life issue. Which chair would we recommend? There's a good reason why the Herman Miller Aeron Chair was such a hit with the dot-com bunch—it's so damn comfortable, hanging your carcass over its frame like a comfy hammock, and keeping you cool at the same time with its vented seating surfaces. With prices that were formerly upwards of $800, you can find them on sale for much less, in a variety of colors.

Silence: Many bloggers are so accustomed to the cacophonous din that is their sound backdrop that this suggestion might not mean much to them. For the rest of us, silence is golden. No blogging in noisy, distracting coffee shops for us. Even listening to the noise of a cooling fan whining away inside that PC all day is tiring. And yes, the tiny fan inside your laptop can be an annoyance, too. There are PCs that are so quiet that they make virtually no noise at all, and we recommend you take a look at one of those. We found one that's got the most powerful processor in the world inside, and it doesn't make a peep. Really, it makes absolutely no sound whatsoever. It's earned the name we gave it—look it up on our network, and you'll see it's aptly named "ChurchMouse."

Kill the telephone: This might sound revolutionary or even rude to you, but it is possible to kill your telephone, making it so that device is there solely for your convenience, and not for the convenience of anyone else. We're all so connected now in so many ways—instant messaging, texting, voicemail, email, and so on—that there's no excuse for letting someone interrupt you with a phone call. Equip your phone with voicemail, and silence it. If someone wants to contact you, and only a voice conversation will do, ask that person to make an appointment with you via email. Politely make it clear to all of your friends, associates, and acquaintances that you are no longer accepting phone calls. Ever. They'll get used to it, and you'll save a boatload of time and free yourself from distraction.

Work at home: Ah, the camaraderie of the workplace! What a huge benefit it is, having your colleagues nearby, always at the ready for you to consult, ask questions, work together, and support each other. But they're also at the ready to distract you, make noise, take you out for long, work-free lunches, ask you "quick questions," and call "quick" meetings that end up taking an hour. Then there's that game of what will you wear today, and what will everyone else wear? It's becoming increasingly clear to us that in an industry such as blogging, the only reason corporate management wants people in an office is so the bosses can lord over their minions and make themselves feel important and useful. Stay home in your pajamas, oh fellow member of the *pajamahadeen*. You'll save time, suffer through fewer distractions, and you will have to take a shower only once a week, whether you need it or not. We're kidding about that last one.

Minimize spam: We could write a whole book about dealing with email and spam, but here's the solution to the spam problem if you haven't figured it out already: Gmail. Google has solved that dilemma with a hefty dose of crowdsourcing. Whenever one of Gmail's tens of millions of users reports spam, everyone else finds out about it. The result? The spam problem is over, gone, kaput. Now, if you're using Gmail, it's a rarity to receive spam. Stuck with a different email account that you can't get rid of for whatever reason? In a few seconds, you can configure Gmail to fetch that account's email through your primary Gmail account, filtering it for spam, too.

Automate everything: Use TextExpander, QuicKeys, Keytext, or the macro utility of your choice to bang out boilerplate text with a couple of keystrokes. Create "droplets" in Photoshop to crop and edit photos to a designated size by using simple drag-and-drop moves. Use NaturallySpeaking to talk to your computer and have it do all the typing for you. Check out the free Google Voice, which can turn all of your voicemail into text, letting you quickly read it in email. Find more ways to automate your life. Automate everything you can, and save time while enhancing your efficiency.

How to Avoid Burnout: Helpful Hints to Bring Back Your Spirit and Enthusiasm

Sometimes a cruel comment from a reader or a dip in traffic can get you bummed. Know when it's time to step away for a while, even if it's for a few minutes. Once I was stuck in a dead-end job with an annoying/controlling boss, and my coping strategy involved walking around for five minutes every time I felt myself reaching my personal boiling point.

Of course, that worked for only about six months, and I eventually had to separate myself from that situation.

If you're dealing with a constant soul-sucking experience, it'll probably cheer you up to start working on that resume. Know when to quit. Sometimes, quitting can be the best career move you ever made. I can think of three instances in my career where quitting at just the perfect time turned into the luckiest moves of my life.

Health Tips for Bloggers

Read the disclaimer on the back of your keyboard! Yeah, it's there for wussy legal reasons, but there's a lot of truth there. I get up and walk around at least once per hour. Drink coffee if you like it, or tea, and don't believe all the nonsense the fear-mongering medical press spouts about how coffee does this or that to you.

Exercise

In the most stressful job I ever had, you know how I made it through every day? I walked 4 miles a day, right in the middle of the day. It took an hour, but it was the most valuable activity I did all day. I even went walking in below-zero (Fahrenheit) temperatures (properly equipped, mind you!). Blogging is a sedentary activity, so you'll need to move around regularly unless you want to end up like those earth-orbiting invalids in the movie *Wall·E*.

Diet

Yeah, I know. Cheetos and Mountain Dew, right? Oh wait, Red Bull. If you're going to eat like that, at least take a multivitamin every day. Contrary to common mythology, pizza is actually a fairly nutritious food. But no, ketchup is not a vegetable.

Sleep

Everyone is different, but you won't be able to stay up all night like you did in college for the rest of your life. I've noticed I get noticeably grouchy and spacy when I haven't gotten enough sleep, so I make it a point to get at least seven hours every night. One suggestion: try not to do anything too exciting right before bed. Another: sleeping pills are a short-term solution. Another: go to bed at the same time every night.

Ten Tips: Besides Posting, What Do You Do to Lure Readers?

1. Fresh ideas
2. Sharp writing
3. Interesting topics
4. Consistent posting
5. Accuracy
6. Humor
7. Promotion
8. Link generosity

9. Context in every post
10. Be a watchdog, not a lapdog

Readers like to click a star rating system. But be careful—if you start off your blog with a star rating system at first, it'll display how only a few people are reading. Best to wait until traffic starts to build before you display any hints about your traffic numbers.

Trade show tip: Don't make too many appointments. Most PR people will try to rope you into meeting with their clients at trade shows, but all that does is lock you up for an hour (or more) when you could be covering breaking news that hasn't been announced yet. When you get a meeting request, ask what will be announced, offering to keep that confidential. If there's nothing newsworthy, politely refuse the meeting. Schedule meetings with your most important sources, but leave yourself plenty of free time to pursue those stories that inevitably pop up at trade shows.

Keep neat notes: When I started my blogs, I didn't keep notes. So far, it's not a problem because it's all fresh in my mind . . . but in six months when, for instance, I want to change my four 125×125 ads to a single 300×250 ad, I may be kicking myself for not leaving myself notes. Granted, the steps are on Pollock's WP-Magazine Theme instructions, but sometimes even rediscovering the answers can be time-consuming. If I were to start a website again, I'd write everything down.

Index

Index

Index

Index